Algorithmic Institutionalism

Algorithmic Institutionalism

The Changing Rules of Social and Political Life

Ricardo F. Mendonça
Fernando Filgueiras
and
Virgílio Almeida

Great Clarendon Street, Oxford, OX2 6DP,
United Kingdom

Oxford University Press is a department of the University of Oxford.
It furthers the University's objective of excellence in research, scholarship,
and education by publishing worldwide. Oxford is a registered trade mark of
Oxford University Press in the UK and in certain other countries

© Ricardo F. Mendonça, Fernando Filgueiras, and Virgílio Almeida 2023

The moral rights of the authors have been asserted

All rights reserved. No part of this publication may be reproduced, stored in
a retrieval system, or transmitted, in any form or by any means, without the
prior permission in writing of Oxford University Press, or as expressly permitted
by law, by licence or under terms agreed with the appropriate reprographics
rights organization. Enquiries concerning reproduction outside the scope of the
above should be sent to the Rights Department, Oxford University Press, at the
address above

You must not circulate this work in any other form
and you must impose this same condition on any acquirer

Published in the United States of America by Oxford University Press
198 Madison Avenue, New York, NY 10016, United States of America

British Library Cataloguing in Publication Data

Data available

Library of Congress Control Number: 2023940918

ISBN 9780192870070

DOI: 10.1093/oso/9780192870070.001.0001

Printed and bound by
CPI Group (UK) Ltd, Croydon, CR0 4YY

Links to third party websites are provided by Oxford in good faith and
for information only. Oxford disclaims any responsibility for the materials
contained in any third party website referenced in this work.

Dedicated to Guilherme, Felipe and Paula, for their support and patience along the way – Ricardo F. Mendonça.

Dedicated to Francisco Gaetani, a great friend and inspiration for the public spirit and for all possible muddling through – Fernando Filgueiras

Dedicated to my family, and especially to my grandchildren, who are sources of joy and hope for the future – Virgílio Almeida

Foreword

What are institutions? We use the term frequently in both our everyday discussions and our academic writings, but what does it mean? Our first thoughts, at least among political scientists, would be of large government buildings with brass plaques that proclaim that they are the parliament, or a ministry. A second thought might be of social institutions such as marriage, or the Church, or even law. We might even think of even more amorphous institutions based on norms or discourses—even a social club or a sports team—that exert influence over individual behaviour because the individuals have learned and accepted the values. But can a few lines of computer code be an institution?

All the versions of institutions mentioned above are familiar, and largely uncontroversial, but Mendonça, Filgueiras, and Almeida have extended our thinking about what an institution is, and what institutions are likely to become. The institutional literature coming out of rational-choice theory emphasizes that institutions are rules that shape the behaviour of individuals (see Ostrom 1991). If we think of algorithms—those lines of code—as institutions, however, to some extent the rules no longer have to be interpreted by individuals, but become self-enforcing.

In this forward to a very important book, I want to reflect on the meaning of algorithmic institutions from the perspective of someone interested in public administration and policy, as well as institutional theory. As the three authors point out, the institutional conception of an algorithm has applications that go well beyond the world of governing, but for me some of the crucial impacts occur in the public sector. This is primarily because this domain, already well populated by institutions, has special requirements of fairness and equity. When the state is dealing with its citizens, it is crucial that it and its agents act *sine irae et studio*. Despite appearances to the contrary, those demands for fairness may not be met by a robotic adherence to a simple formula, no matter how well designed and well intentioned the algorithm may be.

The algorithm has a number of similarities with the more familiar conceptions of institutions. The most important is that the algorithm shapes outputs by organizations, and applies rules to individuals. If we take the public bureaucracy as an example of a 'normal' institution, then the rules by which bureaucrats apply law to individual cases are to some extent analogous to algorithms, and indeed scholars and practitioners who want to limit the autonomy of bureaucrats and bureaucracies have wanted to develop means of ensuring that decisions would follow the letter of the law (McCubbins et al. 1987). An algorithm that replaced the discretion of individuals could provide that inflexibility, but perhaps at some cost to the clients of the program.

The historical element of algorithms as institutions is also analogous to what can be seen in more conventional institutions. Institutions of all types represent solidified preferences, and to some extent are products of their time and place. That can be beneficial in creating stability, but I may also lock in ideas and preferences that are less desirable. For example, we now know that algorithms used in sentencing decisions in courts tend to institutionalize certain familiar negative ideas about offenders, as well as at times some racial attitudes. Thus, the design of these policy solutions must be even more careful than that of other policies.

Although they do reflect historical preferences, institutions do change, sometimes dramatically but more often by gradual steps (see Mahoney and Thelen 2010). Institutions that are composed of humans, not formulae, respond to their successes and failures, and to changes in their environments, to adapt. They may, of course, make mistakes as they learn, but they can make attempts to adapt. Algorithms as institutions may encounter more difficulties in adapting, given that more purposive change will be required, rather than the more organic change in human institutions.

Again, as I am focusing on institutions and activities within the public sector, these difficulties in changing an algorithmic institution become more evident. Most algorithms employed will need some form of legitimation, whether by the legislature or through secondary legislation from the bureaucracy. Changing them will also involve some form of official action, and that may open up the policy area to unwelcome changes, especially when there are powerful political forces that oppose existing patterns of policy. Policy implemented by individuals can change by 'drift', but that which is contained within a formula cannot change so readily.

In addition to the very important issue of policy adaptation, there are some important differences between algorithmic institutions and conventional institutions. One of the paradoxes of institutions and institutional theory has been that, while institutions are designed and shaped by humans, humans also feel themselves bound by them. Those bounds on the members of institutions are largely a function of socialization and learning the values and rules of the institution. Therefore, despite the political issues mentioned above, change may be easier because individuals do not have to be convinced of the appropriateness of the change and resocialized into another set of values.

Perhaps the most crucial difference between algorithms as institutions and other forms of institutions is that in the algorithmic version the important decisions have already been made once the institution has been launched. Institutions are generally described as being important because they shape other decisions, but in this case the construction of the algorithm is the crucial decision, and decisions about individual cases are merely a product of the initial decision. This then provides what may appear to be perfect administration. In most understandings of institutions, individuals devise an institution through their interactions, and later adherents to the institution accept the norms and rules.

In addition, algorithmic institutions are more free-standing. We usually conceptualize institutions as functioning within a field composed of other institutions, and interacting constantly with those other institutions. The public bureaucracy as an institution interacts with political executives, legislatures, and courts. It also interacts with more amorphous institutions such as law and markets. Algorithms, on the other hand, do not readily interact with others. Coordination is always a difficult challenge for organizations in both the public and the private sectors, but this form of decision-making may exacerbate those difficulties.[1]

The free-standing nature of algorithms as institutions means that unfortunately they will be less capable of performing some of the tasks that make other forms of institutions so important. First, an algorithm may not be able to generate stability. While institutions in the usual sense structure interactions and can impose rules for voting that generate stability, algorithms do not allow for such interactions. Nor do they provide means of solving collective-action problems, other than through imposition, while a good deal of thinking (and practical solutions) has been focusing on social norms and bargaining.

One important issue that arises with algorithmic institutions is the extent to which the cases to which the algorithm is applied are sufficiently similar to make the application equitable. The applications may be equal, but may not be equitable. A potential client being denied social benefits, for example, may not be formally eligible, so the machine making the decision may be technically correct in denying the benefits. However, we know from studies of street-level bureaucracy (see Hupe 2019) that human decision-makers do make adjustments and do make decisions that may violate the letter of the law.

---

[1] This may be analogous to the creation of autonomous or quasi-autonomous organizations in the New Public Management. They were designed to act autonomously, did so, and produced major governance problems (Verhoest et al. 2010).

The issues raised about algorithms as institutions point clearly to the need to monitoring them closely, along with other innovations in governing, such as artificial intelligence. These innovations may appear to open new opportunities for equality in decisions, as well as for more effective implementation. But, like all technological innovations, they also have the potential for 'biting back', with unanticipated consequences that undermine the benefits that have been created (Tenner 1997).

To this point I have been discussing the implications of an algorithmic form of institutions for public administration and public policy. There are, however, also important implications for institutional theory that should be considered. The most obvious question is where does one draw a line as to what is an institution? If some rule is accepted and applied within a certain domain, and it persists over time, does that make it an institution? Or is it still only a rule that is a manifestation of an institution? Does the fact that it is an algorithm rather than some other type of rule contribute to, or detract from, its institutional character?

If, as I have throughout, I accept the algorithm as an institution, how does it fit with existing institutional theories? The most obvious connection is with rational-choice versions of institutional theory that depend on rules to structure behaviour, both within and without the institution. The difference is that algorithms are dependent on other explanations for how they are created—the algorithm says nothing about the internal processes of an organization or institution that developed it. We may be able to infer the preferences of the members of the institution, but we cannot discern the process. Is it not important to understand how institutions function, as well as what they produce?

In terms of institutional change, the algorithmic version is more akin to original versions of historical institutionalism that relied on 'punctuated equilibrium' to describe change. This is in contrast to versions that conceptualize change as occurring more readily through incremental means. Thus, the algorithmic view of institutions may sacrifice some of the stability that is usually associated with institutions. Somewhat paradoxically, this version of an institution may be extremely stable while in place, but may not be open to adaptative change, with changes potentially being more radical.

In summary, this book provides a novel and intriguing conception both of institutions and of the formulae that increasingly influence our lives. It certainly makes the reader confront the rapidly changing world in which we live, with algorithmic decision-making being but one of the challenges posed by the digital world. I have examined those changes more as a social scientist interested in public governance, but the implications of this book are far more extensive and worthy of careful consideration and debate.

B. Guy Peters
University of Pittsburgh

References

Hupe, P. (2019). *Research Handbook on Street-Level Bureaucracy*. Cheltenham: Edward Elgar.

McCubbins, M. D., Noll, R. G., and Weingast, B. R. (1987). 'Administrative Procedures as Instruments of Political Control', *Journal of Law, Economics and Organization*, 3: 243–77.

Mahoney, J., and Thelen, K. (2010). 'A Theory of Gradual Institutional Change', in J. Mahoney and K. Thelen (eds), *Explaining Institutional Change: Ambiguity, Agency and Power*. Cambridge: Cambridge University Press.

Ostrom, E. (1991). 'Rational Choice Theory and Institutional Analysis: Toward Complementarity', *American Political Science Review*, 85: 237–43.

Tenner, E. (1997). *Why Things Bite Back: Technology and the Revenge of Unintended Consequences*. New York: Kopf.

Verhoest, K., Roness, P., Verschuere, B., Rubecksen, K., and MacCarthaigh, M. (2010). *Autonomy and Control of State Agencies: Comparing States and Agencies*. Basingstoke: Palgrave Macmillan.

Acknowledgements

We are grateful to an extraordinary collection of colleagues and collaborators from our institutions—namely, the Federal University of Minas Gerais, Federal University of Goiás, Berkman Klein Center for Internet and Society at Harvard University, Institute of Advanced Studies at the University of São Paulo, University of California, Irvine, University of Canberra, and the community of Ostrom Workshop on Political Theory and Policy Analysis at Indiana University. The book was supported by Coordenação de Aperfeiçoamento de Pessoal de Nível Superior (Capes) (88887.370393/2019-00), Fundação de Amparo à Pesquisa do Estado de Minas Gerais (Fapemig) (PPM-00284-17), and Conselho Nacional de Desenvolvimento Científico e Tecnológico (CNPq) (423218/2018-2). We are extremely thankful for this support, as Brazil, our home country, experienced a severe political, sanitary, and economic crisis in the period in which this book was written.

We also express our sincere gratitude to Prof. João Carlos Vieira Magalhães, University of Groningen, for his comments that helped us better frame the book's theoretical approach. We thank Tammi Titsworth, Jennifer Stout, Mateus Canela, and Victória Lima for their support in the revision and preparation of the manuscript. We are particularly grateful to the reviewers assigned by Oxford University Press. Their comments and suggestions helped us enhance the argument through the development of this book. We are also grateful to the impressive editorial work of Oxford University Press, namely to Dominic Byatt, Phoebe Aldridge-Turner, and Raja Dharmaraj, whose work was very fruitful and efficient in making the book a reality.

Contents

Introduction	1
1. Algorithms as Institutions	5
2. Reading Contemporary Issues via the Lens of Algorithmic Institutionalism	26
3. Security in Algorithmic Times	53
4. Redesigning Governments through Algorithmic Systems	79
5. Algorithmic Recommenders	104
6. Algorithms and Politics: From an Epistocratic View to a Democratic Approach	126
Final Remarks: A Needed Agenda	148
References	152
Index	172

Introduction

This book was born of a question that permeated our multidisciplinary conversations about the future of our world intertwined with digital technologies: 'What if algorithms were conceived of as institutions?' We decided to dive into researching the question. What does it mean, however, to think of algorithms as institutions? Why should we do it? How do algorithm-driven processes affect traditional institutions of contemporary life? What are the potential benefits of approaching algorithms through the lens of New Institutionalism? As algorithms become woven into every part of social life, how can society reclaim its share of control on algorithmic decisions? Are there legitimate justifications for autonomous algorithmic decisions? What kind of relations link algorithmic systems with current worldwide democratic crises?

The book did not emerge only from a careful analysis of an extensive multidisciplinary bibliography. It materialized also from our academic research, from our classes, and from our experience in government. It also benefited from many interactions with colleagues from different areas in diverse countries. This is a multidisciplinary book, covering knowledge emanating from political science, computer science, communication studies, and sociology to analyse algorithms' role in constructing human action in contemporary society.

A major point of this book is precisely that we—all of us—are part of a global digital ecosystem mediated by algorithms that have impacts on individual and collective behaviour. Conceiving of algorithms as institutions means that we aim to understand algorithms as sets of formal and informal rules that establish contexts in which human and algorithmic interactions occur. We do not dispute the benefits of algorithms: often, they optimize scarce resources, they provide efficient services at scale, and they create ways to manage the modern world's complexity. However, when we look beyond the facades of technological efficiency and convenience, a more complex reality emerges. In many situations, algorithmic systems reproduce biases or forms of discrimination, increase inequalities, violate human-rights principles, and make decisions that cannot be explained. This book explores cases that show the impact of algorithms on both developed and developing countries.

Algorithmic Institutionalism. Ricardo F. Mendonça, Fernando Filgueiras, and Virgílio Almeida, Oxford University Press.
© Ricardo F. Mendonça, Fernando Filgueiras, and Virgílio Almeida (2023). DOI: 10.1093/oso/9780192870070.003.0001

The central argument of this book is that algorithms are not only changing existent institutions, but can, themselves, be conceived of as institutions in the extent to which they frame contexts of interactions, create pathways to development, inducing or constraining certain behaviours with collective consequences. Algorithms are reshaping the conditions for actions in many contexts, as they structure rules, norms, and meanings grounding social action.

Thinking about algorithms as institutions requires a theory that offers explanations about how they shape human actions in different social and political contexts. In the private and public world, we have algorithmic systems performing different activities and making decisions about different issues in social and political life. Algorithmic systems pervade the way different organizations make decisions and create new contexts for human agency in society. In governments, for example, algorithmic systems make decisions about resource allocation or the auditing of public benefits. In any of these situations, algorithmic systems are used in public or private organizations to optimize their agency capacity for political, commercial, economic, social, or cultural purposes. The pervasiveness of algorithmic systems is a new reality that profoundly affects society and politics, with deep implications in the rules and norms that guide action.

The insight that algorithms may be thought of as institutions is not, however, entirely new. Philip Napoli made this claim explicitly, when he advocated the fruitfulness of institutionalism to analyse changes in media production and consumption with the advancement of social media. Before him, and in a more implicit way, we can track the origins of the insight that algorithms can be read as institutions to Lessig, who argued that 'code is law'. Both authors shed light on the role of coding in the establishment of rules that guide sociotechnical agency.

This book seeks to advance this insight, developing a proper framework for an institutionalist comprehension of the origins, transformations, interactions, and consequences of algorithmic systems. What is different about this book is that it explores the extent to which institutional theory can contribute to make sense of algorithms as new institutions of society. Resorting to institutional theories, the book provides a comprehensive framework that unravels diverse dimensions of the sociopolitical dynamics of algorithmic systems. Its novelty lies, therefore, in its capacity to bring together an insight and many contemporary debates about algorithms into one comprehensive framework.

The framework of *Algorithmic Institutionalism* understands algorithms as institutions, which are designed and created through multiple interactions in sociotechnical networks, thus affecting the distributions of resources through the establishment of power relations. Moreover, the framework draws attention to the historical constitution and transformation of algorithmic systems, to the rules and norms enacted through these systems, to the way social actors play with these rules, and to the discursive nature embeddedness of algorithms. Despite its comprehensiveness, we do not claim that our framework is exhaustive, and we do invite other scholars keen to contribute to this agenda to develop other potential dimensions in which the lenses of institutional theory could help the advancement of an in-depth understanding of the sociopolitical consequences of algorithms.

Besides its comprehensiveness—and openness to future developments—the framework of Algorithmic Institutionalism advanced by this book offers a second contribution. Not only is it complex enough to bring together different dimensions of the phenomenon investigated (that is, algorithmic systems), but it is also flexible enough to be applicable in different levels and for diverse units of analysis. Algorithmic Institutionalism can help the comprehension of specific algorithms, but also of macro scenarios crossed by different algorithms in complex systems. It can be mobilized to make sense of particular technological developments (such as machine-learning algorithms and recommendation systems, for example), of the way certain actors employ algorithms to change their activities (such as governments, judicial courts, or investment firms, for instance), or even of certain areas and policy issues (such as welfare and security, to cite two examples). The framework is flexible to allow different types of analysis at different levels that are relevant to a comprehensive understanding of the way algorithms function as institutions and affect existing institutions. In doing so, it invites a self-reflexive attention to the legitimacy of these institutions, paving the way for a debate about the possibilities and obstacles for the democratization of algorithms.

Throughout the book, we try to explore these multiple possibilities, reaching the political discussion about the democratization of algorithmic systems. The book has three parts. The first part (Chapters 1 and 2) uses the analytical lens of institutional theory to deal with the problems, consequences, and dynamics involved in viewing algorithms as institutions. New Institutionalism makes it possible to expand analytical possibilities to understand and analyse algorithms and the way they are incorporated into the systems that make decisions and shape social behaviour. To further that understanding, we build an analytical framework for analysing algorithms as institutions of modern society.

The second part (Chapters 3 to 5) analyses three cases that demonstrate how algorithms can be viewed as institutions that are built from social dynamics of design, have historical contexts, reflect power relations, have regulatory functions, are susceptible to gaming, and shape and incorporate discursive dynamics of society. Each chapter of this part looks at algorithms in different levels and with different units of analysis on focus, showing the flexibility of the framework developed in the first part.

The third part (Chapter 6 and Concluding Remarks) addresses the challenge of developing approaches to democratize the new political order, influenced by the global expansion of algorithmic decision-making systems in governments and big technology companies. There is a need for new analytical lenses, new assumptions, and new approaches to ensure that interactions between humans and algorithms are legitimate and democratically infused, based on respect for human autonomy. And these new approaches may require revisiting established theories and lost insights to make sense of emerging phenomena.

1
Algorithms as Institutions

On a given day, let us say that a group needs to go from the Harvard campus in Cambridge, MA, to terminal B at Logan Airport in Boston. They are in a hurry and cannot take public transportation, so they decide to use an app from a smartphone to call an Uber. Five minutes later, a car picks them up at Harvard, and it takes half an hour to drop them off at the airport.

Today's algorithms allocate, optimize, and assess the work of large and diverse workforces, and Uber's is no exception. Similar to many other algorithmic-based companies, Uber manages its millions of drivers in cities around the world with algorithms that instruct drivers on which passengers to pick up, the value of the ride, and which route to take.[1] Uber uses dynamic-pricing algorithms to set the price for rides and vehicle-routing algorithms to determine the optimal path for the trip's destination. Facial-recognition algorithms check identities to detect fraud, and other algorithms evaluate drivers' performances. Uber also has algorithmic systems that allow service providers to assign scores to passengers after a ride has been completed. Algorithmic management means that a small number of human managers can oversee thousands of drivers in an optimized mode on a large scale.[2] From the drivers' and customers' perspectives, Uber algorithms are viewed as opaque black boxes: the algorithm organizes different aspects of the transportation from rules, and the only visible elements are the app interfaces that appear on smartphones and the results they show.[3]

Uber is a good example of the sharing economy, with companies driven by data, algorithms, and smartphones. An initial take on the sharing economy must consider the benefits and concerns brought by companies such as Uber, Lyft, Airbnb, and others. Benefits to consumers include customer-friendly features such as the convenience of calling a car and paying by smartphone, low fares, and short waiting times. Among other potential benefits, companies in the sharing economy promote efficiency by lowering search costs and providing consumers with more options. They also enable unemployed individuals to earn some money.

---

[1] Lee et al. (2015).
[2] Lee et al. (2015).
[3] Chen et al. (2015).

While Uber has become extremely popular, concerns abound regarding algorithm-based companies' social and economic impact. To cite one among many issues, the precarious labour condition of Uber drivers makes clear the new forms of exploitation in the contemporary market economy. There is also evidence of racial discrimination among service providers and consumers in the literature, indicating discriminatory bias against passengers with African American names having experienced longer wait times.[4] The opaqueness of Uber's algorithms, such as its surge-pricing algorithm, raises questions about the service's transparency, accountability, fairness, and efficacy.[5]

In addition, Uber—like many other sharing economy companies—has the capacity to monitor and collect data that reflect both driver and passenger activities in detail. Its algorithms' complexity and operations' monitoring technology highlight deep asymmetries in information and power that affect users and providers alike.[6] Uber is the only entity that controls detailed information about its ecosystem: the decision-making process and data used by its algorithms are unavailable to drivers or passengers.

As the use of algorithms to improve both efficiency and accuracy of management processes grows, so do concerns about the impact of this type of automation on the workplace. Algorithms offer powerful opportunities for bureaucratic control, which can reconfigure work relations within organizations. Three dimensions are relevant here.[7] First, worker supervision occurs via restricting and recommending algorithms that impose what must be executed and in what order and time. Second, workers' evaluations are carried out by recording and rating algorithms that identify problems and mistakes made by workers and then assess their performance. The third dimension refers to algorithmic procedures that enforce compliance with labour norms and rules, providing rewards in real time for workers who comply with predefined correct behaviours.

The nature and implications of managing workers through algorithms are not yet clear. If we focus on the Uber-driver scenario, three areas of consistent complaints about working 'for' algorithms have been identified so far: constant surveillance, little transparency, and dehumanization.[8] The intense use of surveillance practices, with algorithms tracking drivers' GPS location and monitoring their speed (along with their acceptance rate of customer requests), is part of the working environment. Drivers are managed

[4] Calo and Rosenblat (2017).
[5] Lee et al. (2015).
[6] Rosenblat and Stark (2016).
[7] Kellogg et al. (2020).
[8] Möhlmann and Henfridsson (2019).

without real knowledge of algorithmic processes, or the data collected about them. They often feel frustrated about the lack of transparency into critical algorithmic management functions such as recruitment, performance management, work allocation, and dismissals.[9] The lack of transparency also leads to feelings of dehumanization related to the algorithmic management process.

These algorithmic systems are human–machine assemblages comprising a vast array of interconnected algorithms that regulate drivers' and customers' actions and behaviours. This Uber scenario illustrates how algorithmic systems participate and become part of everyday life around the world, raising questions to be addressed in this book, such as: How should we conceive of algorithms' social role? Is it possible to control algorithmic systems? What is the human role in automated decision-making? We argue that tackling the challenges associated with the multiple roles played by algorithmic systems requires new social and political lenses that account for the changes they bring to society. Throughout the book, we advance the approach of Algorithmic Institutionalism to make sense of this scenario.

Algorithms

Algorithms are a fundamental concept of computer science.[10] They can be described as finite sequences of instructions or well-defined steps to solve a particular problem, task, or calculation. The term *algorithm* derives from the name of the ninth-century Persian mathematician Muhammad Ibn Musa al-Khwarizmi, who produced a well-defined formal procedure for deriving calculation rules.

The study and use of algorithms are multidisciplinary and have triggered researchers' interest from practically all areas of science, from computer science, mathematics, and engineering to social and political science. Computer scientists tend to focus their work on the design and analysis of algorithms, determining their efficiency, correctness, and optimality from a technical perspective. This means that, given an input to a problem, an algorithm should always produce a solution, so an algorithm's efficiency is measured by the amount of time it needs to find the correct solution.

For every problem, a set of algorithms exists for implementing solutions in different ways. There are several algorithms, for instance, to sort a list of

---

[9] Möhlmann and Henfridsson (2019: 4).
[10] Knuth (1968).

numbers from smallest to largest, such as *quicksort, merge sort, bubble sort,* and *heap sort.*[11] In recent years, remarkable progress has occurred in algorithm design.[12] The progress can be characterized by a focus on efficiency, scalability, and adaptability of algorithms. These hallmarks have enabled the development of new algorithms that can tackle increasingly complex and diverse applications. Several popular algorithms reflect the advancement of the area of algorithm theory and design by aiming at increasingly complex applications, incorporating ideas from fields such as optimization and privacy.

Some examples of popular algorithms that reflect the advancement of the area of algorithm theory and design include the PageRank algorithm, which does link analysis used to rank web pages in search engine results. Travelling salesman problem heuristic is a class of optimization algorithms to find the shortest route between a set of points and locations that must be visited. They are widely used in logistics, planning, and transportation applications. Because of the growth of usage of algorithms in applications with societal impact, explicit considerations of privacy and social values have been incorporated in algorithm design. For example, differential privacy algorithms are designed to provide privacy guarantees for statistical analysis of sensitive data. They add a carefully calibrated amount of noise to the results of data analysis to protect individual privacy while maintaining the accuracy of the analysis.

Advanced algorithms' development is associated with the evolution of computing capacity and big data proliferation. Rather than specifying rules and step-by-step routes that traditional algorithms follow, machine-learning algorithms are software that learn from examples, data, and experience. Machine-learning algorithms are part of a family of artificial intelligence (AI) methods that includes deep learning and reinforcement learning.[13] These algorithms drive modern software embedded in virtual personal assistants, autonomous cars, recommender engines, image and voice recognition tools, and language translation services.

Essentially, a machine-learning algorithm takes data as input and produces a model that represents the patterns the algorithm learned from that data. Based on statistics and probability theory, machine-learning computer programs generate results with some degree of uncertainty about what is useful or optimal. Machine-learning algorithms, also known as self-learning

[11] Kearns and Roth (2020).
[12] Russell and Norvig (2021).
[13] Kelleher (2019).

algorithms, define a process to analyse a data set and identify recurrent data patterns.

Machine learning encompasses two steps—training and inference—with the training process organized into three groups. In the case of supervised machine learning, a system is trained with data that have been labelled. The system then uses this information to predict the categories of new or 'test' data.[14] Without tagged data, unsupervised learning algorithms analyse and cluster unlabelled data sets. Reinforcement learning focuses on learning from experience and lies between unsupervised and supervised learning. Deep-learning algorithms—a subfield of machine-learning algorithms—are artificial neural networks inspired by insights drawn from physiology and neuroscience. Once the model has been trained, the second part of machine-learning algorithms is inference, which refers to the process of using the model to generate new values for the examples.

The concepts presented in this book are applicable to both traditional algorithms and machine-learning algorithms. Both types of algorithms fulfil tasks as elements of rationalization of the organization of society, establishing rules that set contexts of interaction. Our primary emphasis is on high-risk algorithms that may have significant public or impactful consequences, regardless of their classification and regardless of their public or private usage. The use of algorithms in various high-risk areas can have significant consequences on people's lives and fundamental rights. These include essential public and private services, critical infrastructure, educational and vocational training, employment and management of workers, and law enforcement.

Are Algorithms Changing Society?

Software has been incorporated into almost every facet of our lives. On an ordinary day, people meet hundreds of pieces of software with embedded algorithms that drive all types of digital devices and services used for communicating, working, connecting with other people, and consuming goods and services. Algorithms are therefore general-purpose technology that impact on multiple domains of society. 'The promise of algorithms traverses social and political fields globally ranging from the politics of security to that of humanitarian action.'[15]

---

[14] Royal Society (2017).
[15] Aradau and Blanke (2022: 3).

Algorithmic decisions already rule many public and private services, such as human-resources recruiting, mortgage approval, visa processing, and predictive policing. They have been used to make life-changing decisions across the criminal justice system, in welfare distribution, in loan-access systems, and as part of hiring processes. Likewise, social-media platforms use algorithms to control the flow of information to users, potentially swaying social, cultural, and political formation and collective behaviour. Spotify, Twitter, Netflix, YouTube, Facebook, Tinder, and Amazon are just some of the algorithmic platforms that affect billions of lives worldwide, influencing culture, shared values, and identities for different social groups.

Multiple studies have shown how algorithms affect people in many dimensions, such as their mood, political preferences, and sociability.[16] Experimental research results indicate that emotions expressed by other users on Facebook, for example, can influence our own emotions, pointing to massive-scale contagion via social networks.[17] In fact, social-media algorithms can influence peoples' preferences in numerous contexts, from elections to dating.[18] A study on social-media platforms shows that some algorithmic systems have directed users to radical and extremist content, thereby increasing their political bias and contributing to societal polarization.[19] Many modern-day situations entail multiple interactions with apps and digital platforms, a composition in which both humans and algorithms have active participation.[20]

Algorithmic systems could be viewed as agents in determined contexts when they are designed to act autonomously or make decisions on their own. Typically, computational algorithms work as agents; they perform bureaucratic functions, such as classifying and ranking people and data. Patrick Henry Winston, for instance, defines AI algorithms as 'the study of computations that make it possible to perceive, reason, and act'.[21] Stuart Russell defines AI algorithms as agents that perceive a stream of inputs and produce a stream of outputs to realize an objective.[22] This agency condition is attributed to algorithmic systems through rules and procedures embedded in their complex codes. Algorithms are not, however, completely autonomous agents; rather, they are sociotechnical artefacts— or artificial entities—moulded in contexts, and they incorporate rules to

---

[16] Epstein and Robertson (2015).
[17] Kramer (2014).
[18] Agudo and Matute (2021).
[19] Ribeiro et al. (2020).
[20] Neyland (2019).
[21] Winston (1992).
[22] Russell (2019).

influence human behaviour.[23] Social-media algorithms, for instance, exercise their agency when they 'select and prioritize content by translating user activity into the most relevant or trending topics'.[24]

Recommendation algorithms, image-identification algorithms, search engines, routing algorithms, and digital 'agents' such as Alexa are examples of algorithms that narrow or eliminate the need for human involvement in some tasks. Algorithms are deployed at border facilities, for example, to replace human decisions at security operations.[25] Likewise, credit-scoring algorithms are used to assess a loan applicant's suitability. Claudia Aradau and Tobias Blanke speak of an emerging algorithmic reason, which 'renders the conditions of possibility of rolling out algorithms for governing the conducts of individuals and populations, of friends and enemies, of normality and abnormality across social worlds and political boundaries'.[26]

Human agency and machine agency, however, have different characteristics. Both make decisions that lead to individual and collective consequences,[27] but our self-understanding as human agents includes a broad sense of purpose and forms of awareness that are not present in the software pieces that implement algorithmic agency. Humans do not always act on a cost–benefit or rational-choice basis; rather, they are motivated by a wide range of appropriate behaviours.[28]

The case of a chatbot called 'Tay' illustrates some differences in algorithmic agency. The experiment's purpose was to expose the robot to interactions with human users to learn human habits of speech. Less than twenty-four hours after the experiment began, though, the robot began to generate inappropriate tweets, using racist, sexist, and anti-Semitic language.[29] Microsoft then published the following statement: 'Unfortunately, within the first 24 hours of coming online, we became aware of a coordinated effort by some users to abuse Tay's commenting skills to have Tay respond in inappropriate ways.'[30] This experiment clearly shows that the robot was incapable of understanding context and keeping a sense of awareness.

Algorithmic agency is the complex outcome of many layers of interaction, including designers' intentions, feedback from users, and connections with other algorithms, all of which makes it not entirely predictable or knowable.

---

[23] For a deep discussion on the sociology of mundane artefacts, see Latour (1992).
[24] van Poell and van Dijck (2014: 188).
[25] Amoore (2021).
[26] Aradau and Blanke (2022: 3).
[27] Rose and Jones (2005).
[28] March and Olsen (2009).
[29] Wolf et al. (2017).
[30] Kantrowitz (2016).

As described by Nick Seaver, 'algorithmic systems are not standalone little boxes, but massive, networked ones with hundreds of hands reaching into them, tweaking and tuning, swapping out parts and experimenting with new arrangements'.[31] Algorithmic systems include many distinct algorithms, models, mathematical functions, training data, applications, hardware, and networks. They are sociotechnical ensembles that combine technical and social components where social actors and technological artefacts are complexly intertwined.[32]

Large production systems such as Facebook's newsfeed or the YouTube recommendation system use multiple software components, which include both conventional and machine-learning algorithms with different models, massive training data sets, and complex network architectures and functions. They also rely on human interventions, such as a set of criteria for content moderation that reflect business rules, regional culture, and national regulation. Waze is a good example for thinking about algorithmic decision systems' complexities.[33] It shows how daily activities, such as choosing itineraries from A to B, increasingly become automated and delegated to decision-making algorithms. Waze collects real-time data from hundreds of millions of devices and drivers (such as location, driving speed, place of origin and destination, and time of use) and processes them to gain unique spatial knowledge about a city and then deliver personalized directions to drivers. The central role of algorithms in Waze's operation makes it hard for society to dissect and discern Waze's processes and suggestions. As Eran Fisher proposes, the case of algorithmic spatiality introduced by Waze and similar services adds epistemic and political dimensions to the analysis of algorithmic decision-making,[34] but historical, cultural, and social contexts in the urban space are not considered. This lack of embeddedness creates an image of space that clashes with how other major—mostly human—*actants* perceive and experience space. As an example, small towns are dealing with newly created traffic jams caused by the algorithms in navigation services such as Google Maps, Waze, and Apple Maps suggesting shortcuts for commuters through narrow and hilly residential streets.[35]

These algorithms have deep political implications, because they affect the way users experience a shared reality. In Taina Bucher's view, the political dimension of algorithms is related to their capacity to generate new ways of

[31] Seaver (2013).
[32] Green (2021).
[33] Graaf (2018).
[34] Fisher (2022).
[35] Foderaro (2017).

ordering the world.[36] Randy Connolly argues that power is often enacted 'by the construction of meaning through knowledge production and distributed by communication systems'.[37] Along the same vein, David Beer discusses algorithms' power by asking: 'Should we treat them as lines of code, as objects, or should we see them as social processes in which the social world is embodied in the substrate of the code?'[38]

In algorithmically infused societies,[39] the social fabric is co-shaped by layers of algorithmic and human behaviour, so it is necessary to discuss ways of dealing with the potentially harmful, sometimes unexpected, consequences of algorithmic systems. A recent study demonstrated, for instance, how Twitter's automated image-cropping algorithm created cases of representational harm against marginalized groups, especially Black people and women, reinforcing the subordination of some groups along lines of identity,[40] with user agency suggested as a way to avoid racial or gender stereotypes.[41] Kyra Yee and colleagues advocate 'no crop' as a signal that the use of a machine-learning algorithm may not be appropriate for certain tasks if potential risks are high.[42]

Augmenting human agency is not, however, possible or effective to deal with many of the potential problems generated by algorithmic systems. As we will see in Chapter 6, transparency of both the outcomes and the procedures used by algorithmic systems is necessary for promoting accountability.[43] However, explaining the behaviour of real-world algorithmic systems such as search and recommendation platforms may be challenging or even impossible, because of the complexity of interactions between humans and algorithms.

The development of AI algorithms has reached new levels of capability and functionality with technologies such as foundation models, generative models, and language models. These advancements have created new tools and applications across various domains accelerating the use of artificial intelligence and offering new possibilities for interactions between humans and algorithms.[44]

A foundation model is any model trained on vast data sets that can be adapted to diverse applications. Generative AI is a type of model that can

---

[36] Bucher (2018: 20).
[37] Connolly (2020).
[38] Beer (2017).
[39] Wagner et al. (2021).
[40] Yee et al. (2021).
[41] Sweeney (2013).
[42] Yee et al. (2021).
[43] Diakopoulos (2020).
[44] Bommasani (2021).

create content such as text, images, audio, and code, in response to user prompts. It is a set of algorithms powered by large training data sets to generate content that seems realistic or factual but may be biased, inaccurate, or fictitious. Language model is a type of generative AI specializing in the generation of human-like text, used by many applications such as conversion of text to speech, language translation, and chatbots. Owing to the utilization of extensive and unverified training data, language models have the potential to generate content that can give rise to various issues. Examples of such problems include misinformation, discrimination against vulnerable groups, privacy violations, and copyright infringement.

Although language models such as ChatGPT are able to produce coherent and contextually relevant content during dialogues, they raise questions regarding the roles of both humans and algorithms.[45] The interaction between ChatGPT and users showcases a combination of algorithmic agency and human agency. Chatbots possess the capability autonomously to generate responses and engage in conversations without human interference. They exhibit algorithmic agency by comprehending prompts, analysing context, and producing coherent replies. Conversely, humans retain the agency to initiate prompts, ask questions, and provide instructions, thereby influencing the course and substance of the conversation.

Despite the technical opacity of algorithmic systems, humans have dealt with situations in which there was a need to establish forms of regulation and governance for artefacts that were not widely understood or understandable.[46] This has been a central element of how humans deal with many institutions. We argue that—similar to other institutions—today's algorithm-based technologies operate as vectors that create norms and (not necessarily formal) rules for influencing individual behaviour with collective outcomes.[47] Algorithms shape human behaviour by assigning meanings, obligations, permissions, or resources to human actions in opaque ways. They are artefacts created by humans, moulded in institutional contexts, that incorporate norms, rules, standards, and strategies that influence human behaviour and achieve determined goals. As such, institutional theories can offer insights and reflections on how we may contend with today's algorithmically infused societies.[48]

---

[45] Stokel-Walker and Van Noorden (2023).
[46] Just and Latzer (2017).
[47] Epstein and Robertson (2015); Pasquale (2015); O'Neil (2016); Bucher (2018); Zuboff (2019); Amoore (2020); Crawford (2021).
[48] Wagner et al. (2021).

Towards Algorithmic Institutionalism

Algorithms are at the heart of what Roger Silverstone once termed the *textures of experience*.[49] They are embedded in our own existence and in the ways through which we construct and change reality.

The social relevance of algorithms has stimulated a rapid growth in the literature devoted to comprehending them and their political dimensions.[50] Great strides have come from this body of scholarship as it identifies problems, processes, and outcomes of algorithms' power in society. Yet, despite this increasing attention to algorithms, the literature has not advanced an institutional reading of them. To remedy this situation, we build an original contribution about the role that algorithms play and then provide the lens of Algorithmic Institutionalism to make sense of algorithms as institutions.

What does it mean to think of algorithms as institutions? Why should we do it? Conceiving of algorithms as institutions means that we understand them as sets of rules that establish contexts in which individual choices and human interactions occur. These contexts are not simply a background for these actions and interactions but an infrastructure enabling certain courses of action and constraining others.

This idea is not exactly new. When Alan Turing asked if a 'machine can think', he emphasized the need for computers to have a control unit in addition to a data store and an executive unit.[51] The control unit would be computational artefacts—a 'book of rules' that would offer machines a set of instructions to be obeyed correctly. The need for this book of rules stems from the premise that a machine imitates the human mind. According to Turing, humans are intelligent because they store information about the world in memory, calculate possibilities, and act according to rules set by an external authority. These rules fulfil an intermediate function of human action, like institutions.

The foundations grounded by Turing place algorithms as a book of rules that perform control functions, offering action patterns, meaning structures, and grammar to machines. If the agency of machines depends on the book of rules to be performed, then, in the same way, these rules can structure and give meaning to the actions of humans when they interact with these machines. For Turing, these rules were fixed and neutral, as they were technically dictated. However, the advancement of science and technology studies

---

[49] Silverstone (2012).
[50] Rubel et al. (2021).
[51] Turing (1950).

shows that these artefacts are inherently political objects. According to Langdon Winner, technical devices and systems are essential in everyday life and contain possibilities for many ways of ordering human activity.[52] Or, as Lessig puts it, 'code is law', because technology is used to enforce existing rules, regulating human action.[53]

The control function attributed to algorithms as a book of rules, according to Turing, helps to understand how humans shape their actions based on the rules inscribed in computational codes. But, contrary to Turing's thought, this book of rules is not fixed: just as in other institutions, rules in contemporary society are adaptive and dynamically shaped by interactions between humans and machines. The advancement of systems based on machine learning makes these institutions more dynamic, and the rules are moulded, not in a fixed and invariable nature, set in stone, but dynamically by reinforcements and feedbacks that arise from different aspects of their application in society. Thus, algorithms reproduce norms, rules, and strategies for human action in more complex frameworks, influencing individual choices and social behaviour.

This is quite clear when we think about recommendation algorithms. The suggested titles in a streaming platform, for example, affect individual decisions (of what to watch and what not to watch) and have collective implications (in cultural and economic terms, for instance). Another example could be the role algorithms play in framing our interactions in social media and the broader effects of these interactions to politics, culture, and sociability. The affordances of platforms and the way they provide preferential exposure to certain content over others creates communicative contexts that mark what we say and how we do it. Yet another example is how governments use algorithmic systems to implement public policy, essentially performing governmental action and having an impact on society in diverse fields of action. Algorithms can shape the scope of public space, increasing or decreasing reflexivity, and they can operate decisions in a technocratic way, reducing publicity and the democratic character of public decisions.[54]

In the contemporary world, human–machine interactions transpire through multiple interfaces designed to improve the user experience. We interact with different digital interfaces to fulfil our desires, tastes, preferences, or interests, and, behind these interfaces, algorithms incorporate and produce rules, norms, standards, and strategies to achieve a socially designed objective. According to Herbert Simon and Allen Newell, 'an "interface" in

---

[52] Winner (1980).
[53] Lessig (1999).
[54] Eubanks (2018).

today's terms [is] between an "inner" environment, the substance and organization of the artifact itself, and an "outer" environment, the surroundings in which it operates".[55] Algorithms are rationalizing artefacts because they capture the human experience through data and provide attempts to solve problems through outputs applied to social reality. In other words, algorithms are designed with a purpose and can organize different aspects of human life. These interactions can be inclusive or exclusive, more (or less) egalitarian, stereotyped (or not), and they have a direct impact on human action. Algorithms are institutions.

These interactions are at the heart of the power of digital technologies and the figurative reimagining of the world through instruments incorporated into social action. This insight into how algorithms create power contexts stems from theories such as Joseph Weizenbaum's. For him, the power of algorithms emerges from the fact that they create interactions between humans and humans and between humans and machines.[56] Social interactions are rule-governed games. These games imply a language that defines what is allowed, prohibited, and made possible. Computers incorporate the rules to interpret a given phenomenon in the form of data and produce knowledge outputs. How we incorporate technologies has social and political implications, since algorithmic systems, often considered a simple instrument, constitute a language of social action and new meanings and forms of power relations. Tools such as computational systems provide new possibilities for the imaginative reconstruction of the world. However, according to Weizenbaum, the way computational systems designers re-create the world implies the prominence of an instrumental reason.[57]

Philip Napoli was the first to make this link explicit, mobilizing institutional theories to make sense of algorithms.[58] Drawing from Scott,[59] he argued that algorithms have regulative, normative, and cultural–cognitive dimensions, which could be mapped in recent changes in media consumption and production. Napoli claimed that there needed to be a broader effort to mobilize institutional lenses and concepts to understand algorithms and their roles in societies.

A theory that conceives of algorithms as institutions in contemporary society can offer new insights into the interactions between humans and algorithmic systems, as well as into the interactions between different

---

[55] Simon and Newell (1958).
[56] Weizenbaum (1976).
[57] Weizenbaum (1976).
[58] Napoli (2013, 2014).
[59] Scott (2014).

institutions working towards collective goals. Given the significant social, political, economic, and cultural impacts of algorithmic systems, a comprehensive framework is needed to enable a deeper and multifaceted understanding of the social dynamics shaped by algorithms. Moreover, a well-developed institutional approach to algorithms can pave the way for a necessary political discussion towards their democratization.

We see this book as part of this endeavour, advancing the agenda of Algorithmic Institutionalism. At its heart lies the premise that human interactions performed from computational interfaces that comprise different aspects of human life are structured by rules and norms embodied in algorithms. And, because these algorithms are books of rules, they define meanings, organize, and influence human action in society. The rules of interaction are grounded within the algorithms' agency. They do not have the power to define choices made by individuals and collective actions, but they set the boundaries for these choices and actions to happen, just as institutions do. By defining these boundaries, the algorithms frame the choices that individuals can make.

There is a second aspect relevant to understanding algorithms as institutions. How institutions create the rules that establish contexts for actions reveals much about their historical dynamic of interaction, and the stabilization of practices, values, and orders of interaction happens through their institutionalization. Institutions are, in a way, signs of how we shaped the rules of interaction through deliberate decisions or simply taken-for-granted ways of acting. They do not always indicate stabilization, however. Social change is marked by processes of de-institutionalization and re-institutionalization. Ruptures are marked by displacement or erosion of some existing institutions and the creation of new ones. Institutions are, hence, like Janus looking in two opposite directions: they point simultaneously to the past and to the future.[60]

A good example of algorithms' role in de-institutionalization and re-institutionalization processes comes from online dating. Dating can be viewed as an institution, characterized by a set of informal rules and practices. Traditional ways of finding a partner for a date would be to go out and meet someone in person or to connect with them through a recommendation from friends and relatives. Meeting a partner through these methods has declined over time, though, and research shows that Internet meeting has displaced the role that family and friends once played in bringing couples together. As a consequence, platforms and their algorithms have de-institutionalized

---

[60] March and Olsen (1975).

dating processes,[61] with online dating processes offering much larger pools of potential partners compared to the number of people who could be introduced by family and friends. Dating apps such as Tinder, eHarmony, Gindr, Planet Romeo and Match.com offer an additional avenue for LGBTQ communities, with the algorithms for matching people improving over time. Moreover, as in-person contact became risky owing to a global pandemic, people turned to digital environments for human connection, making digital dates the new normal, and algorithms, instead of friends and family, the go-to matchmaker for people looking for partners. The dating process has been re-institutionalized now, with people increasingly trusting dating platforms' algorithms, their new rules and norms defining meanings and organizing human relationships.

Thinking of algorithms as institutions involves capturing the historical dynamic. On the one hand, algorithms embody the values and patterns of interaction currently in vogue. They stabilize and reproduce comprehensions of reality, normative aspirations, and taken-for-granted ways of making decisions. Algorithms tell us much about who we are and how we have arrived at this point. But, on the other hand, algorithms also change existing patterns of interaction, with deep implications for social life. Algorithmic societies challenge established ways of acting and displace traditional social and political institutions. They have changed the way we circulate in city streets, the way we order food, the way we meet other people, and even the way we talk. Algorithmic decisions affect how we make sense of one another and make key decisions about our lives, whether the topic is access to health, jobs, or pensions. They have changed how we experience elections, representation, and political engagement. As institutions, algorithms are constantly in the business of crystallizing certain affordances and patterns of action, while also displacing and re-creating others.

In advancing the approach of Algorithmic Institutionalism, we claim that it is capable not only of diagnosing how algorithms embed, reproduce, reconfigure, and organize power in different arenas but also of highlighting the ways forward to discuss issues related to transparency, justice, governance, and democracy. Algorithmic systems organize power in context, because they are institutions that act in contemporary political dynamics. They perform agency and interact with humans, and the outcomes of these interactions modify society's structure, in turn creating new political orders. Such political

---

[61] Rosenfeld et al. (2019).

orders may be democratic or authoritarian—or epistocratic[62]—depending on how we deal with algorithms and their consequences.

Like other institutions, algorithms do not have the power to determine the future, but they can be open to reflexivity and human agency. And, again like other institutions, algorithms are artefacts designed by humans. Their power depends on the interactions between the system designers, programmers, data analysts, and different organizations—public and private—that guide their constitution. If we are to observe how humans create new power structures mediated by algorithms, we must also understand how various aspects related to the effects of these power structures have an impact on society.

Beyond Attractive Dichotomies

Algorithmic Institutionalism seems particularly productive in reading contemporary power relationships, as it helps us navigate four dichotomies that seem tempting when we think about algorithms.

Animism versus instrumentalism. Algorithms are sometimes conceived of as an autonomous entity that acts, desires, and seeks its own advancement autonomously. As science fiction has made clear, there is an ongoing fear that animated robots and mechanisms of AI may rebel against humans. Animistic views are not, however, restricted to literature. Some often speak of algorithms as fully autonomous agents determining people's choices. Occasionally, they are thought of as if they were agents with their own free will, determining courses of action and, thus, being responsible and morally accountable for the effect they may have. On the other pole of the dichotomy is the conception that algorithms are tools invented by humans, simply reproducing what they are told to do. Most tools are seen as neutral, with outcomes determined by the intentions of the one using them; so, as tools, algorithms cannot be judged morally. Individual intentions can be praised or criticized, but the idea of evaluating a tool according to moral and ethical standards does not make sense.

Algorithmic Institutionalism understands that algorithms are not fully autonomous animated entities, but it does not conceive of them as neutral tools created and employed by humans. Like institutions, algorithms should be thought of as products of human interaction that retroactively affect humans with their affordances and structures. Humans act through

---

[62] Holst (2012); Brennan (2016).

them, but they also are affected by them, as they enable and induce certain behaviours while inhibiting others.

Structure versus agency. While some may think of algorithms as part of the infrastructures of contemporary societies, limiting human agency and determining courses of actions, others frame them as elements of reality that are submitted to human agency and to their choices, intentions, and purposes. Structuralists tend to focus on stability, continuity, and human containment through arrangement whose grounds lie beyond human control. Agent-centric perspectives emphasize creativity, innovation, and human capacity to exert control upon these arrangements.

Algorithmic Institutionalism understands algorithms as elements that provide continuous mediation between structures and humans' capacity to act. Algorithms have a structural dimension as they restrict action and delineate courses of action, but they also promote agency and are affected by action, as humans reinvent ways to interact with systems and with other humans through them. Algorithms are not structures set in stone, but social institutions re-created in, through, and with human action. On the one hand, they condition behaviours, but, on the other, they work as action arenas, where individuals play with their patterns and rules of decision to reinvent outcomes and act strategically.

Collective versus individual. Algorithms cannot be placed only in the box of collective artefacts nor in the box of individual tools. As with any other social institution, algorithms are created and enacted collectively, but they affect individuals in specific ways. In addition—and like other institutions—algorithms suffer the impact of individual actions that may end up producing collective outcomes. They are, therefore, simultaneously collective and individual both in their constitution and in their implications.

Algorithmic Institutionalism understands that algorithms have collective implications via individual effects. They have quite particular consequences to individual lives, but their social impacts are far beyond an aggregation of these individual effects and involve reconfiguring the textures and structures of our collective existence. Building from institutional theories, Algorithmic Institutionalism navigates the micro and macro levels to make sense of algorithms' origins and consequences in the interplay between individuals and collectivities.

Determinism versus novelty. Since the Presocratics, philosophy has dealt with the tension between permanence and change. While determinists believe in causal chains and natural rules that predefine outcomes, those focusing on impermanence and change save some space for serendipity and innovative action in producing unforeseen consequences. If we look at algorithms, a deterministic approach would see them as consequences of causes that can be traced and as holding their futures in their own existence. They would be dots in a continuum, with implications already predefined even if unknown. Looking at algorithms from the lens of novelty, on the other hand, implies acknowledging their potential to take part in unpredictable interactions—between humans, between humans and machines, and between machines.

Algorithmic Institutionalism understands algorithms as historical constructs that derive from previous choices, establishing path dependence. Nevertheless, it does not reduce path dependence to historical determinism and is attentive to the emergence of novelty, which may occur in critical junctures, but also in more continuous processes.[63] Novelty can derive from changes in the context, both from individual agency and from complex interplays between layers of algorithmic decisions and human actions.

Thus, navigating between the poles of these four dichotomies, Algorithmic Institutionalism is particularly capable of dealing with contemporary dilemmas. Like other institutions, algorithms create orders—and stabilizing processes—that are grounded on power relations. As with other institutions, however, algorithms do not exist or govern independently from human action. Humans still play a key role in making political and moral choices, and they must find ways to deal with these structures that set boundaries for their actions. Algorithmic Institutionalism offers a theoretical path and a methodological approach to make sense of these processes.

The Epistemology of Algorithms: Situations, Frames, and Scripts

A proper comprehension of institutions requires an epistemological framework capable of making sense of their ability to influence human behaviour and shape collective outcomes. Long ago, Karl Popper took interest in this direction, developing an approach that understands institutions as providers of situational contexts in which humans are inserted and act. Popper argued that situational analysis was a central element for constructing knowledge in the social sciences.[64] According to him, the work of social reform, carried out by social engineers, depended on creating social technologies.[65] The main

---

[63] Thelen (1999).
[64] Popper (2002b).
[65] Connolly (2020).

task of social engineers was to delineate institutions considered from a functional point of view—as a means to achieve certain goals—and assess them according to their adequacy, efficiency, and simplicity. Popper emphasized that institutions were not mechanical tools but dynamic processes adapting in relation to shifting organisms and situations.[66]

Much of this institutional theory depends on situational logic, which discusses aspects of the design and construction of artefacts representing technologies. The design of institutions responds to problem-solving perspectives through which engineers (social or technological) understand situations and build responses based on action animators. Consideration of action situations is also essential to understanding technologies' impacts on society and their political activity in shaping the rationality of human action.

Situational logic is at the heart of an epistemology of algorithms as institutions. A relevant body of institutional theories recognizes that institutions enable individuals to situate, perceive, identify, and label the concrete interactions in which they are inserted. In other words, institutions offer individuals *frames* with which they organize their experiences in the world.[67]

The notion of frames was first proposed by Gregory Bateson and developed by Erving Goffman.[68] Frames are shared patterns of interpretation mobilized to define a situation, pervading the way actors engage with it. Frames operate through salience and exclusion, shaping how we perceive and experience reality. Goffman's concept of frames starts from the idea that institutionalization depends on organizing principles that govern social events and our subjective engagement with them. Frames are intersubjectively built and updated via the practices of social actors.[69]

Institutions offer not only contexts of action but also frames that define these contexts. In doing so, they provide guidance on how individuals should perceive reality and attribute meaning to the situations in which they are inserted.[70] Algorithms likewise provide frames for action. In some respects, algorithms automate these frames, classifying, labelling, and routinizing situations to place individuals in the world.

In framing the world, institutions also offer action scripts: patterns of action exist, enabling both rationalization and non-reflexive behaviour. Scripts routinize courses of action, and each institution is grounded within these routinized protocols to deal with specific types of situations. Scripts

[66] Popper (2002a).
[67] Hay (2008).
[68] Goffman (1986); Bateson (2000).
[69] Entman (1993); Van Gorp (2006); Mendonça and Simões (2012).
[70] Hay (2008).

are based on frames and work as a 'predetermined, stereotyped sequence of actions that define a well-known situation'.[71] They work like grammars or recipes, structuring preferences, routines, and pathways. Aneesh identifies how algorithmic systems rationalize and reorganize work relationships, creating new scripts for action in society.[72]

As institutions, algorithms are human constructs that intend to carry out the task of social engineering advocated by Popper. They provide frames that indicate how the world should be understood, then script appropriate behaviour. Algorithmic Institutionalism seeks to understand the different frames and scripts embedded in codes that shape sociotechnical systems with social, political, economic, and cultural implications. Sociotechnical systems create social action programmes and cognitive structures that influence—without determining—human behaviour in different situations. In this sense, Algorithmic Institutionalism enables the handling of different analytical lenses aimed at comprehending algorithms' design and rationality, while also looking at the impacts that emerge from social interactions organized by the institutional context generated by them. It is an interdisciplinary effort based on the analysis of algorithms as central institutions of contemporary society.

Concluding Remarks

The expression *social engineers* is used here purposely to link computer science and the social sciences. The design and analysis of algorithms in both fields are connected by the situational premise of knowledge with the objective of producing changes in society. On the one hand, computer scientists collect and process data that frame a situation, defining a problem and addressing it through scripts coded in the design of technological solutions. For example, computer scientists use big data methodologies to understand situations that are mirrored through massive volumes of data to produce classifications, labels, connections, identifications, and perceptions, addressing a problem through mathematical models. On the other hand, social scientists—working with institutionalist lenses—seek to understand frames and scripts mobilized to define social problems, often proposing institutional changes to affect collective outcomes.

Understanding what algorithms are and how they change society's action situations is at the heart of the epistemology of Algorithmic Institutionalism.

---

[71] Schank and Abelson (1977: 41).
[72] Aneesh (2006).

With that in mind, in Chapter 2, we advance an analytical framework for the use of Algorithmic Institutionalism to make sense of contemporary issues. The following chapters aim to apply this analytical framework to cases that reveal different levels of the phenomenon. We begin with a detailed examination of the use of algorithms in a specific area—namely, the field of security (Chapter 3). We then broaden our focus to the employment of algorithms by governments, focusing on their platformization and on the use of algorithmic systems in policymaking (Chapter 4). Finally, we delve into a wide-ranging discussion of recommendation systems, which pervade numerous applications of algorithmic systems (Chapter 5). Chapter 6 then builds on to the big picture to discuss a central element of institutionalism along with a key concern in contemporary scholarship about algorithms: can these institutions be democratized?

2
Reading Contemporary Issues via the Lens of Algorithmic Institutionalism

There is a growing interest in the idea of algorithms as institutions, with different approaches informing the need to build an institutional theory of algorithms.[1] As with any other rationalizing mechanism, algorithms embed different forms of power relations in their attempt to deal with uncertainties. Algorithms absorb, through data, a stream of preferences, ideas, discourses, and behaviours, then produce outputs somehow related to the intended goals of those who design these technologies. Institutions and algorithms are human-created artefacts with the potential to solve problems, shape collective action, and achieve goals. Applied to different areas of human existence, algorithms are designed to make decisions and perform tasks allegedly in more objective, effective, consistent, and reliable ways.

New Institutionalism is a family of social theories that explain society and politics through their institutions. This approach to studying institutions focuses on the constraining and enabling effects of formal and informal rules on the individuals' and groups' behaviour.[2] With this in mind, this chapter advances the understanding of algorithms as institutions, reconstructing the foundations of institutional theories in four different approaches: *sociological institutionalism, rational-choice institutionalism, historical institutionalism,* and *discursive institutionalism*. Drawing from these four approaches, we then present an analytical framework aimed at operationalizing institutional theories to make sense of algorithmic systems. Our framework focuses on six dimensions: institution building and design; historical processes; rules and norms; power relations; gaming; and discursive dimensions.

Institutional Theories

The first and fundamental question that arises when approaching algorithms as institutions is how to define institutions. In political science, institutional

---

[1] Napoli (2013); Ananny (2016); Caplan and boyd (2018).
[2] Peters (2019).

theories claimed to devote more attention to the formal structures that would govern human behaviour.[3] So-called old institutionalism scrutinized the role of laws and formal rules, while adopting a structuralist perspective of power and broad historical approaches in terms of methods.[4]

The behaviourist revolution had important implications in developing political science as an academic field aimed to explain and predict various phenomena related to collective action, political culture, and agents' behaviours in different contexts. From a methodological point of view, behaviourism fostered an empirical turn, mainly driven by experiments. Theoretically, it strengthened anti-normative approaches and methodological individualism, focusing on individuals and their behaviours, rather than broader structures.[5] In behaviourism, institutions were not investigated as central to the understanding of human behaviour because often they were reduced to aggregates of individual preferences.

In response to behaviourism, institutional theories reconceived some of their assumptions, building a middle-range theory that circumscribes the importance of institutions in shaping human behaviour, while advancing in the proposition of more systematic empirical studies. James March and Johan Olsen defined these developments as New Institutionalism.[6] They posited that, while old institutionalism disregarded the role of individuals in the construction of collective processes, behaviourism reduced collective behaviour to individual decisions, neglecting interactions, structures, and the role of social values.

In New Institutionalism, the concept of institution refers to 'a relatively enduring collection of rules and organized practices, embedded in structures of meaning and resources that are relatively invariant in the face of turnover of individuals and relatively resilient to the idiosyncratic preferences and expectations of individuals and changing external circumstances'.[7] Rules and routinized practices provide appropriate codes of behaviour for specific roles in given situations. These structures of meaning are essential to

---

[3] Wilson (1956).
[4] 'Old' institutionalism denotes a formal, descriptive, and legalistic conception of the study of institutions. This institutionalism goes back to the classic work of Montesquieu, defining different natures and attributes of government and how the separation of powers is essential for modern constitutional governments. The old institutionalism is essential in the Anglo-American tradition, especially in the Progressive Movement from the nineteenth to the twentieth centuries. In the United States, Woodrow Wilson and others reinforced the need for reforms in political representation's bureaucracy and structure. We also mention the entire tradition of constitutionalism in continental Europe and its influence in Latin America. Old institutionalism founded the roots of political analysis and the design of institutions by constructing a legalistic, structuralist, holistic, historicist methodology based on normative analysis.
[5] Easton (1965).
[6] March and Olsen (1984).
[7] March and Olsen (2006: 3).

explain, justify, and legitimize behavioural decisions.[8] Norms frame power relations, enabling certain actors access to given resources and possibilities of action. From this perspective, resources are tied to rules, enabling and constraining actors in different ways. As institutions, algorithms incorporate codes of behaviour—expected or produced—aiming at solving a problem or defining situations, frames, and action scripts.

Institutions are external to individual behaviour and articulate how individuals make collective decisions and solve problems. They define grammars of structured power relations, where norms work as prescriptions for actions that should be performed, that are prohibited, or that may take place.[9] In a nutshell, institutions present the rules of the game.[10]

When people play chess, football, or hide and seek, their behaviours are marked by the game's rules, which define the roles, movements that are allowed or prohibited, and elements to be considered by players in selecting their strategies. Rules do not determine the results, but they outline each player's possible courses of action and the resources they may have in different situations. The rules of the game do not establish the outcomes of various interactions in society, either: interactions are subject to crises, uncertainties, or ambiguities, making the determination of behaviour impossible. However, institutions are relevant predictors of behaviour by providing frames, scripts, and situations to actors.

A chess player limited to her king and one pawn has extremely limited resources and possibilities of action, for instance. In the same way, when we think about a given political system's institutions or about a social arrangement (such as a family), we must consider how formal and informal rules shape the boundaries of individual choices and behaviours. For instance, in proportional electoral systems, while an open-list system induces internal competition in parties, closed lists foment a more collective approach, strengthening parties' internal coherence. In another example, different types of families may foster diverse types of rules and expectations, which are then taken for granted in everyday life, thus pervading the division of house chores or the way kids are educated.

Sometimes, rules and norms may be scrutinized and become the focus of struggles or discussions. Children who play hide and seek often spend substantial time discussing the rules that are considered valid and managing conflicts. Members of some families may also eventually challenge the household's division of labour. The extent to which a rule may be questioned,

---

[8] Hay (2008).
[9] Ostrom (2005).
[10] North (1990).

though, depends on several factors, including the nature of the rule, its cultural embeddedness, its normative strength, the equilibria upon which it is sustained, and the relations of power it mediates.

These illustrative examples show how rules—which are somehow external to individuals, although enacted and updated by them—shape the boundaries of individuals' behaviours by outlining what is allowed, prohibited, or enhanced, as well as by distributing roles and resources that matter for the choices that individuals make. New Institutionalism, in its diversity, grasps several dimensions of these complex processes, grounding not only individual behaviours but also their social foundations and collective implications.

Shedding light on these processes, New Institutionalism provides an interesting lens to conceive of what algorithmic systems do and how they work in contemporary societies. Organizing and defining how humans interact with different digital interfaces, or even between artificial agents in highly complex sociotechnical systems, algorithms play a role in the continuous process of norm-making. The corollary of Algorithmic Institutionalism is that the power of algorithms should not be explained as an attribute of agents—of systems or of their designers, for example—nor as an attribute of an external social structure. Instead, the power of algorithms depends on a structuring process that involves complex interactions between humans and machines.

New Institutionalism, however, is not a single theory. Instead, it conveys different approaches to institutions, which have often followed parallel routes, despite the possibility of bridges and cross-fertilizations.[11] The following section presents some veins of New Institutionalism that are relevant to our framework.

Approaches to Institutions and Algorithms

A first step in the understanding of institutional theories is to recognize that institutions can mean many things. Therefore, constructing an analytical framework for Algorithmic Institutionalism requires different institutional approaches that try to explain power relations and how they are shaped.[12] To investigate institutions, we rely on four analytical approaches: sociological, rational choice, historical, and discursive.

---

[11] Thelen (1999).
[12] Hall and Taylor (1996); Thelen (1999); Peters (2019).

Sociological Institutionalism

Sociological institutionalism is the approach of New Institutionalism that addresses institutions as elements for the rationalization and organization of social life. The main area of interest of sociological institutionalism is the institutionalization of *normative order*—that is, the way through which a procedural system encodes the use of power and becomes significant for a given collectivity's members.[13] The normative order means a set of values and perspectives that organize collective goals. These values and perspectives represent organized structures that frame the action parameters of individuals in collective environments.

Philip Selznick's work laid the foundations of sociological institutionalism, focusing on institutionalization and institutional change within organizations.[14] According to Selznick, the role of organizational leadership is to establish and protect a value system created within the institution and reproduced by the organization's members as a structure that precedes actual actions. His work served as the foundation for a whole body of theory dedicated to studying organizations and processes of institutionalization and change, mainly because of the bureaucratic phenomenon.[15]

In the lens of sociological institutionalism, institutions are organized structures that frame action situations, as discussed in Chapter 1.[16] The assumption of theories of sociological institutionalism is a cognitive structure defined within organizations that shapes individuals' rationality. Consistent with the antecedents of Weberian sociology, the rationalization of action and motivation for it not only stem from preferences but also depend on organizational work to create meaning. Institutionalization depends on handling symbols, shaping the collective behaviour and the individuals who are part of it.[17] Sociological institutionalism configures a theoretical body concerned with how and why the members of an institution perceive situations within structures and build frames to make decisions.[18] Organizational structure, when

---

[13] Parsons (1949).
[14] Selznick (1949).
[15] Sociological institutionalism has an important influence on Weberian sociology in its foundations. Sociological institutionalism is related to the process of bureaucratization and rationalization of modern organizations—both public and private—creating hierarchical structures based on command-and-control relations legitimized by law. The bureaucratic phenomenon, as designated here, refers to this rationalization process, ranging from modern industrial organizations and unions to governments and political parties.
[16] Peters (2019).
[17] Meyer and Rowan (1977); Hall and Taylor (1996).
[18] Berger and Luckmann (1967).

institutionalized, is central to explaining why individuals follow organizationally defined scripts.[19]

The rationalization of society stems from its organizational structures' expansion, where institutions emerge in multiple social and political settings. Just as Weber identified a tendency for societies to converge to an iron cage of bureaucracy[20], the work of Paul DiMaggio and Walter Powell further developed an institutionalist reading based on sociology.[21] The thesis of *institutional isomorphism*, in which they worked, claims that institutionalization shapes a collective rationality that defines the process and structure of one organization to those of another. Patterns of organizational change follow a trend towards homogenization within an institutional field that comprises different institutions within which multiple interactions between organizations occur, creating patterns of behaviour. Interactions create organizational networks from which changes occur through mutually dependent relationships of organizations in each field. These connections and relationships of dependence lead to a pattern of change arising from coercion, mimesis, or new normative patterns.[22]

The lens of sociological institutionalism is helpful to make sense of algorithms. Algorithmic systems create action patterns and rationalize diverse organizational fields, producing *isomorphic change*—that is, entities operating in a given field tend to develop similar shapes and structures. Algorithmic systems work as bureaucratic mechanisms that induce changes and institutionalize new macro-structural processes, reflecting isomorphic change.[23] Algorithms are mediators of political and social processes that automate organizations and structure the rationalization of user behaviour by attributing meanings to action.[24] Algorithms control and protect norms, establishing patterns of organizational change in different fields such as traditional media, governments, businesses, and industry. In the algorithm-driven economy, Amazon has control over third-party retailers on its platform, and it also sets the rules for businesses to be accepted, promoted, or removed from the platform.[25] Platform algorithms function as gatekeepers protecting rules and informal norms.

The field of news media offers another example of an isomorphic pattern, where different companies must adapt to patterns of communication

---

[19] Stinchcombe (1997).
[20] Weber (1978).
[21] DiMaggio and Powell (1983).
[22] DiMaggio and Powell (1983).
[23] Caplan and boyd (2018).
[24] Napoli (2014).
[25] Ezrachi and Stucke (2016).

established by platforms such as Facebook.[26] Social-media algorithms restructure newsfeeds, redefining the newsworthiness and strategies of visibility that drive journalism. Algorithms used by digital media platforms re-institutionalized the entire news media field, creating relationships of mutual dependence between organizations and new automated communication standards.[27] In the news media organizational field, the change often occurs through mimesis, where different organizations adjust to a new pattern that is established and institutionalized through algorithms.

Algorithmic systems may be conceived of as managing mechanisms that organize relationships between organizations and individuals, handling symbols and structuring action scripts. Another important example comes from governments' digital transformation processes, which also follow isomorphic patterns. Different governments are digitizing public services, following the symbolic argument, and promising to expand public administration's capacities, efficiency, and liability. Governments are creating platforms with implicit data collection to implement user convenience and personalization. As a result, governments worldwide produce a mimetic pattern of change, exchanging benchmarks and new normative patterns disseminated by international organizations such as the Organization for Economic Cooperation and Development (OECD).

The analysis of algorithms as institutions, under the light of sociological institutionalism, assumes that algorithms represent organizational archetypes, embedding in computational codes the institutional logic of a given organizational field. Algorithms manipulate symbols and build action scripts and broad cognitive structures that can emulate, reconstruct, or crystallize societal structures.

Rational-Choice Institutionalism

Rational-choice institutionalism is a branch of New Institutionalism that approaches institutions as a set of rules that operate as coordinating mechanisms, thus generating diverse forms of equilibria in situations where there are multiple actors seeking to maximize their expected utility.[28] The rationality of institutions lies in the fact that individuals' actions are based on their preferences, which have two properties: completeness and consistency.[29] Completeness means that the individual can express preferences between the

---

[26] Caplan and boyd (2018).
[27] Napoli (2014).
[28] Thelen (1999).
[29] Rabushka and Shepsle (2009).

alternatives offered, ranking and choosing among the offered alternatives and directing their course of action to fulfil their preferences. The consistency property is characterized by the fact that preferences are transitive, following Kenneth Arrow's impossibility theorem.[30] The rationale of institutions lies in the fact that they reduce externalities, transaction costs, and uncertainties, ensuring a process of aggregation of preferences into collective choices.[31]

In this sense, institutions are conceived of as collections of rules that shape incentives and constraints for the individuals' rational behaviour. Individuals form institutions to make collective decisions with the aim of aggregating complex and transitive preferences. Institutions produce some predictability and regularity of outcomes that would benefit all participants in a community by reducing uncertainty across the range of available decisions to social actors.[32] The absence or failure of institutions generates collective irrationality.[33] This assumption of rationality leads rational-choice institutionalism to two fundamental orders of problems: first, how institutions are designed to shape individual behaviours, and, second, how individuals interact with these institutions to fulfil their preferences. In both cases, institutions emerge to shape the interactions among individuals and to generate equilibrium in situations, so as to reduce uncertainties arising from political conflict.

The first order of problems observes the importance of decision rules. To rational-choice institutionalism, institutions are human artefacts for decision-making. Decisions provide individuals with motivations for action that are both positive (incentives) and negative (constraints). Behavioural dynamics are guided by utility maximization, enabling the measurement and modelling of individual behaviour in the context of institutions.[34] According to rational-choice institutionalism, collective decisions depend on rules and procedures that organize decision-making, so changes in decision rules alter the collective decision. In rational-choice institutionalism, decision rules will establish who has the power to make rules as well as when, how, and where. Decision rules define who has the authority to create rules and under what conditions they guide institutional designers' behaviour.[35] There are variations in rational-choice institutionalism—in particular, the difference in

[30] Kenneth Arrow's impossibility theorem is applied to voting systems, where the aim is to produce a collective decision. The theorem reflects that aggregating voter preference orders does not produce a collective preference order. According to Arrow, rather than imposition, the theorem requires non-dictatorship, universality of preferences, independence of irrelevant alternatives, and positive association of social and individual values. The theorem's postulate is that preferences are transitive and social choices are always limited. See Arrow (1950).
[31] Shepsle (1989); North (1990); Ostrom (2005).
[32] Weingast (2002).
[33] Ostrom (1999).
[34] Shepsle (1989).
[35] Buchanan and Tullock (1962).

behaviour models that arise from rule-based conceptions, principal-agent models, and game-theoretical models.[36]

The second order of problems is concerned with understanding how individuals act based on the rationale of institutions. Rational-choice theories assume that preferences are external to institutions, which process these preferences and lead to outcomes. For example, electoral institutions process voter preferences and define electoral results based on rules for counting votes and using them to distribute legislative seats and/or define governments. The main feature of institutions is that they will operate in a regulatory rather than a normative or cognitive way.[37] This regulatory logic means that, in many aspects, institutions follow a systemic logic based on payoffs for individuals, rewarding or punishing them based on the set of rules that regulate power relations.

Rational-choice institutionalism can have different applications for the study of algorithmic systems following the two aforementioned orders of problems. In the first analytical focus, the design of algorithms involves theoretical and experimental corollaries arising from collective action games and dilemmas such as the prisoner's dilemma, the tragedy of the commons, and cooperative games.[38] The rationality of an algorithm, similar to the rationality of an institution, demands Nash equilibria to support decision systems and incorporate users' expected behaviours.[39] In this first order of problems, rational-choice theories make it possible to understand algorithms as human

---

[36] These differences from rational choice institutionalism approaches concern the modelling parameters. Rule-based models seek the empirical significance of institutional rules and procedures in human behaviour. In Ostrom's (1990) study of the governance of the commons, games and interactions depend on empirical postulates collected in different situations of practical action. Principal-agent models refer to interactions between an asset owner—or principal—and an agent delegated to manage the asset on behalf of the principal. Principal-agent models are applied to the study of bureaucratic agents' behaviour, who act on behalf of a principal within democratic regimes, as studies by McCubbins and Schwartz (1984) and Lupia and McCubbins (1994) demonstrate. Finally, game-theoretical models are frameworks for conceiving action situations in competitive relations to understand decisions' optimizations present in several studies, such as in Axelrod (1984) and Scharpf (1997). The differences in the assumptions of formal models in political science configure many internal debates in rational choice, defining a diversity of methodologies to address the phenomenon of institutions.

[37] Scott (2014).

[38] According to John von Neumann and Oskar Morgerstern (2021), games represent frameworks of action situations that allow the mathematical formulation of optimal decisions based on players' interactions. Games signify action situations from which the analyst can draw postulates for individual or collective decision and apply them in formulating empirical significance in real situations. In political science, the most mobilized games are the prisoner's dilemma, the tragedy of the commons, and cooperative games. The prisoner's dilemma is when individual decision-makers work with incentives to create a less-than-optimal decision because of difficulties in cooperation. The tragedy of the commons is a situation where individual decision-makers must manage a shared resource with the expectation that, without holding back the exploitation of that shared resource, it will become extinct and affect the entire community. Cooperative games represent situations of competition between groups of players (coalitions) due to the possibility of external enforcement. Game theory is not limited to these games and has different applications for political science, sociology, economics, biology, and computer science, among others.

[39] Nisan et al. (2007).

constructs designed to decide, orientated by the formalization of interactions that form collective behaviour. Algorithms, as institutions, are designed to optimize problem-solving or task performance.

In the second analytical focus of rational-choice institutionalism, the interaction between humans and digital interfaces is shaped by algorithms and among algorithmic layers in complex algorithmic systems. In this sense, algorithms have the potential to shape collective behaviour, but individuals still play with rules and norms embedded in algorithms to maximize their preferences. Algorithms shape different situations in which individuals interact by reacting to the environment, but individuals act. Understanding the outcomes of these interactions and their consequences is essential to Algorithmic Institutionalism.

An example of an algorithmic system that reflects these two analytical concerns is the Chinese government's Social Credit System.[40] In the first analytical dimension, this system is designed by the government to optimize the moral reform of Chinese society through the expansion of surveillance mechanisms and the definition of rewards and punishments for system users. The system links things such as shopping habits, friends, volunteer work, political positions, and obedience to social norms to produce social credit scores that define access to social goods and government services. Although several references interpreted the development of social credit as an intrinsic characteristic of the political authoritarianism of the Chinese government, it is worth noting that various platforms adopt similar strategies.[41] Examples include algorithmic platforms for financial services and recruiting and hiring services. The Social Credit System modifies interactions in society, making users play with the algorithm to maximize its utility and avoid punishment.

Rational-choice institutionalism drives our attention both to the design of algorithms and to how individuals interact with digital interfaces run on algorithms. Rational-choice theories are a useful tool for analysing the complexities of preference aggregation and the ways through which algorithms guide actions while also being affected by agency.

Historical Institutionalism

Historical institutionalism is an approach focusing on how time, historical sequences, and path dependence shape institutions that affect social, political, and economic behaviour, by above all limiting the options presented as

---

[40] Dai (2020).
[41] Burrell and Fourcade (2021: 225).

viable. It usually starts from the puzzles that emerge from empirical observation; then it defines the situations and frames that guide preferences.[42]

Critical to rational-choice institutionalism, the premise of this approach is that actors' preferences cannot be comprehended or inferred without contextual analysis. While the rational-choice approach uses deductive logic to assign preferences to actors and create formal models, historical institutionalism uses inductive logic, analysing preferences in context.[43] Studies based on historical institutionalism are usually diachronic, with time seen as a fundamental variable to understand preferences.[44] At its core, historical institutionalism pays significant attention to the historical development of institutions and how they are path dependent.

Path dependence is the central concept to understanding historical institutionalism's roots, meaning that an institution's historical development produces inertial dynamics. When an institution is formed, initial choices will influence future possibilities and choices.[45] In historical institutionalism, preferences are endogenous to institutions, shaped by ideas and paths that exert a cognitive motivation for agents. They are shaped within contexts marked by frames. Understanding why individuals behave according to norms means understanding the historically formed cognitive consistency, thereby giving meaning to actions.[46] Agents act not within a rational structure motivated by cost–benefit analysis but within contexts of meaning built over time.[47]

Historical institutionalists see institutions as the legacy of concrete historical processes.[48] Positive feedback explains institutions' formation and changes from initial institutional choices and how this feedback reinforces those choices.[49] This positive feedback is related to increasing returns that create cognitive structures shaping agents' actions. Institutions' historical development depends on these increasing returns and conditions the change process.[50] For example, institutional development drives technological

---

[42] Thelen (1999).
[43] Levi (1997).
[44] Pierson (2004).
[45] Krasner (1988); Skocpol (1992); Pierson (2000); Pierson and Skocpol (2002).
[46] An illustrative example of this is found in the use of algorithms applied to assess an individual's likelihood to relapse into crime. In the United States, the experiments carried out in courts with Correctional Offender Management Profiling for Alternative Sanctions (COMPAS) has produced outcomes that punished black individuals more than white individuals with a similar background. Criminal justice's automation tended to incorporate their path dependence because data typically routed to the initial choices or ideas that structured the institution in its moment (Park 2019).
[47] Steinmo (2019).
[48] Orren and Skowronek (1994).
[49] Pierson (2000).
[50] Zysman (1994).

development, not through evolution but through changes based on increasing returns and historical dynamics.[51] Technological changes usually respect the process of path dependence, depending on positive feedback where agents accommodate their strategies to prevailing patterns.[52] Change arises from processes conditioned by path dependence, where critical junctures often create the conditions for events and actors to make choices that will have legacies and constrain future options.[53] In addition to the approach's initial insights on the role of exogenous factors, such as crises, historical institutionalists complexified their views offering a nuanced perspective that conceives of changes as gradual, with actors exerting pressure for change and endogenous political dynamics taking place within institution.

Historical institutionalism can be an interesting analytical tool to address algorithms' power. A historical institutional reading of the algorithms is premised on how they structure power relations in time, encoding the initial choices and initiating processes of path dependence that influence future behaviour (of both humans and other algorithms). Algorithmic systems embed cognitive structures, reproducing structures and norms by framing business models that produce positive feedbacks and tending to reinforce the initial choices that define paths.

The algorithm's design, following a historical institutionalist reading, will be concerned with understanding the broader historical context that helps comprehend how that institution came to exist, as well as the returns and positive feedback that established developments marked by path dependence. An algorithm incorporates its own path dependence, as its formation (design) and interactions depend on positive feedback and the production of increasing returns to organize cognitive structures from frames. Algorithms' power lies in how they organize cognitive consistency to guide citizens' behaviour.

Individuals' interactions with algorithms, explained in terms of historical institutionalism, will be shaped by historical processes in which algorithms

---

[51] The concept of increasing returns originated from the economy being incorporated into the historical analysis of institutions. Increasing returns are the trend for the actor that is already ahead to go further in the market, industry, or business. On the other hand; actors who lose advantage tend to lose more. Increasing returns are positive feedback mechanisms that operate to reinforce what succeeds or aggravate what loses. The concept of increasing returns is applied to the study of technological changes, showing how positive feedback tends to reinforce the leadership position in markets or industry, amplifying political and market power over time. For example, the political power of technology companies derives from their function as market intermediaries, in which market power is translated into political power because consumers are motivated by the convenience produced by the algorithms. Positive feedback, based on consumer convenience, creates increasing returns and trends to reinforce the market power of some technology industries, such as Silicon Valley's big technical companies (Culpepper and Thelen 2021).
[52] Arthur (1989).
[53] Capoccia (2015).

incorporate changes, adapt to the environment, and produce patterns.[54] Algorithms incorporate these patterns into their design and reproduce an earlier path when it has increasing returns. Subsequent changes to the algorithm are conditioned by this path, which may occur by layering, drift, displacement, or conversion.[55]

Machine-learning, dynamic-programming, recursive, or backtracking algorithms incorporate logic that learns from the past to solve problems and accomplish tasks. Machine-learning algorithms create cognitive consistency with data to produce classifications and, in turn, organize decisions sustained on structured preferences that precede problem solving. Even if an algorithmic system incorporates new practices from critical junctures, its changes tend to be gradual, as choices, rules, and procedures reinforce initial decisions.

Although algorithms change over time, the interactions triggered by the algorithm tend to reiterate the design's initial choices and some of its unexpected consequences. For example, hate speech, misinformation, or disinformation continue to be disseminated on social media even as regulatory changes create layers of control. Corporations that control social-media algorithms are not fully capable of changing the initial choices of the platforms' business model, because hate speech and misinformation are embedded in the way they work. Platforms' content regulation is, hence, inherently and continuously path dependent.

Discursive Institutionalism

Discursive institutionalism encompasses quite different traditions that acknowledge the centrality of discourses in constructing preferences and in the way the normative orientations shaping interactions are enacted. Drawing from John Dryzek, Vivien Schmidt notes that the "'institutionalism" in

---

[54] One of the postulates of algorithms' design is that they must produce optimization to accomplish a previously defined objective. The argument defended here is that rational rules for validating systems do not always depend on optimization; sometimes, they also depend on historical processes that require adapting and changing the algorithm constantly. In this sense, an algorithm is not always a finished solution but depends on temporally constructed patterns. Increasing returns rely on this process.

[55] Institutional change is a common topic in studies of historical institutionalism. Institutions may change as a result of exogenous shocks or critical junctures, or they may change as a result of endogenous developments that have an incremental character. These incremental changes, according to Mahoney and Thelen (2010), can occur from four ideal types. (i) Layering occurs through amendments, revisions, or additions to existing rules. (ii) Drift occurs when rules remain identical, but their effects change because of shifts in external conditions. (iii) Conversion results from actors redirecting institutions to goals and effects that were not at the heart of their initial purposes and foci. (iv) Displacement occurs when new rules replace existing ones. Displacement is a kind of change that may be abrupt and entail a radical shift often featured in leading institutional theories. See also Hacker et al. (2015) and Koning (2016).

discursive institutionalism suggests that this approach is not only about the communication of ideas or "text" but also about the institutional context in which, and through which, ideas are communicated via discourse."[56] Discursive institutionalism points to the power of ideas embodied in discourses.[57] It unravels the relevance of discourses in shaping the rules and patterns that govern human interaction, while also disclosing how the meaning-making interactions of humans affect these same rules and patterns.

The role played by ideas is well documented in institutionalist literature, with relevant contributions coming from historical institutionalism[58] and sociological institutionalism.[59] Discursive institutionalism, however, emphasizes how ideas take shape in and through discourses, which mediate human interaction.[60] Discourses simultaneously constrain and enable human action to the extent in which discourses work as a structural force—delimiting what is conceivable and capable of being expressed—but also as a field of creative action and innovations.[61] Discourses are the common grounds that host and shape our interactions, while also expressing the innovative dimension of agency upon this commonality.

In this sense, discourses are particularly relevant for comprehending stability and change in social reality.[62] On the one hand, they express and enact social values, cultural taken-for-granted meanings, and the power relations of a given context. On the other, they may shed light on these sociopolitical elements and promote change. Discourses are grounded on frames, the shared patterns of interpretation pervading the way social actors define a situation and engage with it.[63] If frames are reproduced and crystalized through their discursive embodiments, they are also challenged by other frames in discursive interactions.

Discursive institutionalism builds on these conceptions to understand the interactive processes through which institutions emerge, continue, or change. According to Schmidt, discursive institutionalism is particularly helpful in *endogenizing* change, 'explaining much of how and why public actors bring about institutional change through public action.'[64] Investigating the meaning-making activities of individuals in their discursive interactions,

---

[56] Schmidt (2008: 5).
[57] Schmidt (2010).
[58] Hall (1992); Pierson (2004).
[59] Scott (2014).
[60] Fairclough (2003); Hay (2008); Schmidt (2008).
[61] Dryzek (2000).
[62] Fairclough (2001).
[63] Gofmann (1986).
[64] Schmidt (2008: 308).

the approach can grasp how actors build public problems and seek to transform contexts in which they act by changing the frames used to define these contexts. More than a set of formal rules, institutions are seen as contingent constructs based on discursive frames, pointing to the complex game between structures and agency.

The approach of discursive institutionalism, therefore, conceives of institutions as the product of social understandings, negotiable and renegotiable in discursive practices. Institutions represent rules based on contingent and contextual understandings that are embodied in discourses.[65] Because institutions are contingent, discursive institutionalism is less attached to the statement of permanence and predictability for society and more linked to the perspective of change. Institutions must adapt and cope with changes in the environment, rather than work as stable foundations set in stone to coordinate or constrain social interactions.[66] In discursive institutionalism, changes in discourse are necessary components of institutional change. By analysing discourses, a person can grasp the dynamic nature of institutions. When someone investigates, for instance, the discursive clashes about climate change within the United Nations, that person can map the tensions, contradictions, trends, and dominant frameworks pervading the decisions taken by this institution.

Algorithms can be read through the lens of discursive institutionalism in at least four ways, because algorithmic experiences are always discursive in some way.[67] First, there are frames embedded in algorithms, shaping understandings about the world. When algorithms reproduce racial bias, for instance, a person can see how certain conceptions of the world are assimilated in allegedly technical ways.[68] Second, algorithms frame the context in which they act, helping to shape how other algorithms and humans will engage with a given situation. They create contexts of meaning and affordances for the actions of other agents (which may or may not be human).[69] Third, algorithms can be seen as arguments in broader

---

[65] Hay (2016).
[66] Fairclough (2001); Schmidt (2011).
[67] Lemos and Pastor (2020).
[68] In many situations, AI algorithms reproduce biases or forms of discrimination, stemming from the lack of diversity in the technology design process. As a result, sexism, racism, and other forms of discrimination are built into the machine-learning algorithms that underlie the technology behind many 'intelligent' systems that shape how we are categorized and advertised. In many instances, these forms of discrimination stem from a computer industry comprised of few women, black people, or people of different sexual orientations, for example. In this regard, see Crawford (2021).
[69] Creating meaning is a central issue in the foundations of New Institutionalism. These meanings define an institution's legitimacy and the terms for individuals' appropriate behaviour in society (March and Olsen 1984). More than games or interactions, or even historical processes and organizations, institutions embody meaning structures for individuals, given frames defined in value systems.

discursive disputes happening in the public sphere.[70] Fourth, algorithms can be challenged by other discourses, which may unearth their structures or point to their possible and actual implications. Essentially, algorithms can be confronted discursively, which may eventually lead to change, regulation, and governance.

Institutionalist Framework to Analyse Algorithmic Systems

The branches of New Institutionalism presented earlier define different ways in which algorithms can be approached as institutions. These approaches are not necessarily conflicting, and the boundaries between them often blur.[71] They are general perspectives that organize different ways to approach how formal and informal rules set by institutions shape power relations and fields of human action.

Conceived of as institutions, algorithmic systems can be approached from the analytical lenses of these perspectives. Drawing from previously introduced concepts, our analytical framework requires attention to six key aspects: institution building and design; historical processes; rules and norms; power relations; gaming; and discursive dimensions. These aspects can, on the one hand, drive a comprehensive and nuanced reading of algorithmic systems in contemporary societies. On the other, they also help us reflect on the novelties that algorithmic societies bring to make sense of contemporary institutions. Looking at institutions sheds light on the role algorithms play, while looking at algorithms sheds light on the need for innovation in institutional theories.

Institution Building and Design

An adequate comprehension of algorithms grounded in Algorithmic Institutionalism must start with the understanding that algorithmic systems are, as with any other institution, built by social actors. Institutions do not exist a priori, above the heads of human beings. They are socially constructed, and, therefore, they carry the marks of their context's relations and intentions.

Furthermore, algorithms' building process involves design. While some social institutions emerge through the stabilization of taken-for-granted

---

[70] Wagner et al. (2021).
[71] Thelen (1999).

patterns of interaction, algorithms are intentionally designed, even if their consequences cannot be fully designed or anticipated. Algorithms are planned as tools for rationalizing decision processes, facing a given context of uncertainties through a series of prescriptions.[72] The fact that they are designed does not make designers fully conscious of all the assumptions embedded in these artefacts. Design happens in social contexts, and taken-for-granted cultural and political factors are always at the kernel of their construction. In addition, design does not assure the complete predictability of results or full human control over the scope of decisions. Algorithms are parts of complex algorithmic systems, shaping human interactions with digital interfaces and interacting with other algorithms and humans, which makes their outputs not completely foreseeable and their design more dynamic than it is often conceived to be.

> [Algorithms] consist of parts that are generally independently produced, often in a distributed fashion. Especially once algorithms materialize as code, they are less a single definable whole but consist of bits and pieces of reusable parts shared across the Internet and embedded in thousands of systems. Codes and algorithms are thus hardly ever the product of a single originator, be it an individual or organization. Their work is global, is distributed, is taken in small steps, and employs workflows that assemble fragments into products through human labour.[73]

Algorithmic Institutionalism requires close scrutiny of these complex processes of institution-building. Who was responsible for the algorithm's development? What were the original purposes for its creation? How did the process of design happen? In which context did it take place? How does this algorithmic piece interact with other algorithms in complex assemblages? Which factors affected these construction processes? What was the role played by humans in many phases of the algorithm's design? More broadly, what is the social context of contemporary algorithmic building?

Historical Processes

A second dimension in an analysis driven by Algorithmic Institutionalism is historical. As with any other institution, a proper comprehension of a given algorithmic system requires the understanding of its place in time. This means that algorithms are artefacts, born in specific contexts and under constant development in historical backgrounds. Algorithms embody paths,

---

[72] Simon (1996).
[73] Aradau and Blanke (2022: 6).

and they are produced, sedimented, and transformed through time. Rather than being ahistorical, they are situated embodiments of social relations in patterns of decision-making. It is not by chance, for instance, that some hiring algorithms have an ableist bias[74] or that algorithms employed in criminal sentencing display deep racial biases.[75]

The historical dimension of Algorithmic Institutionalism suggests special attention given to two concepts derived from institutionalism. The first is *critical junctures*.[76] These are moments of uncertainty in which change is more likely, and actors may be more causally decisive in pointing to a direction for institutional change. *Drift* and *conversion* situations are particularly relevant around these critical junctures.[77] In the former, a given institution is held in place within a shifting context, while, in the latter, actors redirect institutions, significantly altering an institution from its origins. In this sense, algorithms may be transformed or held in place in moments of uncertainty and openness.

The second concept with central relevance to Algorithmic Institutionalism is *path dependence*.[78] Institutions' inertial dynamics show that some choices have implications as they influence future choices. In the context of algorithms, the implications are twofold. First, algorithms' development is marked by path dependence, in which key decisions affect the decisions that follow. Second, algorithms can be considered to be a reification of path dependence. By designing logical sequences, they cannot host reflexivity (generated by doubt) in their process of decision-making. Hence, they build self-fulfilling prophecies, projecting futures that are portraits of the past. The flexibility that algorithmic logics can accommodate is not that of reflexivity, which arises from uncertainty about the next step. With no hesitation, algorithms follow established patterns, thus projecting themselves into the future. For example, dealing with legacy systems is essential for corporations and governments in the process of change and innovation. That is because these old, outdated systems define the initial business rules embedded in sociotechnical systems, which may constrain the system's evolution and reinforce path dependence.[79]

The historical focus of an analysis grounded on Algorithmic Institutionalism may address many relevant questions: What was the historical trajectory

---

[74] More information is available in the 2020 report from the Center for Democracy & Technology (CDT), available at https://cdt.org/wp-content/uploads/2020/12/Plain-Language-Algorithms-in-Hiring-Tests-Make-it-Easier-to-Discriminate-Against-People-with-Disabilities.pdf.
[75] Park (2019); Silva (2022).
[76] Pierson (2004).
[77] Hacker et al. (2015).
[78] Krasner (1988).
[79] Davis (2015).

of an algorithmic system? What values were explicitly and implicitly driving this specific algorithm's design? Did the algorithmic system change over time? If so, how, why, and in which directions? What were the critical junctures that allowed change or were overcome without change? Did some choices in an algorithm's design tend to reproduce themselves through time? How can this algorithmic system project past choices into the construction of futures?

Rules and Norms

The third dimension in the framework of Algorithmic Institutionalism is the mapping of rules and norms that establish the scope of possibilities for individual behaviours and its collective consequences. This is the heart of the analytical framework. As with any other institution, algorithms affect their social context by establishing formal and informal rules that shape (without determining) human behaviour.

There are two possible levels of analysis here. The first focuses on specific algorithms, comprehending their affordances, the possible courses of action they can host, and the types of behaviour they tend to induce or restrict. Matching algorithms, such as the ones used by the dating app Tinder, for instance, tend to induce certain forms of behaviour and the disposal of certain pieces of information to the detriment of others, deeply affecting not only individuals but how love is experienced in contemporary societies.[80] The second level of analysis looks not at a specific algorithm but at the broader algorithmic environment to understand how it is influencing forms of behaviour. This is the case, for instance, of studies pointing to how social media (broadly speaking, not as individual platforms) shape more polarized forms of political contention.[81] It is also the case of several studies showing how racism can be deepened through racial bias embedded in many different types of algorithms, from surveillance artefacts to health-diagnoses tools.[82]

In this third dimension, Algorithmic Institutionalism seeks to address key questions: What formal and informal rules are established or strengthened by this algorithmic system? What types of individual behaviours are induced or restrained by these algorithms? How does this influence happen? Which collective consequences can be observed from these sets of rules? How strong

---

[80] Illouz (2011).
[81] Ohme (2021).
[82] Noble (2018); Benjamin (2019); Silva (2022).

are these rules? What are the mechanisms of enforcement used to sustain them?

Power Relations

Power is at the heart of the Algorithmic Institutionalism's framework and deserves a longer discussion here. The definition of power is marked by intense debates and controversies in the social sciences, because power is multifaceted and intangible. Power has a dual nature, simultaneously constraining and enabling action. It is intrinsically linked to agency, while also revealing deeply rooted structures that shape contexts and actors. Our starting point must consider that algorithms are inserted in relations that exert and enact power in society, with diverse political implications.

Among the many definitions of power, Thomas Hobbes's conception emphasized its coercive nature, conceiving of power as an instrument to ensure obedience.[83] The vertical nature of Hobbes's conception of power is grasped by the expression 'power over'. Expanding the idea of 'power over', Max Weber emphasized the relational nature of power, defining it as 'the probability that one actor within a social relationship will be in a position to carry out his will [sic] despite resistances'.[84] Power is, therefore, an inherently relational capacity and embodies asymmetries. Power relationships depend on the instruments and resources available to agents, such as coercion[85] or the rhetorical ability to deal with ideas and values.[86]

This understanding became more complex as other dimensions of power were disclosed. First Bachrach and Baratz pointed to a second dimension of power, which is the power to avoid action or decisions.[87] The control over the agenda is central to an adequate understanding of how power is exerted. Lukes added a third dimension to the concept, claiming that power often operated in more subtle and invisible ways, shaping individuals' wills through structures and institutions.[88]

Michel Foucault worked on a similar insight through diverse theoretical routes. For him, power has a pervasive nature, shaping the structures that reproduce patterns that give meaning to actions.[89] In doing so, Foucault is

---

[83] Hobbes (1996).
[84] Weber (1978: 53).
[85] Weber (1978).
[86] Lasswell and Kaplan (2017).
[87] Bachrach and Baratz (1962).
[88] Lukes (2005).
[89] Foucault (2008).

also attentive to the generative forces of power. Power is not only a constraint; it 'needs to be considered as a productive network which runs through the whole social body'.[90] Power is not episodic: it transcends and embodies the social body in discourse, knowledge, and regimes of truth. Seeking to explain how power currently works, Foucault advances the concept of *governamentality*, which refers to a rationality based on institutions, procedures, strategies, techniques, and practices used to manage populations, something Foucault saw as the core of contemporary institutions.[91]

These various conceptions of power lead to diverse understandings of the power of algorithmic systems. From a Hobbesian perspective, the power of algorithms lies in a more coercive structure that leads to something like an *algocracy*. This definition of algocracy was created by A. Aneesh to understand transnational virtual spaces where labour relations become coercively constructed in codes and data.[92] The term refers to 'a situation in which algorithm-based systems structure and constrain the opportunities for human participation in, and comprehension of, public decision-making'.[93] John Danaher currently treats the concept as the ability of algorithmic systems to impose a new social order based on coercive mechanisms driven by algorithms.[94] From this perspective, algorithmic systems define a new type of Leviathan, formed of coercive structures associated with the voluntary—although tacit—adherence of people to this new type of order.[95]

A more complex approach to algorithmic power is grounded on Foucault's definition. As algorithmic systems become more pervasive in society, they work as an instrument of population management, amplifying the possibilities of governmentality.[96] Proposed by Antoinette Rouvroy and Thomas Berns, the notion of algorithmic governmentality is based on a rationality that extracts knowledge from individual attitudes, accumulating it to manage populations not on the grounds of statistical means and averages, but through profiling based on the relations between data points.[97] 'The mass processing of data does not aim at the judgment, punishment, and control of past behaviours; on the contrary, it intends to guide future behaviours in order to govern or tame uncertainty'.[98] Focusing on forms of relations and on breaking down subjects into points of data, algorithmic governmentality

[90] Foucault (1980: 119).
[91] Foucault (2008).
[92] Aneesh (2006).
[93] Danaher (2016: 246).
[94] Danaher (2016).
[95] König (2019).
[96] Rouvroy (2018).
[97] Rouvroy and Berns (2013).
[98] Alves and Andrade (2022: 1015).

promotes rarefied processes of subjectivation, which hinder the emergence of active critical subjects.[99]

Also drawing from Foucault, Taina Bucher argues that algorithmic systems govern discourse situations and the construction of knowledge, creating new regimes of truth supported by social media. Algorithmic systems do not have an intrinsic power, as they do not own power as a capacity. Instead, algorithms are 'technologies of government', shaping new forms of knowledge and disruptive ways to discipline.[100] In the same direction, according to David Beer, the power of algorithmic systems does not depend on intrinsic capabilities of these artefacts but on how they are socially constructed, 'attempting to understand how notions of the algorithm move out into the world, how they are framed by the discourse and what they are said to be able to achieve'.[101] The power of algorithms lies in a broader notion of how they change whole structures of communication structure and meaning.

These different approaches to power—and to algorithmic power, more specifically—are important for the understanding of algorithms as institutions. A comprehensive understanding of the power of algorithmic systems must consider their coercive nature, their capacity to influence individual decisions through the narrowing of available alternatives, their effects in the control of public agendas, their consequences over individuals' preferences, desires, and self-conceptions, and their broader social implications in the shape of social relations and rationalities guiding social life. Moreover, a complex notion of algorithmic power must understand power, not as capacity intrinsically owned by technologies, but as relational emergences, which are spread over the social fabric in more or less tacit ways. Furthermore, algorithmic power must be seen as both enabling and restraining, to the extent in which it inhibits certain behaviours and social outcomes, while also promoting other behaviours and social outcomes.

Institutionalism, in its diversity, deals with these diverse dimensions and aspects of power. In broad terms, and as reviewed in this chapter, institutional theories are attentive to the way a relational artefact (that is, institutions) offers rules, scripts, and practices that reduce uncertainty, by restraining the scope of possibilities available to actors while also enabling action. The power of institutions lies in their capacity to frame the contexts in which actants exert agency. Setting contexts for action, institutions establish rules for the distribution of resources, therefore, establishing the boundaries for

---

[99] Alves and Andrade (2022).
[100] Bucher (2018).
[101] Beer (2017: 10).

action (and inaction or the hindrance of the action of others). This framing of contexts is historically embedded and pervaded by power asymmetries and social inequalities. Moreover, the power of institutions pervades socializing processes, thus affecting the construction of identities and the formation of senses of belonging, preferences, and desires. It also affects the way other institutions operate, contributing to a broader weaving of the social fabric.

Different trends of institutional theory reveal various roots of power relations in which institutions are embedded. Rational-choice institutionalism attributes the power of institutions to their capacity to establish equilibriums in the performance of certain functions by adding (negative and positive) incentives to the calculations made by agents.[102] Historical institutionalism argues that institutions embody historical processes and their unstable and temporary balances of power.[103] Sociological institutionalism sheds light on the power that institutions have to legitimize certain practices, values, choices, ideas, and distributions of resources to the detriment of others, thereby stabilizing or challenging existing orders. Lastly, discursive institutionalism emphasizes the power of discourses in framing reality, guiding individual engagement with other actants.[104]

Each of these fronts helps to understand dimensions of the complex power relations in which algorithmic systems are embedded. As noted by Napoli, when thought of as institutions, algorithmic systems are embedded in power relations, which interact with both structure and agency.[105] These systems organize the contexts in which other actants exert their agency, without determining how individuals, for instance, will behave. The power of algorithmic systems, from an institutional lens, resides in how the rules inscribed in algorithms calculate and organize different environments, setting boundaries for human engagement. Algorithms are artefacts that mediate the relationship between humans and between human and systems, assigning roles, classifying people, and hierarchizing interests and different perspectives on the world.[106]

Algorithmic Institutionalism faces the challenge of understanding a complex process of profound change in the rules and norms that guide social interactions. These transformations are clear, for instance, in the emergence

---

[102] North (1990).
[103] Thelen (1999).
[104] Hay (2008); Schmidt (2008).
[105] Napoli (2014).
[106] Napoli (2014).

of novel forms of regulation of human behaviour,[107] of new forms of manipulation and agenda setting,[108] of profound organizational changes on many fronts,[109] of new patterns of governance and governmentality,[110] of the changing understandings of security,[111] and of erosion of democratic institutions.[112] In all these situations, we have power relations.

The power of algorithmic systems implies new practices and new ways of institutionalizing things. As we will see, these power relationships between humans and algorithmic systems imply forms of domination and resistance, acquiescence and manipulation, legitimacy and contestation, which affect social practices through its algorithmic institutions. Algorithms provide humans with actionable insights, ranging from simple calculations to more complex applications that can nudge, manipulate, or manage behaviour.[113]

Looking at these complex phenomena, Algorithmic Institutionalism seeks to address several questions: How does a given algorithm embody power relations? How powerful is an algorithmic system? How does this power work? Have individuals resisted this power? What are the outcomes of these power relations? Are there attempts to control an algorithm's power and make it accountable for its consequences? Are existing relations of power being updated and reshaped by algorithmic systems? How are algorithms' power relations affecting relations of power in contemporary societies?

Gaming

In the business world, *gaming* refers to the act of subverting the intent of rules or laws without technically breaking them, thereby gaining some sort of advantage, such as high credit ratings or access to capital on favourable terms.[114] In broader terms, gaming refers to the strategies and tactics used by users to interact in creative ways with an established order. As rational-choice scholars have long shown, individuals play with rules and may reinvent them through their agency. For institutional theory, this has proven instrumental in challenging analysis that sees only structures' strength, thereby foreseeing some type of institutional determinism. Rules matter and shape action situations, but agency remains an important feature of human existence.

---

[107] Yeung (2018).
[108] Gillespie (2014).
[109] Napoli (2014).
[110] Rouvroy and Berns (2013); Veale and Brass (2019).
[111] Amoore (2014).
[112] Runciman (2018); Keane (2020); Ford (2021).
[113] Ekbia (2015).
[114] Slater (2021).

The fourth dimension of our framework considers how individuals interact with algorithmic systems, affecting their functions and decisions. Individuals may learn how to handle automated mechanisms of decision-making, framing their choices and actions in ways that lead to different types of results that may include getting a more beneficial outcome or simply switching the routes followed by algorithms.[115] Many people manipulate social-media activities to escape from what they understand to be a closed-loop bubble or to provide wrong cues to platforms, trying to protect their privacy.[116] For instance, we may attribute a nonsense rate to a movie in a streaming platform just for the sake of remaining less transparent to algorithms, blurring the algorithms' accuracy, and expanding room for happy accidents. Individuals act and, in doing so, they resist and affect algorithms' power.

Looking at gaming strategies, Algorithmic Institutionalism strives to answer multiple questions: How do individuals deal with algorithmic systems? How do they affect them? Do they intentionally play with the patterns followed by automated artefacts of decision-making? Do individual actions unintentionally affect how a given algorithm works? How can they escape from the scripts predicted by certain algorithms and reinvent them? Does human agency affect a given algorithmic system's outcomes? Does it have a broader impact on the algorithm's structure, reshaping its patterns? In a nutshell, how are people playing with these algorithms?

Discursive Dimensions

The sixth dimension in the framework of Algorithmic Institutionalism requires a close look at discourses, ideas, and meanings. As previously discussed, institutions have a central role in attributing meaning to actors and events. They shape behaviours by framing the situations in which individuals are inserted. Even if discursive institutionalism is the strand of New Institutionalism focused on this aspect, we must acknowledge the importance of meanings, ideas, and discourses cutting across the different approaches from which we draw.

Analysing algorithms' discursive dimension first requires comprehending the frames embedded in a given algorithm or sets of algorithms. The decisions taken by algorithmic systems are always grounded in certain

---

[115] Social-media platforms try to establish ways to control and sanction users who manipulate the algorithms. In general, efforts are made to identify this manipulation of and gaming with algorithms, but sanctions tend to be paternalistic. The platforms use gaming accusations to assert their power and authority, mobilized by the social-media platform's algorithm. In this regard, see Petre et al. (2019).

[116] Mendonça et al. (2023).

worldviews, understanding reality from certain angles (rather than others). This can become clear, for example, in the type of data used by an algorithm or in the way these data are used. If an algorithmic system infers teachers' quality by their students' grades, for instance, it assumes a specific perspective, neglecting many other potentially relevant factors, including how individuals may game these algorithms.[117]

Another discursive dimension of algorithms is related to how they shape the context for other social interactions. Algorithms are not carriers of frames but work as frame-setting structures that interpellate acting entities (human or not) in specific ways. Algorithms help design our interactions' situations. Mapping the way algorithms set the frames through which other actors define a situation and act is an important contribution of Algorithmic Institutionalism.

Third, we should not forget that algorithms can be seen as texts. They are commands that establish patterns of decisions. Algorithms are, therefore, discursive pieces participating in broader discursive interactions occurring in the public sphere. They can be interpreted as arguments, expressing positions in the face of other actors. Their performances are symbolic forms of action with actual consequences in wider discursive processes that constitute the public sphere.

Last, it is important to pay attention to the discursive processes surrounding algorithms. In the public sphere, the dangers and problems of specific algorithms—or of the broader scenario of algorithmic societies—may nurture debates around the topic. As Frank Fischer notes, proper comprehension of political processes requires attention to the discursive contestations surrounding those processes.[118] These debates are at the heart of social problems' construction, playing important roles in the way actors attribute meaning to social phenomena and promote changes.

Now that we have outlined this broad map of discursive dimensions, many questions arise as relevant in the framework of Algorithmic Institutionalism: How does this algorithm frame reality? Which views and values are embedded in an algorithmic text? Who are the audiences of these discourses, and what role do they play in this text? Is the algorithm planned as a polysemic open text, or is it organized as an opaque, closed structure? What are its perlocutionary effects? How does this algorithm set the frames for situations of interaction? Does it establish affordances for actors?

---

[117] O'Neil (2016).
[118] Fischer (2015).

Concluding Remarks

This chapter has sought to advance a framework for scholarship in the field of what we are calling Algorithmic Institutionalism. Drawing from different traditions of New Institutionalism, we advocate that algorithms work as sets of rules, shaping contexts of agency while simultaneously being shaped by agency within historical and discursive contexts, thus affecting power relations.

The framework outlined here draws attention to six key aspects, but it is open enough to welcome different methodological approaches and types of investigations. In addition, it need not be used to analyse sociotechnical systems in their entirety. Investigations focused on specific dimensions of this framework can shed light on different elements of contemporary algorithmic societies. Considering the roles of algorithmic systems in contemporary society, the framework invites reconceptualization in institutional theories. This reconceptualization means updating not only the agendas of research in institutional theory but also how institutions can be conceived.

Our intention in this chapter was to raise a set of relevant foci for a proper understanding of algorithms as institutions. The agendas presented in this framework provide a way to analyse how algorithms are changing contemporary societies, creating new political orders by institutionalizing new practices, meanings, and horizons of action. These changes need to be analysed critically regarding algorithms' growing role.

Keeping this in mind, next we delve into three sets of cases through the lens of Algorithmic Institutionalism. To begin, in Chapter 3 we focus on the employment of algorithms in the field of security.

3
Security in Algorithmic Times

During the carnival of 2020, the city of Salvador radiated joy. An average of sixteen million people gathered in the streets of the capital city of Bahia in Brazil to celebrate the country's most famous holiday. As usual, they packed in *blocos*, which followed the *trio elétricos*,[1] dancing through the streets in ceaseless movement. Salvador's festive parades are known for their capacity to promote a form of anonymity, which is quite important in a carnival. In a context marked by such a high density of people drinking and dancing together, nobody expects others to know who they are, what any particular person is doing, or what someone has done.

Yet, despite the feeling of anonymity, during the 2020 carnival, local police managed to capture forty-two fugitives of the judicial system by using facial recognition technologies (FRTs). The app Face Check allowed the recovery of many pieces of information about individuals registered in a state database in a matter of seconds.[2] Established in 2018, the application was developed by the Secretariat of Public Security of Bahia and initially tested in 2019 in the municipality of Feira de Santana. The application also influenced other technological developments in the state of Bahia. In June 2022, for instance, 1,200 additional cameras were installed in the streets of Salvador at the cost of 665 million Brazilian reais.[3]

This example illustrates a global trend: facial recognition is employed increasingly throughout the world. By the end of 2021, an estimated one billion closed-circuit television (CCTV) cameras were operating around the globe, allowing AI to match images of people across multiple databases containing information about individuals.[4] A report published by Comparitech analysed ninety-nine countries, showing that only six had no evidence of using FRTs. These technologies are used by 70 per cent of governments, and

---

[1] *Trios elétricos* are trucks or trailers with powerful sound equipment hosting bands that are the very heart of Salvador's carnival.
[2] https://www.uol.com.br/carnaval/2020/noticias/redacao/2020/02/26/reconhecimento-facial-por-app-captura-42-foragidos-no-carnaval-de-salvador.htm?cmpid=copiaecola.
[3] Roughly US$128 million, as noted in https://g1.globo.com/ba/bahia/noticia/2022/06/15/mais-de-mil-cameras-sao-instaladas-para-monitoramento-das-ruas-em-salvador-e-regiao-metropolitana.ghtml.
[4] Introna and Nissenbaum (2014).

Algorithmic Institutionalism. Ricardo F. Mendonça, Fernando Filgueiras, and Virgílio Almeida, Oxford University Press.
© Ricardo F. Mendonça, Fernando Filgueiras, and Virgílio Almeida (2023). DOI: 10.1093/oso/9780192870070.003.0004

some do it in more invasive ways. China, Russia, and the United Arab Emirates rank as the top users of FRTs.[5] Since 2019, India has been implementing one of the world's biggest facial recognition systems.[6] In Latin America, the spread of CCTV has also been quick, enabling projects based on FRT.[7]

FRTs are at the heart of contemporary efforts to promote security:[8] 'Nearly 70 per cent of police forces globally have access to some form of FRT', and more than 60 per cent of countries employ it in airports for border control.[9] Together with other biometric technologies that focus on fingerprints, vascular patterns, iris, gait, or speech, FRT aims to identify potential threats, such as potentially dangerous individuals, but also behavioural traits that can indicate intentions and eventual attitudes.

The generalized use of biometric technologies such as FRT is, however, only one of the multiple faces of algorithmic developments in the field of security. Parallel to the use of FRTs, we see expansion of predictive policing technologies,[10] software to assess the chances of recidivism in criminal trials,[11] and lethal autonomous weapons systems (LAWS).[12] Algorithmic systems play an increasing role in the design and enforcement of strategies aimed at promoting security, which has deep implications on how coercion is exerted and how states claim a monopoly on the legitimate use of force in a given territory.

Predictive policing is probably the most eloquent example in this respect.[13] Over time, security policies are designed from a grammar dictated by mathematics and the algorithmic capacity of calculations that shape police action based on this knowledge. Briefly, predictive policing involves the collection of a broad variety of data to estimate, through several correlations, when and where crime is likely to occur, thereby more efficiently employing the existing resources to avoid it.[14] Usually, predictions are made via machine-learning advances and the construction of artificial neural networks. Applying these algorithms in security requires vast amounts of data and robust training bases so that surveillance systems can manage risks, promote anticipation and

---

[5] Bischoff (2022).
[6] https://www.aljazeera.com/news/2019/11/7/privacy-concerns-as-india-readies-facial-recognition-system.
[7] Firmino et al. (2013).
[8] Amoore (2006); Introna and Nissenbaum (2014).
[9] Bischoff (2022).
[10] Brayne (2017); Meijer and Wessels (2019).
[11] Skeem and Lowenkamp (2020); Završnik (2021).
[12] https://www.weforum.org/agenda/2022/05/regulate-non-state-use-arms/#:~:text=Stuart%20Russell&text=An%20emerging%20arms%20race%20between,while%20the%20technology%20rapidly%20advances.
[13] Lyon (2014); McCarthy (2019).
[14] Perry et al. (2013); O'Neil (2016); Meijer and Wessels (2019); Chen et al. (2021).

strategies to mitigate risks, monitor threats, and predict possible futures.[15] Some more recent technologies claim to be able to predict crime one week in advance in a 1,000-foot-wide area, with 90 per cent accuracy.[16]

Tested since 2008 by the Los Angeles Police Department, this strategy grew significantly after 2012, with programmes in major US cities such as Chicago, New Orleans, and New York.[17] Predictive policing has also been deployed in China, Denmark, Germany, India, Japan, the Netherlands, and the United Kingdom.[18] In an encompassing literature review, Meijer and Wessels show that ambivalent and non-conclusive evidence exists regarding predictive policing's efficacy. Their 'preliminary conclusion is that this approach has potential but not all types of crimes can be effectively reduced through predictive policing models and therefore the officers executing these strategies need to adequately use these models'.[19] Ineffectiveness has led to the discontinuation of some predictive policing programmes in US cities such as Palo Alto, Los Angeles, New York, San Francisco, Berkeley, Oakland, Boston, Springfield, Rio Rancho, and Santa Cruz. The European Parliament has also approved the banishment of discriminatory predictive policing.

FRTs and predictive policing illustrate how algorithmic technologies are institutionalizing new security policies in an expanded and comprehensive way, as algorithmic systems embody rules, norms, and standards that shape the action of governments, police departments, and military organizations in alliance with private corporations. This chapter focuses on the analysis of algorithmic systems employed in security under the lens of Algorithmic Institutionalism. We aim to show that the framework advanced in Chapter 2 can provide a fruitful and encompassing perspective to make sense of contemporary phenomena. This chapter also points to the need for updating institutional theories on the grounds of algorithmic societies' context.

We begin with a brief discussion about security and its relationship with technologies. Then we transition to an interpretation of algorithms' deployment for security purposes based on the six categories of Algorithmic Institutionalism. We conclude by pointing to new directions in institutionalism propelled by today's context.

---

[15] Amoore (2014).
[16] Rotaru et al. (2022).
[17] https://www.brennancenter.org/our-work/research-reports/predictive-policing-explained.
[18] McCarthy (2019).
[19] Meijer and Wessels (2019).

Security, Surveillance, and Algorithms

Security is a slippery concept that can be construed in multiple ways. As a normative concept, security works more like a goal that transforms throughout history. As a politically contested concept, its normativity acquires different meanings and can be interpreted along different trajectories. Despite its changing nature, broadly speaking, security can be seen as a key aim in any political order. Since Hobbes's *Leviathan* (published in 1651), security is often seen as the heart of political legitimacy.

According to Baldwin, as the political community's foundation, security is the preservation of acquired values that underpin policies seeking to address threats against individuals, political communities, and the international community.[20] These acquired values are broad, including political and territorial independence alongside the preservation of life and peace, economic prosperity, health, and well-being, among others. Since the 1970s, the United Nations' concept of security has expanded in different directions based on the premise that national security involves various aspects of society covered by the broad umbrella of human rights.[21] Conceived of as the preservation of values acquired by society, security requires restraining threats and preventing future scenarios of destruction and failure of the state. It is not meant to address a past or present event; instead, it is built to face future threats, often requiring the instrumentalization of the present to promote anticipation and adaptation. In the old jargon of realist theories in the field of international relations, states maintain military forces and build weapons to maintain peace in the future. The state must instrumentalize the present to avoid future catastrophic scenarios.

Governments need institutions to promote security, and they may need different strategies to pursue this objective. Despite the wide range of possibilities, identifying individuals properly is essential to this task, and establishing patterns of civil identification makes this clear. To mitigate potential threats—whether against individuals, the community, or the nation—citizens must be identifiable and trackable.[22] A crime against life or property, for instance, must be attributed to someone identified by the state and eventually punished. In the community dimension, in situations such as the Covid-19 pandemic, health security must identify individuals to reduce the virus's spread and identify who has or has not received vaccines. Finally, in the

---

[20] Baldwin (1997).
[21] Human Security Unit (2010).
[22] Amoore (2008).

international arena, the flow of foreigners is controlled, requiring the state to identify and recognize international citizens to contain possible threats.

Institutions play a key role not only in this identification process but also in the definition of an order of appropriate behaviour for the political community.[23] For this reason, surveillance has become a key component of modern societies, grounding forms of social control aimed at avoiding potential threats to the political order and citizens' lives. Foucault has demonstrated how modern institutions discipline bodies through surveillance.[24] His work was particularly relevant to the comprehension of the processes through which institutions of modernity enabled an internalization of mechanisms of surveillance, thus facilitating the maintenance of existing orders. Institutions such as the school, prison, hospital, and family contributed, in different ways, to the disciplined behaviour that individuals felt as though they were being watched all the time. For Foucault, discipline was at the heart of modern subjectivities, which was part of a broader project that promised security through social control.

A growing body of literature emphasizes the part played by algorithmic systems in augmenting strategies of surveillance and discipline. Various digital technologies are employed to predict future scenarios and avoid many types of threats. It is always worth remembering that a myriad of digital technologies are applications originally created for military purposes, usually with security goals. When Alan Turing's anti-Enigma 'Bombe' machine decoded Nazi codes, he provided a powerful piece of evidence about the importance of computational technologies to deal with crises and foster security. Today, individuals' identification is often based on machine vision and predictive systems grounded in machine learning and deep learning, which have emerged as essential tools for security.

The use of these algorithmic systems is not restricted to identification; it also involves coercive actions—whether in urban spaces, using robots, or in the international arena with the growing use of LAWS in conflict situations.[25] In all these situations, algorithms embed the rules, norms, and standards considered relevant to promoting security.

The importance of algorithmic systems in managing bodies for security purposes is in the crux of contemporary debates. Drawing from Foucault, the literature seeks to understand how algorithms change the old metaphor of the panopticon so as actually to allow permanent full observation. Unlike in the original design discussed by Bentham and Foucault, we no longer

---

[23] March and Olsen (2009).
[24] Foucault (1995).
[25] Scharre (2018); Russell (2019).

seem to live in a world in which individuals doubt whether they are being watched. Monitoring has become omnipresent, and individuals now know they are being watched. Machine vision and AI extend the panopticon's engineering and make it ubiquitous in different technologies for surveillance and law enforcement. There is a digital integration of discrete systems in broad surveillance assemblages in which different devices, platforms, and databases converge to enable a more encompassing monitorial system.[26]

In this sense, Rafael Sanches argues that privacy is a luxury that precious few have experienced throughout history and that is becoming even rarer. Mobilizing the notion of *algorithmic governmentality*, Sanches focuses on the role played by the processes of surveillance and datafication in constructing subjectivities, shaping forms of existence that aim to sustain existing orders.[27] Antoinette Rouvroy advanced the concept of algorithmic governmentality to analyse a form of management of behaviours and bodies that is grounded in a technical abstraction of disembeddedness.[28] Encoded in software and based on complex statistical correlations, this form of governance fragments the world and its subjects in data, enabling decisions that shape behaviours in ways that cannot be fully understood. For Rouvroy, algorithmic governmentality would be generated by the developments of capitalism, while also causing many of its transformations:

> algorithmic governmentality would be both a radicalisation and an immune strategy of capitalism and neoliberalism that is 'purified' or 'expurgated' from everything that would bring it into 'crisis', that is, from anything that would interrupt and make it bifurcate: the world itself (replaced purely and simply by digital flows), life (in its untimeliness like birth, interruptiveness like death), subjects (capable of reticence—of not doing what they are capable of doing—and fabulation susceptible to bifurcate the course of things).[29]

Zuboff also emphasizes the economic dimension of surveillance mechanisms.[30] She argues that surveillance capitalism is a new, unprecedented form of economic production that extracts profit from the capture and instrumentalization of behavioural traits. Focusing on the surveillance enacted by technology companies, she claims it resembles authoritarian states to the extent in which this surveillance weakens the possibility of autonomy. The *digital dispossession* propelled by technology companies through algorithmic

[26] Haggerty and Ericson (2000).
[27] Sanches (2019).
[28] Rouvroy (2011, 2016).
[29] Rouvroy (2016: 35).
[30] Zuboff (2019).

systems fragments individuals, rendering selves understandable and profitable. Using individuals as a means to their ends, this form of economic oppression is fed by observation, prediction, and influence over behaviours, deeply weakening free will. Individuals are nothing but sources of data that are extracted and targeted, thus feeding processes aimed at accumulation.

Couldry and Mejias define this process of extracting economic value from individuals through data as *data colonialism*,[31] pinpointing that

> data practices today would represent not just a continuation of colonialism/capitalism, but a distinctive new stage of colonialism that lays the foundations for new developments in capitalism, just as colonialism's original landgrab enabled capitalism's emergence and subsequent centuries of colonial oppression.[32]

Drawing on the work of Simone Browne,[33] they argue that colonialism has systematically employed technologies to surveil Black bodies over the centuries. Similarly, data colonialism applies forms of racial surveillance through algorithmic systems that legitimize the continuous incarceration of the Black population and the racial bias pervading many security policies. Shakir Mohamed, Marie-Therese Png, and William Isaac see this issue through the lens of *algorithmic coloniality* that would reproduce colonial power through algorithmic systems.[34]

At this point, two aspects of our argument should be clear. First, algorithms play an increasing role in how security is conceived of and implemented. Second, this central role has dubious implications that (eventually) can lead to effective policies while also reproducing asymmetries and forms of oppression that are at the base of capitalist forms of accumulation. The ubiquitous and pervasive form of surveillance grounding security strategies—such as the wide employment of FRTs and predictive policing—has deep political implications and affects the idea of autonomous individuals, because algorithmic systems are institutionalized for security proposals.

Despite the growing attention to these phenomena, Algorithmic Institutionalism can shed new light to comprehend it—to the extent in which it offers an encompassing framework—and unravel diverse dimensions of security in algorithmic societies. Conceiving of algorithms as institutions, this framework provides a complex way to comprehend the messy and often

---

[31] Couldry and Mejias (2021).
[32] Couldry and Mejias (2021: 3).
[33] Browne (2015).
[34] Mohamed et al. (2020).

opaque way through which key decisions about security are made today. In what follows, we discuss each of the six dimensions of Algorithmic Institutionalism introduced in Chapter 2: institution building and design; historical processes; rules and norms; power relations; gaming; and discursive dimensions. These discussions show not only how institutional perspectives help us to understand algorithmic security but also how algorithms can push institutional theories in new directions.

Institution Building and Design

Thought of as institutions, algorithmic systems deployed in security can be seen as the production of a complex interplay of agents. As with any other institution, they cannot be attributed to a single motivated agent whose intentions would forge them. Institutions are multifaceted, dynamic arrangements that emerge and change through a series of interactions of differently situated actors.

This is not to deny that there are actors designing institutions and shaping their inceptions on the grounds of certain values and goals. In the field of security, often these initial designers are private technology corporations that aim to sell solutions for diagnosed problems to make profit. Companies such as IBM, Microsoft, Amazon, Google, Hanwang Technology, and Facebook have been important in the development of FRT. Although some of them have paused the sale of their devices and analysis software, the surveillance market is skyrocketing:

> Today, facial recognition technology (FRT) is, for an alarming number of us, a part of everyday life. From opening up our phones and logging into online banking to having our faces scanned against criminal databases, FRT has grown at an exponential rate. Experts have even predicted that the global facial recognition market will more than double from 3.8 billion USD in 2020 to 8.5 billion USD in 2025.[35]

Even now, in the market of predictive policing, companies such as Palantir, HunchLab, and Predpol sell their technologies to many cities. Northpointe (whose name was changed to Equivant in 2017) was the company responsible for designing COMPAS, which was employed by several US state courts to assess the probability of recidivism, thus allegedly making sentencing more objective.

---

[35] Bischoff (2022).

One of the problems generated by security's commodification through the private development of algorithmic systems is that companies cannot make fully transparent the way the product they are selling works in order to keep selling it. The case of COMPAS has come under scrutiny, as convicted criminals have tried to understand how they were assessed, but the algorithmic system sold by Northpointe was protected by copyright, which circumvented the possibility of actually understanding how it worked.[36] Likewise, the systematic purchase of privately designed software by state agencies and departments runs the risk of making the state hostage to companies that develop and update these systems. Moreover, as Helen Margetts has argued, the process ends up establishing shadow bureaucracies, as experts and technicians hired by these companies drive state activities without being submitted to the same types of accountability and scrutiny applied to regular public servants.[37]

Private companies are not, however, the only actors responsible for designing algorithmic systems employed with security aims. The military plays a key role in researching and funding projects of AI employed in security,[38] which has obvious implications in how security is conceived and in setting courses of development for both AI and security.

Universities also play an important role in developing these technologies:

> one of the first crime prediction tools developed in Latin America was created in Chile by the Center of Analysis and Modeling in Security of the University of Chile. […] A new project involving the National University and Quantil, a private company, involves setting-up a crime prediction platform in Bogotá that purposefully avoids reproducing biases and profiling.[39]

In Brazil, the state of Ceará established a partnership with the Federal Institute to develop an application that enabled police forces to correlate facial recognition and different databases. Ceará has high rates of criminality, with 4,788 homicides in 2018.[40] That year, the state created the Superintendence for Research and Public Security Strategy, which fostered convergence and interoperability of different public databases to collect data through surveillance systems and fund developing surveillance technologies to combat crime. Research institutions and non-governmental organizations (NGOs)

---

[36] Angwin et al. (2016); Liptak (2017); Dressel and Farid (2018).
[37] Margetts (2012).
[38] https://cset.georgetown.edu/publication/u-s-military-investments-in-autonomy-and-ai-executive-summary/.
[39] Aguirre et al. (2019).
[40] Aquino (2022). It should be highlighted that Ceará has a population of 9.2 million people.

often have economic interests in developing algorithms used for security, but they may also represent possibilities of scrutiny and debate over these systems' implications. They are a relevant voice in the process of understanding the dilemmas and directions of these institutions' design.

The complexity of algorithmic systems' development is also extremely dependent on individuals who provide or become the data that allow the algorithms' actual work. This is particularly true when we think of AI. The establishment of patterns and correlations that forge the outputs of algorithmic systems are not entirely designed and controlled by developers: they also derive from machine-learning processes that find patterns where designers would have never guessed. When we think, therefore, about the design of contemporary algorithms, we should keep in mind the actual role played by those who do not even know they are contributing to establishing these institutions.

In a certain way, this resembles what we see in most institutions. Institutions are not simply designed; they are enacted in a series of practices that shape how formal rules are interpreted and applied and that reinvent informal rules through action. These individuals may not be fully aware of their agency, but their practices are at the heart of how the institution functions. In the case of algorithmic systems, however, it is not only (and exactly) agency and practice that end up shaping the institution. Biometric data and records of millions of individuals in diverse data sets shape how FRTs and software of predictive policing work. Individuals' transformation and fragmentation into pieces of data nurture machine-learning algorithms that overlap with other machine-learning algorithms in designing intricate AI systems that shape the output in not fully comprehensible ways. This is true not only for individuals who are transformed into data but also for the so-called designers.

This is not to deny that values, interests, and intentions matter and help shape the output. As clearly shown by Tarcízio Silva, evidence abounds of racial bias of algorithmic systems employed in security.[41] Parameters established for the operation of AI systems are not socially detached, even if they should not be read as a transparent translation of individual values and interests. Algorithmic Institutionalism points to this complex encounter of factors shaping institutions' structures.

Moreover, it is not only actors that matter in the process of shaping institutions: context is highly relevant, too. As mentioned, FRTs faced a significant setback in the pandemic because of the need to adapt existing software to the

---

[41] Silva (2022).

use of masks.[42] However, they also needed to conceive of new uses, such as combining FRT with thermography to detect fever in public spaces.[43]

Context is also relevant in institutional theories, as shown by discussions about *institutional isomorphism*,[44] which points to tendencies of homogeneity because of coercive, mimetic, and normative mechanisms. In the field of security, it is impressive how quickly some technologies travel from one context to another. Predictive policing has experienced a boom since 2012, with police departments following each other's cues in rapidly spreading the software. The criticisms and challenges raised against these technologies also raise norms and values that reshape their possibilities in different contexts. After predictive policing's banishment in multiple US cities, the European Union is moving in the same direction. In 2022, leading figures in charge of technological issues in the European Parliament suggested banning the use of AI in predictive policing and the judicial system.[45] The point here is that the design of technologies and their usage are deeply affected by contexts, and many players tend to adopt similar behaviours, imitating one another or rethinking their practices.

Historical Processes

Institutions change over time, and so do algorithmic systems. In the previous section we saw, for instance, how FRTs evolved during the pandemic to cope with the demand for new functions and forms of monitoring. The process of transformation of cybersecurity also illustrates the dynamic nature of algorithmic systems. To protect devices, networks, and data from unauthorized accesses or attempts of destruction, security systems must change constantly. As Khaleel Ahmad and colleagues note:

> Cyber security attacks are growing exponentially. Security specialists must occupy in the lab, concocting new schemes to preserve the resources and to control any new attacks. Therefore, there are various emerging algorithms and techniques viz. DES, AES, IDEA, WAKE, CAST5, Serpent Algorithm, Chaos-Based Cryptography McEliece, Niederreiter, NTRU, Goldreich–Goldwasser–Halevi, Identity Based Encryption, and Attribute Based Encryption.[46]

---

[42] Pollard (2020).
[43] https://www.dermalog.com/news/article/hanover-exhibition-fever-detection/.
[44] DiMaggio and Powell (1983).
[45] https://www.fairtrials.org/articles/news/leading-european-parliament-figures-agree-to-ban-predictive-policing-and-justice-ai/.
[46] Ahmad et al. (2019).

The change observed in institutions—and algorithms—is not, however, reduced to processes of adaption and evolution. Context and usage may drive technologies in radically different directions, reinventing their uses and purposes. Even the Internet itself was created as a military project and ended up deeply altering most dimensions of human existence. Many of the AI technologies developed with military purposes are now employed, for instance, in agriculture for crop and soil monitoring, disease diagnosing, intelligent spraying, and the robotization of many tasks.[47] In Argentinian wheat fields and Brazilian soy fields, drones developed by companies such as Taranis employ computer vision to monitor the appearance of pests quickly: 'The algorithm teaches itself to flag something as small as an individual insect, long before humans would usually identify the problem.'[48]

There are also data sets and algorithms created with different purposes that were incorporated by governments and companies for security purposes. An interesting case is the development of the Córtex system by the Brazilian Secretary of Integrated Operations (Seopi), which is part of the Ministry of Justice. The system tracks car plates with the support of thousands of cameras across the country, accessing diverse confidential data sets that were generated for other purposes. Despite developers' denials, there were accusations that the system could access data from RAIS (the annual report of social information from the Ministry of Economy), thereby providing around 10,000 security-force workers with access to highly pervasive forms of surveillance.[49] This data set was not created for this purpose but eventually could be used to monitor and intimidate citizens. According to Rubens Valente, Seopi was the agency responsible for producing a dossier that monitored police officers and teachers who would be tagged as *antifas* under Jair Bolsonaro's presidency.[50]

Understanding algorithms through institutional lenses requires paying attention to their shifting nature. Institutions are not set in stone; they change over time, establishing new patterns, rules, and functions. They face different contextual challenges and are pushed in different directions by diverse actors who enact these institutions through their practices. Situated actors continuously re-create institutions, and the same is true for algorithmic systems. They are pushed in different directions by the practices of—and pieces of data extracted from—agents. In this process, changing institutions also affect the same practices by which they are enacted. War in times of

[47] Talaviya et al. (2020).
[48] Allen (2019).
[49] Rebello (2020).
[50] Valente (2020).

autonomous weapons and AI, for instance, is something completely different from medieval battles and early twentieth-century conflicts.

Our point here is that algorithms should be read as historical constructs that reveal elements of societies. They are not abstractions floating around and above our existences. They embody patterns of behaviour, viewpoints, and norms taken for granted. And this is not necessarily because they are designed in certain ways; this is because AI is also a product of its context. In the field of security, an enormous amount of evidence shows, for example, how algorithmic systems re-enact racial asymmetries.

FRTs are often far more successful at identifying White people, which has led many Black individuals to be accused of crimes. 'A growing body of research exposes divergent error rates across demographic groups, with the poorest accuracy consistently found in subjects who are female, Black, and 18–30 years old.'[51] The case of Robert Julian-Borchak Williams—wrongly arrested in Detroit because of a faulty match from a facial recognition algorithm—is one among many famous cases.[52] In the previously mentioned case of the security assemblage of Ceará (Brazil), the American actor Michael B. Jordan had his image included in a list of wanted suspects for a massacre in the city of Fortaleza. This happened in January 2022, even though the actor had been in Brazil only in 2018, and in a different state. Still in Brazil, 80 per cent of the individuals found to be wrongly imprisoned by facial recognition mistakes in the state of Rio de Janeiro are Black.[53]

The use of facial recognition systems at airports in Canada has also discriminated against Muslims based on racialized databases,[54] and risk assessment algorithms have been criticized for crystallizing racial bias, as shown in a well-known report from *ProPublica*.[55]

This racial bias, or at least the difficulty in challenging algorithmic systems' racial consequences, is deeply connected to historical factors. Bias can derive from algorithms' design, how they are trained, or an alleged valorization of accuracy regardless of social implications. The case of predictive policing is particularly relevant here. Record rates of crimes committed by Black individuals leads to increased surveillance of Black neighbourhoods, thus strengthening the rates of identified crimes committed by Black individuals. O'Neil explains that an algorithm's fairness may require less

---

[51] Najibi (2020).
[52] Hill (2020).
[53] EBC (2022).
[54] Gidaris (2020).
[55] Angwin et al. (2016).

accuracy—which can involve, for instance, the non-consideration of low-risk offences—to challenge this vicious cycle.

Institutionalism helps make sense of it through the notion of path dependence, as past situations are the very basis of the calculations of probable futures.[56] Security systems use data from the past to design the present and act to achieve an allegedly safer future.[57] This future is, however, based on prophecies that reify and reproduce the past,[58] with existing biases replicated under the disguise of objective measures.[59] Path dependence shows the difficulty of interrupting these cycles, which has deep moral implications. Think, for instance, of LAWS, whose use is growing in military situations. Working with past data and discriminatory and colonialist knowledge bases, these systems are programmed to identify threatening situations and decide whether to eliminate them.[60] The implications of these algorithmic technologies for human rights is challenging and requires new frameworks in international law.[61]

Rules and Norms

Institutions are sets of rules and norms that structure some relations.[62] They configure arenas of interaction, shaping behaviours and thus moulding collective outcomes. They set frames and scripts that inform choices and strategies. Algorithmic systems employed in security also clearly operate in this way: they establish formal and informal rules, marking behaviours and social processes. But FRTs and predictive policing are not mere tools that can promote effective surveillance; they become ingrained in the fabric of society, affecting relations of sociability, the way individuals experience the city, and security forces' actions.

As in any other institution, some of the rules enacted by security algorithmic systems are formal and visible. The War on Terror after 9/11, for instance, pushed many explicit changes in the way border control is exerted and in laws that allowed what previously would have been seen as privacy violations. The Intelligence Reform, the Terrorism Prevention Act of 2004, and the USA PATRIOT Act formally changed rules of how data could be accessed and

---

[56] Pierson (2004).
[57] Lyon (2014).
[58] Završnik (2019); Brayne (2021).
[59] Noble (2018); Joyce et al. (2021).
[60] Scharre (2018).
[61] Donahoe and Metzger (2019).
[62] North (1990).

processed with the goal of protecting the 'free world'.[63] Since then, the power of algorithms to mine gigantic volumes of data has grown exponentially, and the Snowden affair exposed the US NSA's pervasive capacity to monitor individual lives.[64] Colliding email exchanges, social-media behaviour, and FRTs can impede someone from boarding a plane if that person is placed on a 'no-fly' list, for instance.

The examples of COMPAS and predictive policing also show algorithms' impact on establishing formal rules that lead to decisions and actions. Many judges can legally run software that looks at risk assessment to ground their decisions on how much time someone should spend in jail. Police forces have their logistics reorganized and activities restructured by algorithmic decisions that indicate areas of the city that should be targeted. In many situations, predictive technologies define and change action scripts within security policies, ensuring discretion for police action through choices made by surveillance assemblages.[65]

Algorithmic systems employed in security, however, have a broader capacity to establish informal rules and norms that shape behaviour. Some argue, for instance, that FRTs can lead to more altruistic behaviours because individuals tend to do good when they feel they are being observed.[66] Jon Elster cleverly theorized about the civilizing force of hypocrisy,[67] for instance. Yet FRTs also can lead to anxiety, fear, and segmentation of communities and groups that occupy different areas of the city. Some people feel safer circulating in hyper-monitored areas, but others may feel frightened because of their history of interactions with police forces. Race is definitely a key variable in the way algorithmic systems applied in security may reinforce urban spatial cleavages.

Hence, informal rules nurtured by algorithmic systems may naturalize social differences and justify them under the facade of objective decisions. Black and Latino neighbourhoods may be targeted more often by police operations under the justification that algorithms point to them as violent areas, even if part of this violence is generated by the interaction with police forces, and the 'peacefulness' of some neighbourhoods may be derived from the absence of police monitoring. In interacting with other institutions, algorithms establish patterns of occupation of urban space and grammars of social interaction, indicating, for instance, who should be feared or trusted.

---

[63] Jonas and Harper (2006).
[64] Margulies (2016).
[65] Brayne (2021).
[66] Van Rompay et al. (2009).
[67] Elster (2000).

Power Relations

As is the case with other types of institutions shaping and framing contexts of interactions, algorithmic systems have political consequences. They pervade power relations in societies, justifying some of them, naturalizing others, establishing new ones, and even displacing some of the existing relations of power. Whether in the algorithms' ability to define action scripts for security forces or in the fact that algorithms outline self-fulfilling prophecies, they affect collective choices and set parameters for individual behaviours.

In the field of security, algorithms primarily shape and institutionalize technocratic forms of power. They conceal decision-making's political nature through depersonalized, opaque, and often uncritical processes that are seen as apolitical. Security measures with deep implications on individual lives and on society are justified as if they were not human based. And yet these decisions benefit some social actors to the detriment of others, grounding social hierarchies.

In previous sections, we argued that algorithmic systems employed in security frequently reproduce racial biases, thereby naturalizing, justifying, and reinforcing racial asymmetries. As is the case with other institutions, algorithms not only reflect rational inequalities but play active roles in their enactment and construction. As argued by Couldry and Mejias, in dialogue with Safiya Noble and Ruha Benjamin, algorithms

> reproduce and amplify racial differentiation under a dangerous veneer of objectivity and scientific truth (Noble, 2018, p. 24; Benjamin, 2019, pp. 5–6). The result poorly serves 'multiracial democracy' (Noble, 2018, p. 186) and facilitates racial modes of social control (Benjamin, 2019, p. 6).[68]

In the field of security, the political implications of algorithms are particularly salient because we are dealing with matters of life and death. Decisions based on algorithms can lead to imprisonment, persecution, and physical harm. Those affected by these decisions are often incapable of effectively confronting them.[69] Algorithmic systems frequently lead to violations of individual rights in contexts that tend to restrain the possibilities of accountability. Gerards argues, for instance, that security algorithms affect privacy rights, freedom of expression, the right to non-discrimination, and procedural rights of equal treatment in courts.[70]

---

[68] Couldry and Mejias (2021); see also Noble (2018); Benjamin (2019).
[69] Matthews et al. (2019); Metz and Satariano (2020).
[70] Gerards (2019).

The non-transparent power of surveillance technologies and security algorithms can be a straight road to forms of authoritarianism in many contexts. It is not by chance that China and Russia led the development of implementing FRTs. Neither is it by chance that wannabe autocrats show interest in spyware that lets them keep a close eye on their citizens. It is worth mentioning the spyware Pegasus, for instance, developed in 2011 by the Israeli company NSO. The technology explores flaws in operating systems to gain full access to private devices, consistently cracking encrypted communications without their users' knowledge. The software allows access to everything stored in a device, along with its camera and microphone.

The spyware has been used by many countries to fight terrorists, drug dealers, and global child-abuse rings. However, it also has been used to persecute political adversaries:

> Mexico deployed the software not just against gangsters but also against journalists and political dissidents. The United Arab Emirates used the software to hack the phone of a civil rights activist whom the government threw in jail. Saudi Arabia used it against women's rights activists and, according to a lawsuit filed by a Saudi dissident, to spy on communications with Jamal Khashoggi, a columnist for *The Washington Post*, whom Saudi operatives killed and dismembered in Istanbul in 2018.[71]

According to Valença, the Bolsonaro clan in Brazil tried to purchase the software in addition to NSO's other cyberweapons that allow pervasive forms of espionage.[72] The software has been sold to Modi's India, Orbán's Hungary, and Szydło's Poland, and its use to spy on social activists, journalists, and adversaries has been denounced in several contexts.[73] These cases show the dangers this software represents to democracies, as authoritarian governments may use algorithmic systems to persecute adversaries. John Keane recently warned about the role played by algorithmic systems in enabling new despotic governments to conduct more precise and surgical forms of surveillance and persecution, which are in tune with the age of communicative abundance.[74]

---

[71] Bergman and Mazzetti (2022).
[72] Valença (2021).
[73] Bergman and Mazzetti (2022).
[74] Keane (2020).

There is yet a second level of political relations pervading technology like Pegasus's deployment. There is evidence that Israel has used access to the technology as diplomatic currency:

> Countries like Mexico and Panama have shifted their positions toward Israel in key votes at the United Nations after winning access to Pegasus. *Times*' reporting also reveals how sales of Pegasus played an unseen but critical role in securing the support of Arab nations in Israel's campaign against Iran and even in negotiating the Abraham Accords, the 2020 diplomatic agreements that normalized relations between Israel and some of its longtime Arab adversaries.[75]

Still, in the diplomatic arena, NSO's technological developments have led to conflicts between the US and Israel. Pegasus did not have the ability to spy on US-based phones, but NSO created another software, named Phantom, that could—and that should be sold only to American governmental agencies. The controversy around Phantom ended with the consideration of NSO as a danger to national security, precluding it from buying supplies from American companies. Israeli officials have recently warned the White House security advisor that the weakening of NSO may strengthen Russian and Chinese hacking companies and, hence, these countries' geopolitical influence.

The NSO case illustrates some of the many dimensions in which algorithmic systems employed in security affect power relations, with deep implications not only for individual ordinary lives but also for the organization of security forces and for the construction and displacement of alignments in international arenas.

Gaming

At this point, it should be clear that different forms of power are exerted through algorithmic systems and pervade such systems' operations. These institutions frame settings of interaction, pervading power relations. From the lenses of institutionalist theories, however, institutions are not mere abstract rules and norms; they are enacted, reproduced, and displaced by agents whose practices may crystallize, update, or challenge extant rules. An important point for an institutionalist understanding of algorithms is how individuals interact with algorithmic technologies and change their functions and actions; that is, how individuals play with algorithms to expand their utility function or prevent algorithms from acting on their subjectivities.

---

[75] Bergman and Mazzetti (2022).

In the case of security policies, expanding surveillance in all dimensions of everyday life has led to different forms of human reaction to this new emerging institutional apparatus. Defining individuals—or regions— accurately and situating them within clusters is a key dimension in the way that the power of algorithms employed in security is enacted. Through algorithmic systems, security forces collect data on how individuals and other machines behave, feel, think, and make decisions: 'Linked together or analyzed separately, these data points constitute a new virtual identity, a digital self that is now more tangible, authoritative, and demonstrable, more fixed and provable than our analog selves.'[76] Algorithmic systems help locate given individuals or groups of individuals with precision to foresee courses of action and intervene appropriately (whatever appropriately means): 'We are ranked, categorized and scored in hundreds of models, on the basis of our revealed preferences and patterns.'[77]

Among the many attempts to resist or reframe algorithms' pervasive power,[78] we highlight some ordinary practices by which individuals seek to thwart being fully identified. Citizens often play with algorithms to hinder their capacity to promote identification. In the *infrapolitics*[79] of ordinary life, some citizens occasionally try to avoid being recognized and may even engage in strategies of disidentification to deceive algorithmic systems. Disidentification is a political action that aims to confront an order of social control.[80] In algorithmically shaped societies, this represents a relevant way to confront the power of algorithms employed in security.[81] By denying the naturalness of a place attributed to oneself, a person may resist algorithms' power.

There are different types of practices in the repertoire of disidentification in the face of algorithmic systems. Anonymization is the first and most frequent tactic adopted by individuals. To remain partially anonymous, some use browsers in incognito mode, for example, or use the dark web to escape constraints imposed by platform algorithms.

Another central tactic of contention involves deceiving algorithms. This is clear, for instance, when individuals choose to spell words differently to avoid automated responses that can range from censorship to unpleasant results returned. Writing with dots between letters or with numbers in the middle of

---

[76] Harcourt (2015: 1).
[77] O'Neil (2016: 63).
[78] Alnemr (2021).
[79] Scott (1990).
[80] Rancière (1999).
[81] Završnik (2019).

some words is a frequent strategy to remain below the radar.[82] Deception is also clear when individuals pretend to have liked something or intentionally go after something they dislike just to confuse algorithms about their real interests and tastes. Sometimes individuals know how an algorithm operates and react intentionally by altering the streams of information input to alter the streams of output.

Last, some forms of resistance can hinder biometric data collection, which is particularly important in the area of security. Strategies adopted by individuals to disidentify bodies include the use of masks, caps, helmets, or even make-up and other artefacts that may thwart facial recognition sensors. Artist and scholar Zach Blas, for instance, designed a series of masks as a means of resistance against facial recognition algorithms to promote what he called *informatic invisibility*.[83] Another tactic sometimes used is the hindering or even destruction of sensors. Individuals in public demonstrations in Hong Kong, for instance, confronted sensors, with different activists painting cameras to avoid being identified.

From the lens of Algorithmic Institutionalism, the agency of individuals to affect algorithms from within is key, because, as previously discussed, the outcomes of algorithmic systems are generated by an overlap of intervening factors. By playing with the rules, norms, scripts, and frames embedded in these institutions, individuals interact and perform a role in enacting and reinventing them. As in the case of other institutions, algorithmic systems can be seen as capable of exerting restraining forces, but they also depend heavily on the agency of actors that are not fully determined by these restraining forces.

Discursive Dimensions

Employing Algorithmic Institutionalism to think of algorithms in the field of security requires attention to their discursive dimensions. As Chapter 2 discussed, there are at least four ways to articulate algorithms and discursive institutionalism: algorithms are grounded on discursive frames with particular comprehensions about the world; algorithmic systems frame contexts of action in which other interactions take place; algorithms are arguments in broader discursive disputes; and algorithms are often discussed in the public sphere.

---

[82] Mendonça et al. (2021).
[83] De Vries and Schinkel (2019).

The three initial possibilities were covered in the previous sections. We have discussed how FRTs, predictive policing, and risk-assessment software used by courts frame reality in certain ways, often naturalizing, for instance, racial biases. Algorithms are grounded in particular ways to understand reality, and, in this sense, the lines of codes end up offering practical arguments about how the world should be seen and how it should work. In defining certain neighbourhoods as more dangerous than others through a specific way to define what 'danger' is and how it should be measured, algorithms warrant certain courses of action and justify feelings and behaviours of different sorts. They are arguments with strong perlocutionary effects, as extremely concrete things are done through them. They make J. L. Austin's famous claim quite clear: we do things with words.[84] In contrast to many other forms of argumentative expression, however, arguments presented through algorithmic functions seem less visible. They are often not perceived as discourses justifying certain perspectives and courses of action, which conceal their argumentative nature, posing new challenges to the public sphere.

In addition, many security-aimed algorithmic systems frame reality in ways that undermine trust, feeding a general sense that anyone is a potential threat and that the lack of surveillance will necessarily lead to crime and violence. In doing so, algorithmic systems employed in security frame other contexts of action, setting affordances, rules, and norms that mark many interactions. From border control to everyday surveillance, several contexts of interactions have been affected by these technologies. A study about implementing FRTs in the favela of Jacarezinho in the city of Rio de Janeiro raises concerns about how this technology will affect a context deeply marked by violence. Jacarezinho was the stage of a massacre with at least twenty-eight deaths during a police operation in 2021. Implemented in 2022, the system may add injury to harm in an overly stigmatized community, shaping many interactions between the community's dwellers and other citizens. Interestingly, the system

> serves only as a repressive use of police power and strengthens the production of evidence to support police innocence in trial settings. The data is not made available to eventual victims of excesses in the use of violence and human rights violations by the historically repressive state security forces.[85]

Because these previous points have been covered in other sections, we must focus here on the fourth one: algorithms are often challenged and

---

[84] Austin (2001).
[85] Alves et al. (2022).

supported by other discourses in the public sphere. There are growing controversies around surveillance assemblages in the public sphere, and more attention is directed to these assemblages. The case of LAWS is quite illustrative in this respect. On the one hand, there are voices in the public sphere supporting LAWS, especially in the industry that develops these devices, which are revolutionizing warfare.[86] They argue that LAWS demand fewer resources, reduce casualties, and enlarge the battlefield to cover previously inaccessible areas.[87] For some, killer robots would be more ethical in avoiding unnecessary harm: 'Several military experts and roboticists have argued that autonomous weapons systems should not only be regarded as morally acceptable, but that they would in fact be ethically preferable to human fighters.'[88]

On the other hand, there are several opposing voices regarding the use of LAWS. The risks, they argue, are manifold. LAWS would represent new dangers to human rights and international stability, and their use would run the risk of nurturing terrorism and rogue states by potentially enabling a small number of individuals to inflict extremely large-scale casualties at a low cost, either intentionally or accidentally.[89] The risk also exists for radical transformations of the scale of harm potentially inflicted through software changes. Hence, many push for the banning of LAWS, arguing that regulation will not be able to restrain the potential hazards. In 2015, an open letter published by the International Joint Conference on Artificial Intelligence advocated the banning of autonomous weapons.[90] The letter was signed by prominent robotics scholars and endorsed by individuals as diverse as Jack Dorsey, Stephen Hawking, Noam Chomsky, Elon Musk, and Steve Wozniak. At the top of the list of authors signing the letter was Stuart Russell, a Berkeley computer scientist who has been one of the main voices noting the dangers of autonomous weapons. In one of his articles, he warns that non-state actors can now develop home-made autonomous weapons, as technologies have developed far more quickly than states' capacity to sign a banning treaty or at least anti-proliferation agreements.[91] Throughout the world, initiatives such as StopKillerRobots seek to mobilize and call for action against the destructive power of autonomous weapons, nurturing debates in the public sphere.[92]

---

[86] Javorsky et al. (2019).
[87] Thurnher (2012); Byrnes (2014); Etzioni and Etzioni (2017).
[88] Etzioni and Etzioni (2017: 255).
[89] Arkin et al. (2019).
[90] http://futureoflife.org/open-letter-autonomous-weapons/.
[91] Russell (2022).
[92] https://www.stopkillerrobots.org/.

The same can be said for discourses around facial recognition, predictive policing, and risk-assessment software. The public sphere is flooded by opinions and evaluations of these technologies' benefits and risks. Some claim that these algorithmic-based technologies are important for security, preventing attacks, optimizing resources, and avoiding impunity. They would make the police and courts more intelligent and capable of preventing harm, instead of simply repressing crime or letting a judge alone evaluate if they think someone has a chance of recidivism.[93] Yet many voices point to these technologies' ineffectiveness and risks, drawing attention to their social and ethical implications.

As pushback grows against these technologies, requests for bans resound. For instance, as mentioned previously, many cities that implemented projects based on FRTs and predictive policing either aborted these projects or put them on hold. In 2021, the EU passed a nonbinding resolution banning facial recognition, signalling the need to prohibit the technology.[94] In the US, more than twenty states and cities have banned FRTs,[95] and, in India, resistance to FRTs is growing in some of the world's most surveilled places.[96] Minorities, students, and public servants lead the struggle against the fast spread of CCTV cameras in cities such as Hyderabad and New Delhi, where police have used these systems to monitor protests: a prevailing fear is that the technology could end up targeting the rights of Muslims, Dalits, transgender people, and other marginalized groups. In Brazil, initiatives such as #SaiDaMinhaCara[97] and #TireMeuRostoDaSuaMira aim to mobilize civil society against facial recognition.

If we step back to gain perspective on all these cases' details, the point that interests us here is that algorithmic systems emerge and develop within discursive networks that can push them in different directions. Discourse is at the heart of the creation and unfolding of these technologies. The public sphere can shed light on dangerous elements of these technologies, pointing to the need for changes, prohibitions, and regulations that affect the shape of these institutions and their consequences. Discourses are not illusory abstractions but sets of embodied practices that have consequences on other practices. Institutions—and thus algorithms—are pervaded by concrete discourses that embody these institutions and may push these institutions in different directions.

---

[93] Kehl et al. (2017); Meijer and Wessels (2019).
[94] Li (2021).
[95] Dave (2022).
[96] *Al Jazeera* (2022).
[97] https://tecmasters.com.br/iniciativa-banir-reconhecimento-facial-publicos/.

Concluding Remarks

This chapter sought to apply the framework developed in Chapter 2 to make sense of algorithmic systems employed in security. By conceiving of algorithms as institutions, Algorithmic Institutionalism points to six dimensions worth consideration, thereby providing a complex matrix to make sense of diverse phenomena, such as FRTs, predictive policing, risk-assessment software, and LAWS.

The chapter started with an encompassing definition of security, then demonstrated the growing relevance of algorithmic systems in many fields of security. To delve into these various phenomena, we discussed the following points:

- The design of security assemblages happens through a complex process in which governments, corporations, universities, and individuals interact. We have also shown the presence of institutional isomorphism in security assemblages, as some technologies—like FRTs—travel fast from one context to another.
- Security assemblages are historical and reflect the values and bias of the contexts from which they emerge, as shown by the reproduction of racial injustices in automated decisions. Path dependence reinforces the inertial nature of these institutions, which raises many dilemmas if we think of FRTs and LAWS.
- Algorithms employed in security enact, stabilize, and challenge norms and rules, thus shaping many social interactions. Informal rules nurtured by security assemblages may naturalize social differences, as shown by projects of predictive policing.
- Security assemblages institutionalize technocratic forms of power. The non-transparent power of surveillance technologies and security algorithms can lead to authoritarianism.
- Individuals play with the power of algorithms, reinventing the structures that shape their agency. In the case of security assemblages, there are many attempts to deceive algorithms and hinder their capacity to identify individuals in micro forms of everyday resistance.
- Security assemblages can be seen as arguments that frame comprehensions about risk and security. There are also important debates around these algorithms, as exemplified by the attempts to problematize the development of LAWS.

The framework of Algorithmic Institutionalism has paved a useful way to understand algorithms, which are usually thought of in rather abstract ways.

The long tradition of analysis of institutions has shown some ways forward, mapping diverse facets of contemporary issues. FRTs, predictive policing, risk-assessment software, and LAWS have deep implications in many arenas of interaction, marking the way we institutionalize policies to prevent risks and promote safety.

The traditional figure of Hobbes's Leviathan is that of the monster composed of the union of all individuals. This monster holds in one hand the sword representing the monopoly of the means of violence and in the other the sceptre that represents the law. The artefacts built into the industrial complexes of surveillance reflect political choices, but algorithmic technologies employed in security build a new type of Leviathan. Private corporations have a key role in shaping it and capitalize on surveillance assemblages for different purposes, making them ubiquitous tools with varied consequences for polities. Perhaps the representation of this new Leviathan is that of an algorithm composed of everyone's personal profiles, with a sword and sceptre in its design.

In this sense, this chapter has advanced in its second main goal: if institutionalism indicates ways forward to make sense of algorithms, the reality of algorithmic systems also points to the need to update institutional theories on the grounds of the context of algorithmic societies. The chapter points to at least three aspects in which the analysis of algorithms suggests relevant updates in institutional approaches.

First, as discussed in the section devoted to design, while individuals remain central to the configuration of institutions, they affect their shape not only through practices but also (and mainly) through their fragmentation in data pieces that nurture machine-learning developments in often unpredictable ways. This adds an extra layer of complexity to institutional design, making reflexive control over institutions more difficult.

Second, there are important distinctions in how discourses operate within and across these institutions. If algorithms play a role as arguments in the public sphere, they emerge as a cyphered argument that warrants certain positions and courses of action without frequently being perceived as an argument. Algorithms have clear perlocutionary effects but are rarely read in their locutionary and illocutionary dimensions. Moreover, even when we move to a more traditional conception of the public sphere and focus on attempts to vocalize pros and cons of algorithmic systems employed in security, we enter a realm of highly specialized technical language that is hard to translate to everyday natural language, surrounded by secrets derived both from the market and from national security preoccupations. It is, therefore, extremely difficult to sustain informed public conversations about the ways through which these algorithmic systems affect societies.

Third, and finally, algorithms are changing the way we think of traditional institutions that are central to security. States and central powers are somehow damaged by the swarming power that can be manifested through algorithmic systems, as the case of home-made autonomous weapons makes clear. The level of decentralization and uncontrollable developments seems unprecedented, posing difficult questions as to how institutional authority is exerted. Curiously, the technical progress fostered by security purposes at the same time represents one of the major challenges to the security of existing institutions.

And the field of security points to just one tiny facade of the many challenges that institutions are facing. As we will see in Chapters 4 and 5, there are many layers relevant to an appropriate comprehension of the institutional roles played by algorithms and the dilemmas that emerge from contemporary societies.

4
Redesigning Governments through Algorithmic Systems

When the World Health Organization (WHO) declared the coronavirus outbreak a pandemic on 11 March 2020, many saw their lives turned upside down. Suddenly, many became aware of a danger they could not see but that was so strong that it could shut borders and abruptly slow down major global economic activities. Stay-at-home orders, lockdowns, and quarantines were adopted in most countries, changing the routines of workers, students, and families in fundamental ways.

Governments had to cope with this colossal catastrophe and invent rapid solutions to old and new problems in a moving context. Digital innovations acquired prominence on many fronts, with remote work, remote medicine, and online teaching, for instance, suddenly at the heart of everyday life, paving the way forward in these difficult days but also creating new problems and demands for public administration.

Another area that required speedy digital innovation was social assistance. As the economy suffered the consequences of the pandemic, many lost their sources of income. This was particularly dramatic in countries with high levels of informal work. In Brazil, for instance, around 40 per cent of the occupied population had no job security or stable source of revenue in 2020. That year, 24.1 per cent of 210 million Brazilians lived in poverty, making less than US$5.50 per day.[1]

Like many other countries, Brazil implemented an emergency strategy to deal with the rapid impoverishment of an already poor population. The country's National Congress approved Auxílio Brasil to ensure a minimum income for the most vulnerable citizens, in an attempt to mitigate the harsh impacts of the economic crisis. Initially, the programme foresaw monthly transfers of 600 reais (roughly US$120) to informal workers and individual contributors to the National Institute of Social Security (INSS). In 2020, 66 million Brazilians—around 32 per cent of the population—received this emergency relief payment.

---

[1] Gandra (2021).

Algorithmic Institutionalism. Ricardo F. Mendonça, Fernando Filgueiras, and Virgílio Almeida, Oxford University Press.
© Ricardo F. Mendonça, Fernando Filgueiras, and Virgílio Almeida (2023). DOI: 10.1093/oso/9780192870070.003.0005

In addition to the economic difficulties of implementing a programme that cost more than US$60 billion, policymakers faced a huge task: they had to design a programme capable of finding those in need and of developing solutions actually to get the money to these individuals. Previous initiatives, such as Bolsa Família, were helpful in the process.[2] They were, however, insufficient to deal with the amount of information required to establish speedy emergency relief. As a result, new platforms and apps were created, and algorithmic systems played a key role in sorting through a huge amount of data to decide who was entitled to the benefit by crossing and pairing different databases and public records. After the algorithmic decision had been made about who was entitled to the benefit, the government authorized Caixa Econômica Federal—a public bank—to pay the money to the nominated citizens. Then another algorithmic system audited the implementation, red-flagging some cases and indicating inconsistencies. This same auditing algorithm made recommendations to citizens who received an improper payment to return it without the application fines or legal proceedings, thus encouraging appropriate behaviour by beneficiaries.

This example shows the scope and relevance of algorithmic systems in contemporary policymaking. Algorithms are used in many important decisions with life-and-death implications: from healthcare to social assistance, security to education, and environmental compliance to urban mobility, algorithms are at the centre of the design, implementation, and evaluation of many current policies around the world.[3] In parallel, the pandemic has accelerated the growing platformization of governments, incorporating more algorithmic systems to perform different tasks and make decisions on various aspects of public policy.

Algorithms are not, however, mere tools in the process of policymaking. They are changing public policy significantly and are at the heart of administrative reforms spread by different international organizations, modifying the way governments work. Even if they may sometimes enable the continuation of long-sought goals, they do so by altering the way governments work and think to carry out the tasks of administration.[4] Governments go through a platformization process, incorporating algorithms for decision-making and

---

[2] The former was a national award-winning social policy established in Brazil in 2003 by the Lula administration, while the latter is a data set with information about families in situations of poverty.
[3] Giest (2017); Henderson et al. (2021).
[4] Investigating social policies and algorithmic systems employed to manage the access to welfare benefits, Eubanks (2018) argues that these systems can be understood as a *digital poorhouse* that further develops attempts to exclude the poor that have been implemented since the nineteenth century. In the same direction, Aradau and Blanke (2022) emphasize how the focus on changes may obscure the perception that algorithmic reason often continues previously existent forms of exclusion.

automating administrative tasks. Algorithms are a central part of the efforts to rationalize decision-making through big data, thus playing a role in the reorganization of operational tasks.

Here, we deal with the idea of algorithms as institutions in the context of government platformization and how algorithmic systems are transforming governments. We start with a brief introduction on government platformization, then make sense of it through the framework of Algorithmic Institutionalism introduced in Chapter 2.

Government Platformization

The possibilities for using algorithmic systems in public policy are grounded in the expansion of the computing infrastructure to process a gigantic variety and volume of data with extraordinary speed of collection and enormous capacity of storage. Governments are major data collectors and data producers in different aspects of individuals' lives. This enables the increasing automation of public administration in the context of governments' platformization.

According to Michael Veale and Irina Brass, there are two main ways in which algorithmic systems are incorporated into public administration and public policy:

> Automation systems attempt to increase the quantity or efficiency of routine public sector operations through computation [...] [while] augmentation systems [are grounded on the] belief that machine learning does not just help cheapen or hasten decision-making but can improve it.[5]

While the former expands the capacity of what is already done by replicating existing tasks and models, the latter focuses on new possibilities, mobilizing various data sources to do things differently. It is on the grounds of these promises that several countries have experienced a growing trend towards government platformization.[6] Public administration is changing its institutional and organizational aspects with the use of platforms, as digital technologies mediate the performance of public organizations,[7] and algorithmic systems are used as tools to achieve policy objectives.[8]

---

[5] Veale and Brass (2019: 4–5).
[6] Platforms are virtual spaces that offer services in an integrated way and establish models of interaction and connection with different types of users (Frischmann and Selinger, 2018).
[7] Dunleavy et al. (2006).
[8] Filgueiras and Almeida (2021).

Algorithmic systems provide a redesigning of governments, amplifying the flows of input data collected on platforms and fostering new standards of knowledge production, new dynamics of formulation of solutions to public problems, and different operational standards that affect policy implementation.

Governmental platforms can produce several benefits for society. First, they promote the integration of public services, avoiding the agencification of public administration.[9] Second, they can generate a more efficient delivery of services, rationalizing processes and facilitating the dynamics of policy implementation. Third, platformization expands states' capacities for policy design in an informed and evidence-based manner. Fourth, platforms may provide greater public integrity, as different actions are performed with less human intervention, institutionalizing compliance rules and barriers to corrupt behaviour.[10]

Platforms incorporate algorithmic systems to transform public-decision architecture and government operations that underpin policy implementation. The Gov.uk and the Gov.br platforms—respectively the British and Brazilian government platforms—incorporate the entire structure of public service delivered to users. Using data inputs from users' interactions with these platforms, governments may try to anticipate citizens' demands and change implementation processes to optimize their policy agenda.[11] In this sense, policy goals may change along the way, as algorithmic systems work to anticipate citizen demands and produce a stream of outputs that make it easier to achieve policy objectives and deliver services to society.[12] Algorithmic systems are incorporated to facilitate various government operations, transforming, in turn, the entire organizational and institutional logic of public policy, along with bureaucratic dynamics and the modes of interaction between governments and citizens.

Despite their potential benefits, such changes also lead to new risks for society. Peter Henderson and collaborators point out that algorithms should be effective, reliable, and fair to be employed in public policy.[13] However, contemporary scholarship in the field shows how these values are difficult to achieve. One of the problems linked to the platformization of public

---

[9] Agencification is the creation of semi-autonomous agencies to implement public-policy tasks. Agencification is a consequence of public-administration reforms that adopted the new public-management paradigm, producing a fragmentation of the public service that led to deep coordination problems. In this regard, see Verhoest (2013).
[10] We understand public integrity as the alignment and adherence of public managers' behaviour consistent with ethical values, principles, and rules that prioritize the public interest.
[11] Hood and Margetts (2007).
[12] Giest (2017).
[13] Henderson et al. (2021).

administration is the danger of data leaks.[14] Another is the exclusion of segments of the population owing to digital divides, but it is only one among the many ways in which algorithmic systems can lead to the crystallization of inequalities and injustices. A well-known case from the area of healthcare shows how racial injustice can be nurtured by biased decisions made by algorithmic systems. In 2019, Obermeyer and colleagues analysed an algorithm employed in US hospitals to rank patients according to their expected health needs.[15] The study showed that, 'at the same level of algorithm-predicted risk, Blacks have significantly more illness burden than Whites'.[16] This means that Whites who were designated for a specific type of treatment were in better condition than Blacks considered in need of that same treatment. The main reason for this bias was the centrality of expenditures in the calculus made to design health conditions: since less money is usually spent on Black patients, the algorithm reproduced this pattern in a feedback loop of injustice.

Among potential benefits and risks, algorithms gradually occupy an institutional space in governments, changing different aspects of public administration and policy. As new institutions that shape governments, they work as decision systems that play key roles in defining what is allowed, prevented, facilitated, or hindered, thus shaping individual human behaviours with collective outcomes. The algorithmization of policymaking represents a new technocratic standard in which essential decisions are both made automatically and mediated by machines.[17]

In this sense, such algorithmization comprises a new set of analytical interests for institutional theory. By playing different roles in policymaking, algorithmic systems change how norms are established, transform the operational strategies of governments, and create new forms of interaction between governments and social actors. In the following sections, we analyse different layers of changes through the lens of Algorithmic Institutionalism.

Institution Building and Design: Why Are Governments Being Algorithmically Redesigned?

On 15 September 2008, Lehman Brothers' bankruptcy was announced. It was a key event in the so-called subprime crisis in which major financial institutions were left with worthless investments owing to the burst of a

---

[14] Chatterjee and Sokol (2021).
[15] Obermeyer et al. (2019).
[16] Obermeyer et al. (2019: 448).
[17] Danaher (2016), Meijer et al. (2021).

housing bubble. The financial earthquake unfolding from the bankruptcy of Lehman Brothers had a cascading effect, leading to a global crisis that forced the US Federal Reserve and the European Central Bank to inject hundreds of billions of dollars and euros into the financial market. The crisis took global proportions, with devastating effects on the economies at both the centre and the periphery of capitalism. The US public debt jumped from 55 to 100 per cent of GDP in a short time. Direct public spending on infrastructure, job creation, and rescue programmes for large companies, such as General Motors, totalled around US$750 billion.[18]

This global economic crisis, often compared to the one in 1929, forced different governments worldwide to formulate solutions and interventions. More than 400 million people became unemployed around the world because of this crisis, requiring government responses that, on the one hand, reinforced austerity measures and, on the other, created social policies aimed at helping the most vulnerable people.

One of the major initiatives—motivated by austerity policies—was to make reforms to increase public-sector productivity, cutting public spending, increasing integrity, and defining global standards of government operations. Digital transformation emerged as a broad consensus to redesign governments to achieve their policy purposes in the context of fiscal turbulence. The crisis and the advancement of technologies therefore created the conditions for institutional changes.[19] This window of opportunity led to the institutionalization of new practices, frameworks, and action scripts for bureaucrats, fundamentally changing various aspects of policymaking and public administration.

In the late 1990s, for example, Estonia faced the bankruptcy of its financial system and produced an austerity policy that involved digitizing the entire governmental structure with the support of the banking system.[20] Similar experiences diffused among other governments, with the support of several organizations, including not only the OECD but also the World Bank and the World Economic Forum. Since that time, they have disseminated governance reforms to promote the digitization of public services, increasing data collection, processing, and sharing across government agencies and private actors. Technology experts designed the strategies, provided benchmarks, and reviewed the consolidated solutions. Algorithmic systems were incorporated in the institutional design of policies and administrative operations, automating procedures and creating new practices for decision-making.

---

[18] Sorkin (2010).
[19] Dunleavy and Margetts (2013).
[20] Kattel and Mergel (2019).

In the concept of digital government as disseminated by the OECD, among others, governments should be: *digital by design*, using digital technologies to rethink and re-engineer public-sector processes, simplify procedures, and create new channels of communication and engagement with stakeholders; *data-driven*, conceiving of data as a strategic asset and establishing mechanisms of governance, access, sharing, and reuse to improve decision-making and service delivery; *platformized*, deploying platforms, standards, and services to help teams focus on user needs in the design and delivery of services; *open by default*, with data and processes available to the public, facilitating stakeholder participation and involvement; *user-driven*, attributing a central role to people's needs and conveniences in the shaping of processes, services, and policies; and *proactive*, by adopting mechanisms that enable this to happen, anticipating people's needs and responding to them rapidly.[21]

The OECD promoted the concept of digital transformation and proposals aimed at redesigning government architecture, with broad impacts on the way governments formulate, decide, implement, and evaluate public policy. The institutional design diffused is technocratic, based on a conception of knowledge supported by data and on models that change the entire policy cycle. The adoption of algorithmic systems in public policy and administration is diffused by international organizations and designed in practice in partnership with industry, which designs algorithmic institutions through trial and error and accuracy testing of mathematical models to agency optimization. In this way, the adoption of digital governments impacts directly on state institutions, modifies the set of rules, and promotes government re-engineering not considering political issues of fairness and policy effectiveness.

Driven by the idea of digital transformation, with governmental responses to economic crises in the background, government platformization provides the insertion of algorithmic systems within the institutional work of the state, defining through algorithms the government's operating rules and strategies of the bureaucracy, along with the definition of incentives and constraints in the regulatory framework. The adoption of algorithmic systems encodes procedures for bureaucratic agents, rearranging various bureaucratic practices.[22] The algorithmization of bureaucratic organizations is embedded further in changes in work routines, streamlining many processes and altering the logic of organizational work.

Such algorithms are designed as bureaucratic action scripts, changing decision procedures to deal with a huge volume of data and reframing the way

---

[21] OECD (2014).
[22] Meijer et al. (2021).

problems are built and known. Algorithms also allow new ways to think about solutions, as different alternatives can be formulated and simulated, thereby also affecting implementation scripts. The institutional design of different public policies has been shaped by algorithms diffused in a new knowledge dynamic.

As already argued, the institutional redesign of governments by adopting algorithmic systems as solutions to different policy problems has been disseminated by many international organizations, and this diffusion process in turn shaped coordinated organizational convergences in a growing transformation of governments into platforms. From the critical juncture of the 2008 crisis, the idea of digital transformation was built as a solution, fostering institutional redesign through algorithmic systems with international organizations' support.

Technology companies—and their data infrastructures—also played a substantial role in this transformation. In China, for instance, partnership with large technology companies such as Huawei or Tencent was at the heart of the government's platformization. The Chinese state controls the data infrastructure and strategically encourages digital development by incorporating different algorithmic systems developed by partner companies and applied to governments.[23] The design of the algorithmic systems employed in this deep reformulation of governments is embedded in power structures, which opens the pathways for such transformations.

As corporations play a crucial role in reconfiguring public administration, states may be redesigned on the grounds of interests and perspectives that have not been submitted to public scrutiny. Market interests and technical choices that may benefit some actors to the detriment of others therefore can reshape existing institutions through these emerging algorithmic institutions. In this sense, the complex and shifting relations between public and private interests acquire another layer of complexity in configuring contemporary political institutions.

Historical Processes: New or Old Governments?

Understanding algorithms through institutional lenses requires paying attention to their dynamic nature. Institutions are not set in stone; they change over time, establishing new patterns, rules, and functions. These changes are

---

[23] Hong (2017).

not fully arbitrary, however, as they are inserted in broader historical processes. Understanding the historical contexts is essential to understanding the shaping of preferences in these continuous transformations.

Digitization reforms are not a kind of 'big bang' of new government technologies; rather, they are part of incremental processes based on trial and error. Choices made are not necessarily the best ones but the ones possible at specific political moments.[24] Let us return to the case of Auxilio Brasil in Brazil to illustrate this point.

When assigning aid based on specific parameters and information, the programme's definition of the target population was problematic, concerning the institutional framework. The law that supports the programme includes informal workers, individual micro-entrepreneurs, and individual contributors to the social security system, in addition to those enrolled in CadÚnico, as eligible to receive emergency aid. CadÚnico is an extensive database containing information on the most vulnerable people in Brazil and had been constituted in previous welfare programmes.

When Auxilio Brasil was implemented in the pandemic, the algorithmic systems that decided who was entitled to it were only possible owing to the existing infrastructure in other governmental programmes.[25] Such infrastructure set the boundaries of possibility, clearly showing the dynamics of path dependence. Databases, for instance, are not simply collections of data points: data are always produced through processes that involve choices grounded on sociopolitical interpretative frameworks.[26] Algorithms are used in public policies to classify and distinguish people based on databases that can reproduce stories of exclusion and injustice. In the Auxílio Brasil, different exclusion processes were reproduced, including digitally illiterate people, problems with public records, and biases about choices between who would or would not benefit from the programme.

Policy implementation is always a struggle for the realization of an idea.[27] Another example occurred with the adoption of an algorithmic system to make decisions about the British education system. The pandemic brought an enormous challenge to the policy of access to higher education in the UK, causing the government to look for alternatives to select students and ensure the education system's continuity. An algorithmic system that replaced the A-level grade to allocate students automatically to universities failed because it reproduced gender, ethnic, and racial biases. The result was criticism and

---

[24] Lindblom (1984).
[25] Cardoso (2020).
[26] Amoore (2014); Couldry and Mejias (2019); Joyce et al. (2021).
[27] Wilson (1989).

distrust in relation to the algorithmic system.[28] Negative feedback eventually led to its abandonment.

In these two examples, we have situations in which databases tell stories about people and reinforce previous choices in public policies. In both cases, algorithmic systems shaped collective decisions on the grounds of pre-existing conceptions, naturalizing and strengthening them. If algorithmic systems are sometimes presented as disruptive innovations, they often fail to promote actual change in collective choices as they are frequently locked in situations of path dependence, which is essential for a proper understanding of algorithmic decisions.[29]

Following the trend of platformization and institutional redesigning, many governments expect that algorithmic systems will revolutionize policy processes. Innovation, however, will not always represent a rupture: more often, it makes similar things in a different way. Indeed, positive feedback can explain the formation of institutions based on algorithmic systems, considering the increasing returns to austerity policies. Positive feedback is the enhancement or amplification of an effect by its own influence on the process that gave rise to it. The adoption of algorithmic systems can therefore reinforce elements of the historical contexts that led to them through the changes they promote in existing institutions of public administration.[30]

Reading government platformization through the lens of historical institutionalism, we can see its dependence on increasing returns and positive feedbacks. Algorithmic systems may expand citizens' trust in the functioning of public organizations, and the consumption of public services creates a logic of convenience that shapes citizens' acceptance of the process of institutional change.[31] These positive feedback loops nourish a historical pathway in which algorithmic systems become convenient, facilitating access to public services and enabling a trajectory of increasing returns and constant changes in the structure of contemporary governments. This logic of convenience creates a political power that frames the influence of technology companies in contemporary political economy.[32]

Positive feedback, deriving from the rationalization of activities and the increasing convenience of services, reinforces the institutional choices embedded in algorithmic systems applied to public policy. In addition, they create cognitive structures that shape agents' choices.[33] The employment of

[28] https://www.bbc.com/news/explainers-53807730.
[29] Eubanks (2018); Wenzelburger et al. (2022).
[30] Wenzelburger et al. (2022).
[31] Wenzelburger et al. (2022).
[32] Culpepper and Thelen (2021).
[33] Zysman (1994).

algorithmic systems in public policy is based on the expectation of increasing returns. In the case of government redesigning through algorithmic systems, the increasing returns—related to cost reduction, citizens' convenience, global alignment with international organizations, and rationalization of processes—foster policy change and frames bureaucratic actions.

Path dependence is referred to as a 'social process that exhibits positive feedback [...] in which outcomes in the early stages of a sequence feed on themselves, and once-possible outcomes become increasingly unreachable over time'.[34] Positive feedback explains the institutional change and path dependence. For example, in Auxílio Brasil, one of the biggest challenges was to identify the target population of the aid, considering the breadth of the formulated policy. The crossing of several databases made it possible to identify the beneficiaries, but it is estimated that the programme left out eight million vulnerable people owing to problems with the databases.[35] The institutionalization of algorithmic systems through government platforms resulted in positive feedback that fuelled increasing returns, which support a growing platformization of governments. However, this pathway was incapable of challenging injustices and forms of exclusion, because the problem is related more to how these algorithmic systems deploy austerity policies than social justice ones. The algorithmic systems employed tend to reproduce existing social injustices, thus crystallizing them.

What becomes evident, then, is that the 2008 financial crisis created a critical juncture that initiated change, paving an institutional path contextualized by algorithmic systems that was in tune with the broader context of the emergence of austerity policies. Government platformization reproduced a complex political economy in which algorithmic systems gradually institutionalized new practices concerning a new way of working in public administration. The increasing returns and contextualization of change arise from new patterns of interaction between citizens and algorithmic systems, paving the way for this innovation process. This does not mean, however, that situations of injustice or exclusion were challenged. On the contrary, digital transformation promotes changes based on algorithmic systems operating as institutions sustained on interactions between service consumers and governments, not citizens and their rights.

Algorithmic systems do not pass unscathed to policy design and implementation problems; rather, they reproduce previous choices in contexts that challenge the redesign of governments. The design of algorithmic systems is

---

[34] Pierson (2004: 21).
[35] https://oglobo.globo.com/economia/os-invisiveis-do-auxilio-brasil-turbinado-25552755.

inserted in contexts of political, economic, and social disputes that are shaped over time. The introduction of algorithmic systems in policy situations does not operate in a vacuum or at zero point: algorithmic systems are shaped in historical contexts, which often explain the policies' alleged successes or failures.

Rules and Norms: Regulation by Design

In the processes of redesigning governments through algorithmic systems, special attention is given to regulatory policy. Algorithmic systems open new avenues and pathways for the attempts of controlling and restricting some activities and behaviours as ways used by governments to deliver policy outcomes. Government platformization facilitates data collection, processing, and sharing to increase the capacity of state actors to implement regulatory policy and to change its scope and reach. Organizations such as the OECD and the World Bank are stimulating the use of digital technologies to promote 'smarter' and more effective regulatory policies that can nudge and affect actors' behaviour in society with normative interventions designed to achieve a given intent.[36]

Thought of as a set of norms that seeks to shape actors' behaviours, whether to produce compliance, steer the economy, or generate social control, regulation needs the input of information that will be processed by the government so that it can craft norms. Regulating the CO_2 emissions into the atmosphere, for example, requires governments to monitor various activities, producing data and strategically imposing a set of expected behaviours to achieve policy outcomes. The same situation occurred in the attempts of social control during the pandemic, in which governments monitored the flow of people and sought to impose rules of behaviour that avoided urban mobility and, consequently, the transmission of the virus.

Algorithmic systems make it possible for governments to process enormous flows of data and use them to calculate and nudge expected behaviours without noise.[37] This has led to *algorithmic regulation*, which 'refers to regulatory governance systems that use algorithmic decision-making',[38] establishing new ways to manage risk and influence individual and collective behaviours.

[36] Gunningham and Sinclair (2019).
[37] Sunstein (2022).
[38] Yeung (2018: 507).

According to Yeung, algorithmic regulation changes the architecture of individual choice, as it makes informal rules that affect the individual's environment to create monitoring possibilities by understanding population trends.[39] Governments gradually simulate responses to different policy alternatives and use algorithmic systems to detect fraud and corruption, thus ensuring reliability and compliance in the use of public resources.[40] Algorithmic systems institutionalize different issues and regulatory practices in different policy domains—that is, algorithms become regulatory institutions.

Georgia, for example, has introduced extensive use of blockchain to implement various government operations since 2016. Among these operations, property registration was transferred to the digital world through blockchain technology.[41] The same movement was made in Ghana, with the uninterruptable and secure registration of land titles by blockchain.[42] In countries such as Georgia and Ghana, blockchain algorithms deploy an essential regulatory function with significant development effects. One of the main barriers to development identified by international organizations such as the World Bank is the lack of institutionalization of property rights; so, blockchain has the potential to support regulatory functions to promote development. The property regulatory functions performed by blockchain algorithms supposedly change the behaviour of political and economic actors, institutionalizing property rights and greater financial security, ensuring the conditions for development.

Another example is Renovabio in Brazil, whose objective is to encourage the production of biofuels. Renovabio is a regulatory policy that sets annual national decarbonization targets for the fuel sector to encourage increased production of biofuels in the country's transport energy matrix. The entire process of this regulatory policy is based on an algorithmic system that uses smart contracts to address the positive environmental externalities of biofuel production on the financial market. An algorithmic system certifies biofuel production and carbon emission data by diverse databases, assigning each biofuel producer and importer an Energy-Environmental Efficiency Score. The score reflects the calculation of the individual contribution of each producing agent to mitigate a specific amount of greenhouse gases in terms of tons of CO_2 equivalent. Certification creates the opportunity for producers

---

[39] Yeung (2017).
[40] Lima and Delen (2020).
[41] Snip (2017).
[42] Matinde (2017).

to trade shares and encourages the production of biofuels, increasing profits and generating decarbonization credits.[43]

Algorithmic regulation incorporates and produces informal rules, including the architecture of the systems, the choice of databases that will be used, and the consequences concerning outputs produced. Algorithmic regulation intentionally seeks to create political and economic opportunities and nudge a framework of appropriate behaviours, all while establishing informal rules that affect patterns of action. The legitimacy of this technique of control is, however, highly controversial, owing to the lack of transparency in many cases and the dangers of active and passive manipulation.[44] The legitimacy of algorithmic regulation is also criticized for how it advances surveillance mechanisms and produces selective choices that may end up reinforcing inequalities.[45]

In a nutshell, algorithmic systems can embed the entire regulatory governance design in them, using data to monitor risks and compliance and nudging actors' behaviours through incentives and constraints. However, algorithmic systems regulate behaviours in often opaque ways, creating a technocratic regulation based on direct or indirect forms of influence with the support of surveillance systems. Regulation by algorithms means that they institutionalize new rules for different social actors, affecting their strategies. Algorithms, therefore, work as institutions, because they put rules in place for human agency in different situations.

Power Relations: Towards a Technocratic Political World

India is a country that has lived with poverty and hunger for a long time. Despite the advances in social protection—about 415 million people have risen out this situation between 2005 and 2021—poverty and hunger persist. According to the Multidimensional Poverty Index, in 2021, poverty affected, about 16.4 per cent of the population or about 230.739 million people.[46]

Algorithmic systems make decisions that have a direct impact on people, and they can have diverse implications that arise from technocratic power.

---

[43] https://www.gov.br/anp/pt-br/assuntos/renovabio.
[44] Active and passive manipulation, according to Yeung, are distinct ways in which algorithms manipulate human behaviour to accomplish regulatory governance goals. Active manipulation is based on experimental logic, where the algorithm actively nudges action elements to change results. Passive manipulation is one in which the nudge relies on deception, exploiting a cognitive weakness to nudge desired behaviours. In this regard, see Yeung (2017).
[45] Yeung (2017).
[46] United Nations Development Program and Oxford Poverty and Human Development Initiative (2023).

The 12-digit Aadhaar unique identification system implemented in Dumka, India, for example, manages social benefit allocation in a single system, using facial-recognition algorithms to identify citizens and make decisions. Unfortunately, flaws in the Aadhaar system have doomed some people to starvation and lack of help in disasters.[47] Each person is required to have this identification number to access social benefits, and it is linked to biometric data and used in various social protection operations. Failures in collecting biometric data and flaws in the algorithmic system can compromise welfare policies in India:

> The Indian government argued that this system would revolutionise welfare: computerised checks would stop fraudsters from siphoning off other people's benefits, allowing more money to reach the poor. But campaigners say its design is flawed and it is riddled with technological glitches. They argue it has become a Kafkaesque nightmare that has caused misery for the very people it claims to protect. Despite the serious concerns raised by economists and poverty experts, the system kept on growing and is now involved in access to anything from a pension to medical reimbursements or disaster emergency relief.[48]

Algorithmic systems such as Aadhaar are shaping new forms of technocratic relations of power. Technocratic power in public policy reduces the possibilities of human mediation and control, strengthening given conditions and hindering attempts to promote actual change. As many previous illustrations make clear, algorithmic systems have deep implications in the establishment and maintenance of relations of power, producing a technicization of social relations. They may be instruments of rationalization, like many other institutions, but they also make the Weberian iron cage of bureaucracy stronger and less porous to contestations.[49] Applied as mechanisms for rationalizing bureaucracy, algorithmic systems change the logic of power as they influence human behaviour inside and outside governments and the state. In this sense, they affect government institutions, creating new dynamics between diverse actors in the process of policymaking.

The way algorithmic systems applied to policymaking impact on power relations is multifaceted. The first aspect of these new power relations is organizational. The digital transformation of governments created an unprecedented process of institutional isomorphism, with the platformization of

---

[47] Ratcliffe (2019).
[48] Ratcliffe (2019).
[49] Weber (1978).

several governments.⁵⁰ The diffusion of digital transformation toolkits has promoted a conception of digital governments by design, fostering processes of mimesis and similar normative structures. This process of institutional isomorphism driven by algorithmic systems affects a global power dynamic that shapes the action of public administrations and creates new dynamics of policy steered by data and the capacity to influence situations, scripts, and frames.

As a result, in many parts of the world, government platforms homogenize and automate many of the public-service transactions, using data channels common to all government agencies, thus fostering data interoperability. Although platforms intend to personalize the provision of public services for each citizen, the transactions are constituted in an impersonal way that do not respect many differences, as individuals are transformed into mere data points.

An interesting example comes from Australia. In trying to automate social welfare, the federal government created Robodebt, an algorithmic system designed to calculate and collect welfare overpayment from citizens. Starting its operation in July 2016, Robodebt made recommendations that ended up causing severe distress to citizens and to the welfare agency's staff. Robodebt's mode of operation has been found to be illegal by Australian courts and has been investigated by the Commonwealth Ombudsman and three Senate committees. Investigations by these committees considered 470,000 of the debts had been recovered illegally, in a manner that negatively affected debt notice recipients' physical and mental health, forcing the Australian government to return AUS$1.8 billion to citizens.⁵¹

The second aspect of these new power relations is political. Algorithmic systems enable a political dynamic based on a new structure of knowledge, supported by data and calculations of the courses of action in society.⁵² This new knowledge structure solidifies a technical conception of governments, hiding power dynamics under the veil of non-personal decision-making and mathematical efficiency. In doing so, the platformization of governments promotes technocratic actors and forms power. Technocracy is a form of organization of power legitimized in politics by expertise and technical excellence, forming empowered bureaucratic elites.⁵³ Technocracy builds

---

[50] DiMaggio and Powell (1983).
[51] Rinta-Kahila et al. (2022).
[52] Amoore (2014).
[53] Fischer (1990); Centeno (1993).

its power based on the distrust of the alleged irrationality of democratic participation and is legitimized by the rationality of technique.[54]

A third aspect of the new structures of power has an epistemic nature. The power to know actors' preferences and create regulation based on induced behaviours frames a novel dynamic between actors and institutions in the policy process that is marked by opacity. Algorithmic systems reinforce the power of state bureaucracies to shape their interventions in an impersonal way, allegedly bypassing differences and making decisions that affect people by technical criteria that is legitimized by the calculation of possibilities and prediction of the future.

In government bureaucracies, algorithmic systems impose action scripts that restrict the possibilities of discretionary decisions taken by bureaucratic agents. The process of institutional isomorphism reduces the margins of resistance or sabotage on the part of bureaucrats, since the tendency is for algorithms to inhibit their previous liberty to make some decisions. For example, public service performed by chatbots removes decision-making power from street-level bureaucrats. On the other hand, outside the bureaucracy, algorithmic systems interact with citizens and companies, creating different action situations that shape the chances for policy success or failure.

In 2019, for instance, the 'Report of the Special Rapporteur on Extreme Poverty and Human Rights', written by Philip Alston, a human-rights lawyer, was presented at the United Nations General Assembly. The report shows that the constitution of a digital welfare state is globally underway. Such a system uses data and algorithms to automate, predict, identify, surveil, detect, target, and punish the poor. This digital welfare state uses several layers of algorithmic systems for digital identification and automated programmes to assess eligibility as well as to calculate and pay benefits, preventing fraud and detecting risks.

Examples abound of digital welfare systems being implemented without due consideration of the human rights of beneficiaries.[55] Virginia Eubanks sees the emergence of digital poorhouses as algorithmic systems establish new forms of exclusion and punishment of those in need.[56] Philip Alston's report shows how governments worldwide have silently transformed the dynamics of access to social rights, creating the need for a new body of rights—digital rights—to protect the most vulnerable people in the face of new digital technologies.[57]

---

[54] Caramani (2017).
[55] United Nations (2019).
[56] Eubanks (2018).
[57] United Nations (2019).

Gaming: In Deception, We Trust

From the perspective of Algorithmic Institutionalism, algorithmic systems are not the only actants establishing new forms of power and strengthening existing ones. Individuals interact with them, in the process through which routines and actions may be reproduced or changed. There are, therefore, many possibilities of playing with algorithms of government platforms.

The interaction of humans with governments is institutionalized in rules, which enable different forms of gaming. An essential precept in public policies is that they generate winners and losers, allocating scarce resources. Citizens often modulate their behaviour to obtain some reward when interacting with governments. When this interaction is mediated by algorithms, there may be novel possibilities of gaming. Just as the Australian government designed Robodebt to balance the budget by clawing back AUS$2.3 billion in welfare overpayments, citizens also build behaviour patterns to resist governments.

Resistance to the power of algorithms mainly occurs through anonymization, deception, and invisibility. These are possible ways of evading the implicit or explicit surveillance used by algorithms to implement organizational tasks or make policy decisions, but they are not always possible to use. Government platforms require forms of identification from citizens so that they can access public services and produce data that feed their algorithms, but government platforms reduce the margins of resistance because anonymization and invisibility are not possible as public services will require identification prior to delivery. Furthermore, anonymization and invisibility imply that people put aside rights or possibilities of rewards, preventing them from enjoying public goods or from participating in collective choices.

The alternative for individuals to play with algorithmic systems involved in public policy is to deceive the ones aiming for a hidden or undeserved benefit or to avoid some consequence for their private life. Citizens may try to deceive platforms to satisfy their interests.

In the UK, for instance, a report by the Competition and Markets Authority identified how sellers on different platforms deviate from market regulations imposed by the government, finding ways to deceive buyers through pricing algorithms. In doing so, sellers produce collusion and threaten economic competition in markets. The report found, for example, that Uber users are willing to pay along a certain path or how Uber determined people would pay more fees the lower their phone battery was.[58] In Australia, deception was

---

[58] Competition & Markets Authority (2021).

used widely against algorithmic systems employed by the government during the Covid-19 pandemic, leading to economic fraud. According to Levi and Smith, the algorithmic systems created new opportunities for deception, establishing new action options between citizens and institutions.[59]

Another example to be mentioned comes from Denmark, a country that has advanced the idea of digital transformation, digitizing public services, and using data in public policy. The Danish government has identified that many welfare benefit payments are incorrectly distributed because citizens adopt deceiving behaviours and play with algorithms to get those benefits by tampering with eligibility requirements. The government's response was the constitution of a new system that amplifies government surveillance to audit eligibility criteria for welfare programmes, verifying changes in citizens' personal circumstances and controlling their ongoing benefits.[60] An essential routine of this algorithmic system is to identify deception and enforce consequences once frauds have been detected. According to the organization Algorithm Watch, the Danish government built a surveillance behemoth, amplifying surveillance against citizens who benefit (or not) from the welfare state.[61]

One alternative is to build algorithmic systems solely to identify deception, creating new layers in platforms to ensure significant data and information integrity while protecting the use of the public-service platform.[62] These algorithms reduce the margins of resistance—which are not always legitimate—to the power of government platforms. From the lens of Algorithmic Institutionalism, the interaction between algorithmic systems and users is essential, because it defines the outcomes of these new institutional arrangements.

Discursive Dimensions: Ideas and their Places

Four orders of issues are necessary for comprehending the discursive dimension of algorithmic systems employed in policymaking. The first is related to how algorithmic systems are grounded in discursive frames that reflect existing interpretations and values. Second, algorithmic systems frame action contexts in which discourses are formulated. Third, algorithms may be seen as arguments in broader political disputes. Fourth, the outcomes of

---

[59] Levi and Smith (2021).
[60] Deloitte (2016).
[61] Kayser-Bril (2020).
[62] Karuna et al. (2018).

algorithmic systems are often discussed in the public sphere, promoting broader social changes or frameworks.

The first order of issues can be exemplified by the aforementioned advancement of government platformization. The algorithmic systems adopted are marked by particular ways of understanding reality, reproducing notions such as 'best practices', efficiency, and austerity that are strong in the contexts from which they have emerged. They embody discourses of merit and impersonality in the way they operate, promoting certain worldviews. The ability that algorithmic systems must automate and increase government capacity is a discursively constructed reality with the potential to change societies.[63]

Every year in Davos, Switzerland, political and economic elites from various countries meet to exchange information and lobby for different ways of approaching policy problems. The World Economic Forum is a non-profit international organization that gathers diverse interest groups to organize and reform economic development agendas. Since 2013, the World Economic Forum has shaped a digital economy agenda, including issues of digital government and models of platformization.[64] There is a strong belief among the participants of the forum that digital governments shape policies and services in more efficient ways. The role of international organizations is essential in constructing discourses that promote the adoption of these systems, as these discourses converge in a broad idea of digital transformation, making them the basis for institutional changes. Public-policy solutions are shaped on the grounds of discursively created and shared ideas that are embedded in the codes of algorithmic systems.[65]

The second issue is grounded in the understanding of the world surrounding the emergence of algorithmic systems in public policy. Algorithmic systems frame contexts of action that justify discourses. For example, when algorithmic systems process various databases to audit welfare benefits, as in Denmark or Australia, they substantiate and frame austerity discourses and the fight against fraud and corruption. In doing so, these algorithmic systems set the boundaries for the possible actions of both citizens and state bureaucrats. The interplay between them in the request, allocation, and verification of welfare benefits establishes the possibilities available to different actors and the limits constraining them. Moreover, algorithmic systems may have broader implications in the configuration of geopolitical contexts of interaction. Latin American countries, for instance, suffer from chronic problems of fraud and corruption. The adoption of algorithmic systems in different

---

[63] OECD (2014).
[64] https://initiatives.weforum.org/digital-transformation/hom.
[65] Béland (2019).

public-administration routines has supported a discourse of public integrity, producing dividends for Latin American countries, as defended by the Latin American Development Bank (CAF).[66]

The third issue is how algorithmic systems may be seen as arguments in broader political disputes. Computer codes create a reality from policies implemented by governments to say who is eligible for public goods and rights, what obligations citizens and companies have, and how to define and encourage forms of appropriate behaviour expected from citizens, companies, and bureaucrats, all of which enables the achievement of policy objectives.

Algorithmic systems employed in governments foster a technocratic argument of neutral and depoliticized treatment of citizens as consumers of public services. For example, the use of machine-learning algorithms in policy evaluation underpins an evidence-based policy discourse, promoting the conception that it is possible to know rationally the causes of policy problems and, therefore, to build more effective interventions. The use of machine learning in policy evaluation results in scientific conception of public problems, disregarding the fact that problems are politically constructed.[67]

The fourth issue concerns how the outcomes and procedures of algorithmic systems underlie discourses in the public sphere, which is flooded by opinions and evaluations of the benefits and risks of algorithmic systems, transforming them into hot topics in many discursive arenas. Several organizations discuss the impacts of algorithmic systems on public policy, and the analysis of these impacts has been the basis for initiatives such as the Open Government Partnership both to create discussion networks about the impacts of algorithms on human rights and to strengthen algorithmic transparency, making systems more accountable to citizens.[68] Civil society organizations create critical perspectives that have the potential to influence the behaviour of policymakers and change several aspects of adopting algorithmic systems in governments. The way the public sphere frames discourses on algorithms is essential to provide feedback on technological development in governments and guide possible changes and perspectives.[69]

When Edward Snowden blew the whistle on the National Security Agency (NSA) in 2012, it became clear that the NSA was spying on American and foreign citizens and authorities, raising many concerns about privacy. Secret

---

[66] Santiso (2021).
[67] Kreif and DiazOrdaz (2019).
[68] https://www.opengovpartnership.org/about/partnerships-and-coalitions/open-algorithms-network/.
[69] Nguyen and Hekman (2022).

documents show that the Prism system mined data and gave the US government access to emails, chats, and a wide range of data from nine Internet operators.[70] The Prism system was accompanied by another algorithmic system—Boundless Informant—which organized all espionage metadata.

The NSA scandal resulted in various protests and public discussions against surveillance systems to pressure governments to implement privacy laws.[71] Owing to widespread movements associated with other scandals, such as Cambridge Analytica, the debate on privacy in the digital world and rules and policies for data protection have advanced in several countries, including Germany, Brazil, China, Denmark, Japan, and several European countries via GDPR. New regulations are linked directly to the debate around algorithmic systems.

Discourses are not abstract conceptions of reality but sets of practices that have broader collective consequences and direct institutional impact. Institutions are pervaded by discourses that ground them and that shape their effects on society. Like other institutions, algorithmic systems employed in public policy are shaped in complex discursive arenas that tend to create perlocutionary arguments promoting institutional change and defining solutions to complex public problems. Algorithmic systems' adoption into public policy embodies, therefore, the institutional work of governments according to their ability to capture the discourses that shape public problems as well as the discourses that engender solutions to complex problems.

Concluding Remarks

Algorithmic Institutionalism is interested in how algorithmic systems are changing institutions and reshaping forms of interaction and power relations in society. The institutional analysis of algorithmic systems employed in public administration and policymaking sheds light on relevant changes in contemporary societies.

This chapter started with a broad discussion about government platformization, which allowed us to discuss many implications of algorithmic systems' deployment in policymaking. We then demonstrated the growing relevance of algorithmic systems in the reconfiguration of bureaucracies, the rationalization of policymaking, and the ambivalent transformation of the

---

[70] Black (2013).
[71] Gabbatt (2014).

exercise of power in public service. To understand this phenomenon, we applied the framework of Algorithmic Institutionalism to

- The design of algorithmic policymaking and the institutional isomorphism that marks the platformization of governments;
- The historical nature of these systems and the implications of path dependence;
- The way algorithmic systems stabilize and challenge the norms and rules shaping the behaviour of different political actors;
- The power that algorithmic systems deployed in policymaking have in framing contexts of interaction;
- The way individuals play with this power, reinventing the structures that shape their agency; and
- The discursive nature of these institutions and the discursive processes that mark their developments.

Conceiving of algorithms as institutions, we argued that technological innovation does not represent a kind of big bang but a process of redesigning government operations that can impact on society in multiple ways. Algorithmic systems can improve governments' capacity to design and implement public policy, but this redesign takes place in complex political situations. Innovation is not a linear progressive process but a multifaceted one marked by specific goals, trials, and errors, crossed by values and worldviews. The idea of digital transformation is motivated by rationalizing bureaucratic activities on a global scale in response to crisis situations. The process of institutional isomorphism stimulated by international organizations sedimented and encouraged a new institutional reality in which algorithms assume the role of organizing and constituting authority to impose norms, rules, and decisions on individuals.

Policy development is path dependent, as previous choices shape present decisions and future projections.[72] Applying algorithmic systems in policymaking frequently means reinforcing certain values and pathways that are extremely difficult to change in the future, as such systems often imply self-fulfilling prophecies through their feedback loops. Crystallizing algorithmic systems in the policy cycle potentially raises new democratic deficits, but this does not mean citizens are without agency. Algorithmic systems interact with citizens in complex ways: on the one hand, algorithmic systems with hyper-nudge structures can create forms of manipulation and surveillance

[72] Pierson (2004).

that reduce citizens' autonomy, and, on the other, citizens can devise ways to deceive and resist algorithms' power. In this complex interchange, bureaucratic activities and regulatory policies shift, thereby affecting the fabric of everyday life by establishing norms, rules, and patterns of actions that have ambivalent consequences on democratic processes.

In this sense, we argue that algorithmic systems have become new types of institutions that organize the strategic level of public policies. First, algorithmic systems change the logic of problem identification based on data. They also change the logic of agenda-setting and the way social attention to problems emerges. Algorithmic systems shape and support decision-making about policies and different government actions. They automate implementation tasks and preset policy evaluation; that is, algorithmic systems incrementally organize and shape public action in complex contexts, establishing norms, rules, and frames that enable and promote certain behaviours while constraining others. Algorithms are institutions that shape collective actions cutting across the whole policy process and are, therefore, transforming other institutions.

Conceiving of algorithms as new institutions of contemporary society, Algorithmic Institutionalism makes it possible to identify the situations and frames that guide their design and construction; the interactions that shape their outputs; the innovative contexts and organizational changes promoted by algorithms; the way they foster new patterns of authority based on technique, which can create new rules and strategies that shape actors' practical action; the structures of political power and the resistance to them; and the discourses pervading all these processes.

If institutional lenses shed light on algorithmic systems and point to their impacts in contemporary societies, furthermore, we can follow the inverse route and think about ways in which algorithms employed in policy processes provide new paths for the development of institutionalism. The first aspect in this regard has to do with institutional design. The platformization of governments takes path dependence and institutional isomorphism to another level, establishing routes for technological development that are relatively detached from national contexts of policymaking and more dependent on processes pursued by other states and fostered by international organizations.

In addition, the algorithmization of policymaking poses new challenges to democratic institutions broadly speaking. In times of big data, evidence-based policymaking can curtail the conditions for the exercise of citizenship, reducing citizens to data points whose relations can provide information for governments, but who cannot actually express their preferences or understand the grounds upon which decisions were taken.

Third, social and political dynamics based on algorithmic systems may affect processes and dynamics through which existing institutions change. Although institutional theories have evolved from the model of punctuated equilibrium to more encompassing frameworks capable of grasping the continuous ways in which institutions change, they have not fully addressed the role that diverse forms of agency can play in changing broader institutional contexts. Algorithmic developments can be very disruptive, undermining the existing contexts that ground broader institutional assemblages. They can represent a gigantic exogenous shock, but also an endogenous force pervading other dynamics of institutional change. Digital technologies in government represent a significant challenge for existing institutions in various ways.

In the next chapter, we will use the framework of Algorithmic Institutionalism to make sense of a broader dimension of algorithmic systems, running across at the centre of many areas and social practices of algorithmic societies, including those discussed in the previous chapters. Algorithms of recommendation are at the crux of many of transformations we have been discussing and point to a wider comprehension of the social and political implications of algorithmic systems. After that, we will then advocate the need to democratize algorithms. Reading algorithms as institutions not only has descriptive implications but raises moral demands for a democratization of these systems.

5
Algorithmic Recommenders

Niterói is a city located 13 kilometres across Guanabara Bay from Rio de Janeiro. It offers magnificent views of Sugarloaf Mountain, Christ the Redeemer, and other local landmarks. The story of MM, who lives in Niterói, can help us understand the role of social media in the 2018 election of Jair Bolsonaro, the right-wing former president of Brazil. MM are the initials of one of the heads of Mr Bolsonaro's political party in Niterói. He attributed to YouTube his ability to recruit supporters for the party.

MM's story begins one day when he was browsing YouTube and got a suggestion for a video by a right-wing blogger. Out of curiosity, he accepted the suggestion, watched the video, and followed this by watching the other recommended videos, which played one after the other. MM's story is not so different from other supporters of Bolsonaro's candidacy. The political influence of YouTube in Brazil grew significantly during the 2018 presidential campaign, and, in the following years, the platform became a home for extremist videos, far-right influencers, and right-wing political actors.[1]

Although recommendation algorithms have a low probability of changing any individual's behaviour, their impact on group behaviour may not be trivial when we look at the aggregate level.[2] The YouTube recommendation algorithm determines which videos the site plays after the one currently being watched. It also makes suggestions of videos when users query the platform with keywords. The algorithm is a central piece of YouTube's architecture, which aims to maintain user engagement with the platform, keeping users watching videos or interacting with comments. According to YouTube, recommendations are responsible for about 70 per cent of the total time users spend on the site.[3]

However, YouTube's recommendation algorithm has been widely criticized for promoting inflammatory, extremist content and conspiracy theories that tend to increase user engagement, and the presence of right-wing channels in YouTube has given rise to concerns about the impact its recommendation algorithm has on elections and democracy. A report by the Pew Research

[1] Fisher and Taub (2019).
[2] Benn and Lazar (2022).
[3] Solsman (2018).

Algorithmic Institutionalism. Ricardo F. Mendonça, Fernando Filgueiras, and Virgílio Almeida, Oxford University Press.
© Ricardo F. Mendonça, Fernando Filgueiras, and Virgílio Almeida (2023). DOI: 10.1093/oso/9780192870070.003.0006

Center shows that YouTube is the most used social-media platform in the US,[4] with citizens of Brazil, Indonesia, Germany, Pakistan, the UK, and the US in the top ranks of YouTube users based on audience sizes. Many studies have examined the role of YouTube's recommendation algorithm in promoting extreme content and user radicalization.[5] Brendan Nyhan's study finds that, when people are already watching radical content, the algorithm recommends other videos from alternative and extremist channels.[6]

As noticed by Hosseinmardi, the high visibility of radical content on the platform may stem from a complex combination of causes, both technological and sociological, that extends beyond the scope of YouTube's algorithms.[7] However, YouTube's role in political campaigns illustrates how recommendation algorithms are institutionalizing new practices and ideas in political processes around the world, generating concerns about the influence of social-media platforms on extremism.

YouTube is only one among many platforms that point to the growing power of recommendation algorithms. Such algorithms seem to be everywhere: they suggest the food we crave, the streets we could choose to avoid traffic, the music we listen to while running, the stocks a company should buy or sell in each day, and even the person with whom we may fall in love.

As an example, B and her husband C matched on Tinder in Bangalore, India. B stayed there for a few days for work, and the couple-to-be was not able to meet before she returned to Mumbai, but they stayed in touch until she went back to Bangalore a couple of months later. She was not accustomed to exchanging confidences with someone she did not know personally, but C seemed like a nice person, and B relished the online conversations. When B returned to Bangalore for a long period of work, they finally met in person, and the relationship developed into a marriage a few months later. India is now the second-largest market for dating apps after the US. Such apps represent a revolution in the process of finding a potential partner, moving away from the old tradition of arranged marriage to a more Western, modern style of dating.[8]

Online dating services rely on algorithmic recommenders to perform a kind of social recommendation. They have different requirements, and the outcomes are not determined by one user receiving a good recommendation

---

[4] Perrin and Anderson (2019).
[5] Ribeiro et al. (2020).
[6] Nyhan (2021).
[7] Hosseinmardi et al. (2021).
[8] Rajvanshi (2022).

but rather by both parties of the interaction accepting it. Compared to recommendations for products, services, music, videos, and news, the problem of finding romance with data is a more difficult two-sided matching problem.[9] Algorithmic dating platforms have rules that govern dating moves, such as who is allowed to initiate communication, how many profiles a person can see per day, and how much information people's profiles display. For example, on Tinder, everyone can make the first move, while, on Bumble, only women can initiate communication.[10] Design choices specify the algorithms that implement the rules that shape user behaviour. In fact, as institutions, algorithms define and limit the set of choices individuals can make in online dating environments.

Approaching online dating recommenders as institutions broadens the scope of analysis of algorithmic systems and their interactions with other institutions. For example, marriage is an institution comprised of many complex layers of formal and informal rules that influence the behaviour of partners and of other social actors towards them.[11] The dating process is one of the informal rules associated with marriage that encompasses the courtship movements each party makes to get to know the other partner better. The dating process shapes social and cultural specificities through informal rules that establish what is allowed or prohibited in a social relationship. These rules constitute the context of dating, which may evolve into a marriage, with all its affective and legal implications.

The advent of online dating platforms with algorithmic recommenders impacts on the institution of marriage with unanticipated consequences that range from interracial marriage rates to the marriages' overall stability. A study shows that, for heterosexual couples in the US, online connections have become the most popular way for couples to meet, displacing what an affective relationship means and how it happens.[12] To put it differently, online dating recommenders are changing the rules and norms of very intimate layers of human existence. They are emerging as institutions, reshaping the context of human action in diverse ways.

Given the central importance of recommenders in algorithmic societies, this chapter explores the potential for analysing recommendation systems through the lens of Algorithmic Institutionalism. We explore different forms of relations enacted by algorithmic recommenders that impact on collective and individual behaviour. These relations are associated with preferences,

---

[9] Rosenfeld et al. (2019).
[10] Gilbert (2022).
[11] Allen (2005).
[12] Rosenfeld et al. (2019).

autonomy, and values that implicitly make evident the pervasiveness and power of recommenders.

Recommending Choices, Re-Institutionalizing Life

Algorithmic recommenders are systems aimed at generating meaningful recommendations for content or products that might interest a given set of users. There are also algorithmic recommendation tools for specific areas, such as computer science, health, and psychology.[13] Algorithmic recommenders are a central vector of the global digital infrastructure, becoming indispensable tools for living and working in the digital world and its information abundance. The main function of algorithmic recommendation systems is to estimate a *utility function* that automatically and mathematically predicts, ranks, and presents the user's top preferences for a specific content or product.[14] In terms of our work, algorithmic recommendation systems also perform institutional roles and can be seen as contemporary forms of institutions.

Recommenders shed light on products and resources, sorting them and creating cognitive shortcuts for those needing to make decisions. In doing so, they disseminate ideas and shape decisions, which explains why they have become a key component of contemporary problems, such as the dissemination of disinformation in political elections, pandemics, and wars.[15] As with other institutions, algorithmic recommenders have ambivalent consequences in society, as they pervade different human interactions.

The rationality of institutions lies in the assumption that individuals act based on their preferences, which are essential because they modulate human behaviour and decision-making. Algorithmic recommendation systems operate by aggregating data to calculate individual preferences and produce outputs that allow systems to recommend alternatives, whether they are products, political content, opinions, information, cultural content, or affective relationships. Algorithmic recommenders connect human preferences with the choices they make, constituting what will be the object of human attention and rationalization. Put another way, when recommending something, algorithmic systems frame the object of attention and organize different human action situations accordingly.

---

[13] Melville and Sindhwani (2017); Roy and Dutta (2022).
[14] Schrage (2020).
[15] West and Bergstrom (2021).

Algorithmic recommenders transform data into relevant suggestions by finding, calculating, and ranking correlations and patterns for users. These suggestions rationalize individual choices, offering humans what, when, where, how, and why to choose. There are two predominant filtering approaches to designing algorithmic recommenders: collaborative and content-based.

Collaborative filtering is the process of predicting a user's interests by identifying preferences and information from other users.[16] The intuition behind collaborative filtering relies on the observation that, if two users have similar tastes about one product, then they are likely to have similar tastes in other products as well. The correlation measured between pairs of users has been recognized as a good proxy for high-quality predictions and recommendations. Algorithmic recommendation systems based on collaborative filtering keep track of each item a user has rated or liked, then find the users who are good predictors. Based on the preferences of these good predictors, the system finds new items to recommend.[17]

The approach of content-based filtering relies on the properties and characteristics of items to model user interests and generate recommendations. Content-based algorithmic recommenders analyse a user's past behaviour by identifying the properties and characteristics of items the user has interacted with to predict new items that match that user's preferences. In general, the three primary data sources used by the recommendation algorithms are system users, items or content to be recommended, and interactions between users and items.

Ultimately, a crucial role of algorithmic recommendation systems is to provide information so that a user makes informed choices. For example, in any democratic society, news recommenders should provide users with the information they need to make meaningful political choices. Schrage points out the essential characteristics used by recommenders to capture the context for a human choice:

> Algorithmic recommenders calculate relationships between people, prices, purchases, preferences, personality, items, images, artists, features, characteristics, metadata, melodies, rankings, ratings, talents, clicks, swipes, taps, tags, texts, locations, moments in time, times of day—that might better inform and improve human choice.[18]

---

[16] Cobbe and Singh (2019).
[17] Ekstrand et al. (2011).
[18] Schrage (2020: 109).

Recommender systems are a central piece of services in the digital economy. They select, filter, and personalize information across social media, news aggregators, music and video streaming, online dating, online shopping, online ad targeting, and other services.[19] They 'help' people navigate the information deluge from YouTube, TikTok, Netflix, Amazon, Spotify, Facebook, and Twitter. Netflix's algorithmic recommender system, for example, helps its users find videos to watch, but it is not only one algorithm; rather, it is a collection of different algorithms serving different use cases to offer services and experience on the Netflix platform. The recommender shows something attractive to users, and its power is evidenced by the fact that it influences choice for about 80 per cent of the hours streamed on Netflix.[20] At YouTube, approximately 70 per cent of all watch time spent on the site is driven by the platform's recommender system.[21] That is, the algorithmic system frames most of what, when, and how users will choose their interactions with the platform.

With the increasing importance of algorithmic recommenders, there is a need to recognize its ethical and societal consequences. For example, depending on their design, news recommendation algorithms risk creating enclosed spaces that separate users from different ideas and viewpoints. They risk pushing people to social and political polarization, with serious negative effects on democratic institutions.[22] As an institution in the entertainment environment, algorithmic recommenders impact directly on users' tastes and consumption, re-engineering cultural processes.[23] Algorithmic recommenders hold the power to influence people when they are trusted by users, but, in most cases, algorithmic recommenders do not provide any documentation or tools that help us understand how they work and capture our attention and trust.

In an encompassing analysis of automated influence driven by algorithms, Claire Benn and Seth Lazar show the role of algorithmic recommenders over human opinions, beliefs, and desires. According to them,

> automated influence has funnelled people towards human manipulators because the recommendation algorithms that serve us products, services, and especially content are optimized to sustain user engagement; and content produced by manipulators is, by its nature, deeply engaging to the manipulated.[24]

---

[19] Stray et al. (2022).
[20] Gomez-Uribe and Hunt (2015).
[21] Solsman (2018).
[22] Milano et al. (2020).
[23] Gaw (2021).
[24] Benn and Lazar (2022).

The capacity of algorithmic recommenders to influence and shape opinion in the context of social media—through control of the feed, for instance—can have an impact on democracy via the dissemination of disinformation, conspiracy theories, and hate speech.

The growing presence of algorithmic recommenders in contemporary society gives rise to concerns about the power of dominant digital platforms and their capacity to influence political, social, and economic issues in different parts of the world. To enhance our capacity to understand the role of algorithmic recommendation systems in influencing and changing individual behaviours in society, we need an encompassing framework, such as the one provided by Algorithmic Institutionalism and its six dimensions developed in Chapter 2. Briefly, the framework focuses on institution building and design; historical processes; rules and norms; power relations; gaming; and discursive dimensions. Along each dimension of the framework, we explore the potential benefits of viewing recommenders as institutions in the context of practical examples drawn from real-world situations.

Institution Building and Design

An essential characteristic of modern organizations is that they operate in contexts of bounded rationality. According to Simon, preferences drive human choice and limit rationality, because they depend on what people pay attention to and how much information they must decide on and choose from alternatives. Human decisions are not necessarily those that maximize a utility function but rather the most satisfactory ones in each context.[25] When Simon imagined the importance of algorithms for modern organizations, the objective was that these algorithms should be utility-maximizing mechanisms that handle the most significant possible volume of information in a way that exceeds human decision-making capacity.

Competing for human attention and rationalizing human choices are a central pillar of modern industry, and both concepts rely on decision-making and instrumentalization tools. Algorithmic recommenders have become essential mechanisms for increasing returns in markets, governments, e-commerce, and political communication. Algorithmic recommendation systems are pervasive, because they shape the objects of human attention, expanding the available information and leading people to decide, thus

---

[25] Simon (1976).

facilitating the achievement of increasing returns, political influence, and impact on online business.

Attention battles are at the heart of the algorithm design process. As Shoshana Zuboff points out, information is abundant, but attention is a valuable resource for companies to maximize their profits.[26] Recommender algorithms are institutions designed around systems that monitor behavioural data to compete for consumer attention. Algorithmic recommenders operate with machine-learning systems to produce predictions on what people will click on based on their search input and past activities. Ranking and recommendation algorithms are at the heart of search engines, because they classify the information the user needs, defining a hierarchy of attention. By shaping the attention of consumers and citizens, algorithmic recommenders have become the instruments of commercial and business model innovation. Regarding the role of algorithmic systems in the development of new business models, Moshe Vardi makes the following alert:

> The biggest problem that computing faces today is not that AI technology is unethical—though machine bias is a serious issue—but that AI technology is used by large and powerful corporations to support a business model that is, arguably, unethical.[27]

The technology industry designs algorithmic recommenders as a tool to compete for attention, making these algorithms pervasive in different areas of business and government.

Recommendation systems are, in fact, designed in the context of this competition for consumer attention. Industries use them to increase returns and expand political influence with the argument of consumer convenience, with the technology industry designing algorithmic recommenders to instrumentalize this consumer attention and rationalize their choices.[28]

The design of algorithmic recommenders based on collaborative filtering approaches works by identifying patterns across users. The algorithms recommend content based on what similar users have consumed or interacted with,[29] and thus vast amounts of data are essential to train recommender algorithms to derive solutions via statistical methods. This class of recommendation algorithms relies on massive amounts of social data collected from different platforms such as Facebook, Google, Amazon, and TikTok.

---

[26] Zuboff (2019).
[27] Vardi (2022).
[28] Baeza-Yates and Fayyad (2021).
[29] Cobbe and Singh (2019).

Then behavioural information such as social relationships, user-to-user interactions, shopping habits, and communication patterns are extracted and transformed into digital data.[30] The process of data extraction is defined by Sadowski as data 'taken without meaningful consent and fair compensation for the producers and sources of data'.[31] Nick Couldry and Ulises Mejias argue that the current practices of data collection resemble colonial modes of exploitation, characterized by the dispossession of resources to generate a new fuel for the growth of global capitalism.[32] From an institutional perspective, the process of designing and building algorithmic recommenders is situated in a broader context of data colonialism, characterized by unremunerated extraction of behavioural information.

Recommender systems are specific institutions that reflect new power dynamics within contemporary capitalism. Within the attention economy, algorithmic recommendation systems perform essential elements, making algorithms pervasive in industry, markets, and governments, because they classify and hierarchize information, create political and social biases, and transform the public communication process. As institutions, they emerge by mediating knowledge and influencing citizen and consumer behaviour. They are designed in complex processes pervaded by economic interests, political views, and individual activities.

Historical Process

Several distinct contexts shape the evolution of institutions. Algorithms, like other institutions, change over time in response to pressures and demands on specific issues raised by society and businesses. An interesting illustration from the area of healthcare sheds light on this topic, with our example highlighting a historical process that describes the evolution of an allocation algorithm for kidney transplant.[33]

Alice and Bob are two hypothetical patients on the kidney transplant waiting list in the United States. They are clinically equivalent, so the question is, which patient will be recommended to receive a donated organ? It is a life-and-death question. Based on a complex set of medical data that integrate many parameters from both donor and recipient—and moral and ethical criteria—an algorithm decides which patient on the list should receive the

---

[30] Verdegem (2022).
[31] Sadowski (2019).
[32] Couldry and Mejias (2019).
[33] Robinson (2022b).

donated kidney. The algorithm then calculates each patient's allocation score, which in turn is used to rank the patients.

The algorithm, though, should not be evaluated only by its technical accuracy in the score calculation. Suppose, for example, that the algorithm calculates the score with fifteen decimal places, and the difference between Alice and Bob's score is in the thirteenth place.[34] Should this tiny difference decide the future of Alice's life? Does this minimal variation represent a medical opinion about Bob's and Alice's health condition? Answers to these types of questions indicate that the decision cannot be made on technical details alone. This is an ethical and moral decision that should be constructed via a collaborative decision-making process that includes representatives from doctors, technicians, and the community affected by organ transplants.

In 1984, the US Congress passed the National Organ Transplant Act to create a system to match organs with recipients. Similarly, the United Network for Organ Sharing (UNOS) was formally incorporated as an independent, non-profit organization to meet the growing demand for transplants nationwide.[35] UNOS maintains the digital system that recommends recipients when an organ becomes available. In 2003, UNOS initiated a review process of the kidney transplant algorithm. There was discontent about the algorithm's objectives and design, with some people concerned about ageism, and some about the algorithm's complexity, which made it difficult for physicians and patients to understand the calculations. One of the revisions focused on maximizing the number of life years recipients gained from the transplant, but other factors, such as equity based on race and age, also had to be considered. The review process, including a series of public meetings, hearings, and debates with different groups in different parts of the US, lasted for ten years, until people accepted a tolerable compromise on the final form of the algorithm that went into effect at the end of 2014.

Multiple lessons can be learned from studying the evolution of the kidney allocation algorithm. Viewed as an institution, the algorithm evolved to reduce uncertainty by establishing transparent rules that are understood and accepted by all, although it created different social dilemmas along the way. Nevertheless, the evolution of UNOS illustrates the historical process of developing a recommendation algorithmic system and how it defines values, rules, metrics, and goals for the kidney allocation process that shapes human lives.

---

[34] Robinson (2022b).
[35] https://unos.org/about/.

The kidney allocation algorithm opens a series of new questions about algorithms' use in life-and-death situations. Should algorithms be used to make decisions in situations characterized by ethical dilemmas? Who should audit the performance of algorithms that decide who lives and who dies? These are questions whose answers should not focus on technical aspects of the code—they require a moral and social understanding of the problem, as they have to do with the algorithm's social role as well. It is not about the technology; it concerns the algorithm's ethical values as an institution. Our point here is that the institutionalist framework creates a social context that surrounds the algorithm, where society has a role in interacting with developers to construct rules and norms for the ethical decisions involved in life-and-death decisions achieved through algorithms. And such a role becomes more prominent in critical junctures, as crises often work as exogenous shocks, opening room for agency. Individuals' interactions with the algorithmic system shape physician preferences and have an impact on patients in different ways, with many ethical dilemmas.

As a result of the historical development process, the logic of algorithms and the parameters that decide a patient's life are transparent and publicly disclosed. The governance of the algorithmic system tracks its performance, establishes audits by third-party organizations, and publishes detailed reports about the algorithm and the transplant system. UNOS is one of the most comprehensive healthcare oversight programmes in the US, and it is governed by policies that aim to improve participation, transparency, and auditing. Allocation rules are transparent and explained in plain English. Every organ-allocation decision and the algorithm's performance data are subject to audits prepared by third-party monitoring that shows how the rules are working out, with full participation from the transplant community.

The historical dimension of the kidney allocation algorithm shows how time and the demands of society shape different groups' behaviour. During the history of altering the algorithm, path dependencies established initial conditions that led to negative impacts of the algorithm, such as racial/ethnic disparities in access to kidney transplant. The formation of the initial committee in charge of specifying the algorithm was judging people 'in accordance with its own middle-class suburban value system: scouts, Sunday school, Red Cross'.[36] The reference points to suggestions that the committee had been biased in favour of white applicants.[37] Historical institutionalism pays significant attention to the historical development of institutions and

---

[36] Robinson (2022a).
[37] Robinson (2022a).

their path dependence. Like other institutions, algorithms must be analysed in the context in which they are assumed to play their role. An algorithm designed to make decisions on critical matters cannot be developed detached from its social context.

Rules and Norms

Social-media platforms were created to connect people and facilitate online communication. In their construction, they started from an almost literal conception of freedom of expression. In principle, people can manifest, say, or elaborate on any subject via social media. Algorithmic recommendation systems take these expressions as input data and organize which posts will be visible to whom, how, and when. A post written on social media can be recommended and gain visibility to go 'viral', or become a hidden expression in the multitude of messages written by different people every day. What determines this visibility or invisibility of posts are rules embedded in recommendation algorithms that shape influencers' and audiences' roles and perceptions about public opinion.

As algorithms permeate our lives, their features and affordances play a critical role: they structure and frame spaces within which human interactions take place. Algorithmic recommendation systems, like other institutions, make use of formal and informal rules to influence user beliefs and values.[38] Newsfeed algorithms and search engines, for instance, affect how we perceive reality and influence our behaviour by suggesting news, videos, songs, content, products, and social connections.

The media ecosystem has multiple levels of organization that involve a variety of media companies and digital technology platforms.[39] Algorithmic recommenders act as institutions relative to the primary organizational level, which is composed of media companies, by filtering the communicative abundance.[40] They also influence the political life of several countries with democratic regimes. On the one hand, recommendation algorithms inform citizens about the processes in which they make meaningful political choices, but, on the other, news recommenders may generate filter bubbles and echo chambers.[41] The potential negative effect of news recommenders was clearly

---

[38] Napoli (2013).
[39] Jepperson (1991).
[40] Keane (2013).
[41] Helberger (2019); Cinelli et al (2021). For a critical view of the literature on echo chambers, see Bruns (2019).

stated by a UK regulator, which argued that there is 'a risk that recommendations are used in a manner that narrows citizens' exposure to different points of view, by reinforcing their past habits or those of their friends'.[42]

Social-media platforms have become the object of political dispute, because the framework of total freedom of expression also makes these platforms an instrument to spread disinformation and hate speech. Many civil-society actors, legislators, and regulators are calling for action by platforms to create content-governance mechanisms and initiatives to reduce the spread of disinformation. Some platforms maintain their recommendation systems with the same objectives of producing engagement and monetizing user posts, but combat disinformation by creating red flags that send content to moderators. If the content is considered false or misleading, Twitter may hide the post to prevent it from having a broad reach—the platform can even disable likes, retweets, and shares to hide the post.

Algorithmic recommendation systems work as mechanisms to give visibility and monetize user posts, as well as to control posted content to modulate user behaviour.[43] Such mechanisms are incorporated into terms of use, which define a set of rules of appropriate user behaviour. Recommender algorithms shape these rules, representing potential advances in defence of the public interest. However, how these rules are shaped and work exacerbate existing problems, such as algorithm opacity, complicating outstanding issues of fairness and justice and obscuring the political nature behind certain decisions.[44]

Like other institutions, algorithmic recommendation systems in social media embed rules of appropriate behaviour based on socially constructed values. They can even drive rules of appropriate user behaviour on their platforms in the context of interaction mediated by other algorithms.

Power, Preferences, and Autonomy in the Age of Recommenders

Recommendation algorithms are particularly powerful institutions owing to their ability to make some alternatives more visible than others. It is not by chance that recommenders are a key element in the business model of some of the most powerful tech corporations, including Meta, Alphabet,

---

[42] OFCOM (2012).
[43] Bucher (2012).
[44] Gorwa et al. (2020).

and Amazon. By reducing the range of potential alternatives and suggesting other choices to users, recommenders provide ways to navigate saturated informational ecosystems.

In the contemporary world, it would be unfeasible, even impossible, to find relevant content, products, and services without algorithmic tools that make content visible. By learning what we might like and might want to know right now, recommenders help shape what we will like and will know in the future. Based on trillions of data points fed daily into technology platforms, algorithmic systems are used to micro-target, recommend, and influence users.

The power of the dominant digital platforms makes this point clear owing to the centrality of recommenders. Facebook's algorithms for recommending posts and ads, for example, were designed to make people engage with as much content for as much time as possible. One of the algorithm's main goals is to increase engagement to generate more revenue from the online advertising market. On TikTok, the first thing users see when they open the app is the 'For You' page, with a feed suggested by the algorithmic recommender based on videos the user has already watched or interacted with. TikTok is a platform of targeted content and loose ties that relies fundamentally on algorithmic recommendation systems. On Instagram and YouTube, social recommendation by algorithms is an eye-catching part of the user experience.

At this point, it is important to highlight that visibility is a fundamentally critical part of understanding the power of algorithmic recommenders. The design of algorithmic recommenders aims to create spaces of *constructed visibility*, where big technology platforms exploit business opportunities, collect personal data from users and customers, and exercise their power accordingly[45]. Recommendation algorithms frame reality in certain ways, making some things visible and rendering others invisible.

Michel Foucault argues that power is associated with the notion of making things seeable in specific ways.[46] Algorithmic recommenders are a means to shed light on specific pieces of information immersed in the limitless, almost infinite, online space. Because of the immense variety of items available in online stores and on streaming platforms, customers must resort to algorithmic recommendation systems, because they give visibility to items that will help them make their choices. Hence, these choices are restrained

---

[45] Airoldi (2022).
[46] Rajchman (1991); Foucault (1995).

and marked by the suggestions users come across. An interesting illustration of this form of restraint is identified by Tufekci in an article about recommendation algorithms during Donald Trump's administration.

> The YouTube algorithmic recommender started to recommend and autoplay videos for her that featured white supremacist rants, Holocaust deniers, and other disturbing content. This is a case where the algorithm created a space for right-wing ideas by making related videos visible. A well-mapped yet unintended consequence of the effort to maximize user engagement on platforms has been the strengthening of many extremist groups, which have acquired more visibility as a result.[47]

The power of algorithmic recommendation is also related to the pleasure and convenience derived from the visibility it produces. In an interview, Foucault notes:

> What makes power hold good, what makes it accepted, is simply the fact that it does not only weigh on us as a force that says no; it also traverses and produces things, it induces pleasure, forms knowledge, produces discourse.[48]

Algorithmic recommenders are designed to induce pleasure, show pointers to different forms of knowledge, and provide choices. They are inducers of engagement, triggering desires and wishes. Harcourt talks about a virtual seduction by recommenders, where the algorithms seduce us into buying the most recent smartphone, downloading the newest application, viewing an attractive picture, or watching a cute short video, creating possibilities that fill out our dreams, tastes, and ambitions.[49] Based on data collected from our previous digital experience, algorithmic systems recommend things to us we did not even know we wanted.

Aligned with Foucault's vision of power, the combination of pleasure, desire, convenience, and efficiency transforms algorithmic recommenders into powerful elements in the construction of visibility. And, in doing so, algorithmic recommenders operate as institutions establishing the boundaries for agency. The power of recommendation involves an undermining in an individual's decision-making power that can be deleterious to human autonomy and agency.[50] Sometimes, we even speak of this manipulation as

---

[47] Tufekci (2018).
[48] Foucault (1979).
[49] Harcourt (2015: 122).
[50] Varshney (2020).

thwarting our liberty to select alternatives in a human–algorithm interaction. On their work on automated influence, Benn and Lazar argue:

> The worst kind of manipulation in our digital lives right now is being conducted by some of the people who use social media, and they are enabled and empowered by the newsfeed algorithms that drive people towards more sensational, extreme, and polarizing content.[51]

The growing presence of algorithmic recommenders in contemporary society gives rise to concerns about the power of digital platforms and their capacity to influence political, social, and economic issues in different parts of the world by disseminating disinformation, spreading extremist and harmful content, or exploiting an individual user's specific vulnerabilities. In addition, recommendation algorithms facilitate echo chambers, making it harder for individuals to perceive the limits and problems of the communicative ecosystem in into which they have been drawn.

In the US's turbulent 2020 election, much of the political conflict took place on social media, with disinformation being a vital resource in shaping public opinion about electoral results.[52] Algorithmic recommendation systems incorporated in social media such as Facebook, Twitter, TikTok, YouTube, and Instagram modulate which actors will be more visible than others, which posts will generate more engagement, what will be seen by different groups, and what will be rendered invisible to other groups. This algorithm-promoted visibility, which is necessarily fragmented and susceptible to polarization, has affected the fabric of public discussion and, in a way, the electoral process.

And this issue is not restricted to the political world. Algorithmic recommenders—and the influencers that become visible through them—are also present in marketing initiatives, where companies associate their brand with influencers' content, likes, and visibility. From their hair to the clothes they wear, from their drinks to the car they drive, influencers expand brands' presence, amplifying the possibility of commerce.

A study by Panpan Wang and Qian Huang shows that digital influencers live up to their name and influence consumer engagement and purchase behaviour in online social commerce communities.[53] They also exercise power in society by engaging people in environmental behaviour and participation. By promoting pro-climate content that advocates sustainability,

---
[51] Benn and Lazar (2022: 143).
[52] Aral and Eckles (2019).
[53] Wang and Huang (2022).

for example, influencers have promoted offline engagement for the environmental cause.[54]

At the heart of the new power dynamics emerging in digital interactions, algorithmic recommendation systems define visibility and engagement mechanisms, outlining, in turn, who exercises power and under what conditions. As institutions, recommendation algorithms shape the power relations in society, setting contexts for preference formation, fragmenting the access to expressions of preference, and giving a set of actors additional strength to influence preferences and behaviours.

Gaming

Similar to other institutional contexts, *gaming the system* refers to situations in which users interact with an algorithmic system to foster certain types of outcomes without resorting to frontal attacks, such as hacking.[55] Those who are gaming algorithms use various strategies and practices to subvert rules and norms to gain visibility, avoid censorship, inflate content's reputation, promote *happy accidents*, or simply puzzle algorithms to make them work at suboptimal levels. When someone rates positively a film that they dislike, or intentionally seeks out songs or food they are not really willing to consume, they can confuse recommenders, thus paving the way for less precise predictions and possible surprises. Quite often, individuals neglect dimensions of their own tastes to deceive algorithms with the purpose of being less transparent to recommendation systems and, hence, somehow less enclosed in their own previous tastes.

Gaming is also clear when social actors organize concerted actions to promote the visibility of certain content on digital platforms. Eric Drott investigated, for instance, how fake streams, listening bots, and click farms affect a changing music economy.[56] Rumours continue to grow about celebrities playing with a platform's algorithms to boost their tracks (and revenues).

A recent illustration occurred when Anitta became the first Brazilian singer to reach the number one spot on Spotify with her song 'Envolver'. According to some music experts, the hit can be partially 'attributed to fans gaming the platform's algorithms in ways that potentially broke Spotify's terms and conditions'.[57] Fandoms may also have political purposes for gaming an algorithm.

[54] Dekoninck and Schmuck (2022).
[55] Cotter (2019).
[56] Drott (2020).
[57] Marasciulo (2022).

Emily Wharton argues, for instance, that Spotify's pride lists are essential to LGBTQ identities, so they get significant engagement from groups willing to promote the visibility of their idols to manifest their pride.[58] Another example of social actors organizing for purposeful gaming is the coordinated action of political groups in India that made particular political hashtags appear on Twitter's trending topics list during the 2019 Indian general election.[59]

Automated bots are often employed artificially to increase reputation metrics of content to game recommendation algorithms. By inflating metrics for specific content, such as likes, views, and shares, bots attempt to increase the likelihood of content being recommended or having its position improved in content rankings to increase content visibility.[60] These actions can be harmless or even politically empowering in some contexts, but they often manipulate audiences and can have consequences such as the dissemination of disinformation and extremist content. By giving visibility to fake news and hate speech, bots help create toxic online spaces that contaminate political discourses.

For instance, a study by Portland Communication on the use of Twitter in some African nations correlated the rise of fake news and the use of bots in politics, changing the dynamics of elections in some countries.[61] Social bots have been deployed to influence opinion and votes, creating climates of opinion, and the Portland report shows that Twitter bots account for more than 20 per cent of influencers in countries such as Lesotho and Kenya.

The analysis of how users and businesses attempt to game recommendation systems through the lens of Algorithmic Institutionalism lets us highlight the interaction of algorithms with other critical societal institutions such as elections. It also shows the importance of discussing how society should create mechanisms institutionally to limit negative actions via algorithmic recommenders.

Discursive Dimensions

The discursive dimension of Algorithmic Institutionalism can be explored through links between algorithms, institutions, and discourse. As Nelson Phillips states, 'institutions are not just social constructions, but social constructions constituted through discourse'.[62] Discourses characterize ways

---

[58] Wharton (2020).
[59] Jakesch et al. (2021).
[60] Cobbe and Singh (2019).
[61] *Portland Communications* (2018).
[62] Phillips et al. (2004).

of making sense of reality, and algorithms—like other institutions—enact certain interpretative frames while also being deeply affected by publicly available discourses.

Recommendation algorithms have worked as arguments in discursive disputes about the mass violence against the Rohingya in Myanmar in 2017, for example. A report prepared by Amnesty International analyses the combination of Meta's business practices and the content-shaping algorithms that led to discrimination and violence against the Rohingya people.[63] Facebook's newsfeed, Twitter's timeline, and YouTube's recommender system are examples of content-shaping algorithms designed to serve the content that users see online.[64] In this case, Meta's algorithms framed the reality of ethnic conflicts in Myanmar by amplifying posts that incited violence and discrimination against the Rohingya people. The number of posts and their viral dissemination reverberated across different regions of the country, creating a sense that everyone in Myanmar shared anti-Rohingya sentiments. This is a case where recommendation algorithms set ground elements for comprehensions of a global ethnic and religious conflict. Specifically, they framed a context for the campaign of ethnic cleansing against Rohingya Muslims in Myanmar.

The allocation algorithm for kidney transplants covered earlier in this chapter shows another way to articulate discursive institutionalism. It results from the role of algorithms in framing the context for patients, families, experts, formal institutions (that is, UNOS), and software involved in the process of organizing the organ transplant waiting list. The discourse about the kidney allocation algorithm shows the story of a governance process aimed at achieving public interest with the participation of multiple stakeholders who represent different perspectives in a context where stakes are high.[65] The design and development process of the kidney allocation algorithm contemplated the key characteristics to gain trust from society. Participation, transparency, accountability, fairness, and multi-stakeholder governance played a role in the construction of the system's discursive dimension, which helped create a perception of trustworthiness in the kidney allocation algorithm[66].

Recommendation algorithms frame political discourses by, in many situations, spreading hate or promoting polarization. Digital platforms are contexts where humans coexist with algorithms, creating the interactions

---

[63] *Amnesty International* (2022).
[64] Huszár et al. (2022).
[65] Robinson (2022b).
[66] *Lancet* Editorial (2016).

that mould political opinions. Social-media platforms have played an influential role in political discourse by intensifying political polarization.[67] Several studies have shed light on the relationship between digital platforms and different forms of political polarization—for example, Fernando Santos and colleagues analyse the link recommendation algorithms that make suggestions for new connections (such as friends or followers) to social network users.[68] These algorithmic suggestions lead to the formation of closed, integrated, like-minded groups that are less vulnerable to different viewpoints. Another study published by *Science* shows that

> Social media technology employs popularity-based algorithms that tailor content to maximize user engagement, increasing sectarianism within homogeneous networks (SM), in part because of the contagious power of content that elicits sectarian fear or indignation.[69]

Social media platforms are not the root causes of political polarization, but the effects of their algorithms do exacerbate it.[70] In their calculations of probabilities and relationships, algorithms incorporate the political discourse and mould scripts for human action. Recommendation algorithms are therefore at the heart of discussions about sociotechnical systems owing to their pervasiveness in contemporary societies.

Concluding Remarks

This chapter has explored recommendation systems through the lenses of Algorithmic Institutionalism. A salient feature of algorithmic recommenders, like other institutions, concerns their ability to influence individual and collective behaviour in modern societies.

Drawing from different cases, such as the role of social media's algorithms in the dissemination of disinformation and in the radicalization of some political users, or the wide use of dating apps, we have argued that algorithms, like other institutions, are shaping new practices and contexts of interaction, affecting the way humans do many things: from political mobilization to the construction of affective bonds.

Algorithmic recommenders exercise a special kind of intermediary power: they institutionalize new power relations, with consequences that influence

---

[67] Finkel et al. (2020).
[68] Santos et al. (2021).
[69] Finkel et al. (2020).
[70] Finkel et al. (2020).

other institutions in politics, economy, and government. The analysis of recommendation algorithms in each dimension of our framework can be summarized as follows:

- Algorithmic recommender systems can be viewed as institutions that reflect new power dynamics within contemporary capitalism. They play a powerful role in the attention economy by deciding who or what should be visible in the online space, with impacts in politics, economy, and culture.
- Recommendation algorithms, like other institutions, evolve over time, responding to the pressures and demands of specific issues raised by society. An illustrative example of the historical evolution of a recommendation system can be seen in the allocation algorithm for kidney transplant. Based on demands from different groups, the algorithm underwent various modifications over ten years to meet complaints about ageism and racism. Historical institutionalism shows how time, society's demands, and path dependence shaped the algorithm's behaviour.
- Like other institutions, recommendation algorithms that operate the feeds of social media platform incorporate rules of appropriate behaviour based on socially constructed values. However, the rules that shape behaviour and select content are often opaque, thus hindering the public understanding of the algorithm.
- Algorithmic recommenders build the visibility and engagement of actors in different situations, creating new power relations. Social media influencers influence opinions, desires, and perspectives, meaning they exercise power in society by engaging people with ideas and products that are made visible by algorithms. Making things seeable in a specific way can be conceived of as a form of power.
- Like other institutions, algorithms create disciplinary apparatuses that prescribe participatory norms and rules to shape human interactions with digital platforms. Gaming an algorithm involves various strategies and practices to subvert rules and norms to gain visibility, avoid censorship, or inflate content reputation. One consequence of gaming an algorithmic recommender is the dissemination of disinformation and extremist content for political purposes, which in turn reduces trust in algorithmic systems.
- The notion of an algorithm conveys implicit concepts of objectivity, accuracy, and efficiency that influence interactions between algorithms and humans. Recommendation algorithms frame political discourses,

in many situations spreading hate or promoting polarization. We have illustrated this with the amplification of posts that incited violence and discrimination against the Rohingya in Myanmar in 2017.

Similar to the previous chapters, the discussions raised in Chapter 5 point to a two-way relationship between institutional theories and algorithmic systems. If the former illuminates our comprehension of the latter, the latter points to many agendas and questions that could contribute to the advancement of the former. Algorithmic systems have played a significant role in reshaping institutions to different extents. The impact of these platforms can be seen in various areas, such as elections, public health, news, security, governments, and markets. The pressure and actions stemming from algorithmic platforms, for instance, have led to changes in several institutions, affecting not only how they are transformed but also the pace at which this happens and the directions to which we, as a society, are heading. The various illustrations discussed throughout this chapter about how algorithmic institutions interact with and transform traditional institutions, such as marriage and electoral systems, will open rich research agendas for institutionalist scholars.

Given the impact of algorithmic systems on society, we must now move to our last chapter, which explores the need to democratize algorithmic institutions.

6
Algorithms and Politics
From an Epistocratic View to a Democratic Approach

Democracies face hard times. The signs of democratic erosion are easily felt by citizens across the globe as they witness the weakening of political institutions, the intensification of radicalized forms of political conflict, a growing sense of bewilderment amid narrative wars, and the lack of a wide range of rights. These signs have been extensively mapped by an abundant body of academic literature that points to the multidimensional nature of the crisis.[1] The decline of democracies has economic, social, environmental, political, and epistemic causes and consequences.[2]

Moreover, such a decline is not restricted to the de-democratization of countries but seems to indicate a broader wearying of democracy as a normative horizon to be pursued. As Runciman ironically put it, democracy is no longer the only game in town.[3] There is serious scepticism about democracy's capacity to deal with complex and life-threatening phenomena such as climate emergencies, wars, disinformation, and even the more ordinary decisions of policymaking in extremely complex and fractured societies. There is a well-documented lack of trust in the efficiency and good will of democratic institutions, such as parliaments, courts, the media, political parties, and civil society (including unions, social movements, and NGOs).[4] The dead end seems, sometimes, unavoidable and unsurmountable.

It is in this context that algorithms have become thought of as the grounds for new routes for decision-making. When pointing out the alternatives emerging against democracy, Runciman identified two trends that are strongly related to the algorithmic changes in societies.[5] One of these is the belief in liberated technologies, as if the technical potential to

---

[1] See Crouch (2004); Kurlantzick (2013); Ercan and Gagnon (2014); Greer (2014); Fukuyama (2015); Fischer (2017); Levitsky and Ziblatt (2018); Mounk (2018); Runciman (2018); Avritzer (2019); Curato et al. (2019); Dryzek et al. (2019); Forst (2019); Kalyvas (2019); Norris and Inglehart (2019); Przeworski (2019); Urbinati (2019); Mendonça (2020); Chambers (2021).
[2] Mendonça (2020).
[3] Runciman (2018).
[4] Rosanvallon (2011).
[5] Runciman (2018).

Algorithmic Institutionalism. Ricardo F. Mendonça, Fernando Filgueiras, and Virgílio Almeida, Oxford University Press.
© Ricardo F. Mendonça, Fernando Filgueiras, and Virgílio Almeida (2023). DOI: 10.1093/oso/9780192870070.003.0007

foster horizontal communications would evolve in the direction of participatory processes, grounding anarchical regimes of political decision-making capable to challenge entrenched hierarchies.

A second trend is epistocracy—the idea that good political decisions should be based on knowledge instead of an aggregation of opinions. This goes back to Plato and Stuart Mill, acquiring contemporary momentum in a controversial book written by Jason Brennan, *Against Democracy*.[6] Brennan believes that democracies are incapable of delivering good solutions and advocates epistocratic procedures to protect political communities from the rule of ignorance. In Brennan's view, technical solutions would overcome political disputes, thus enabling a more efficient government.

Runciman is not an advocate of epistocracy, but he notices that epistocratic trends are growing in contemporary polities that experience a simultaneous overpoliticization of issues and attempts to depoliticize areas of social life.[7] In a line of thought also followed by Pierre Rosanvallon, he identifies the rise of discourses that undermine the political and a quest for technical solutions that present themselves as objective and apolitical.

Curiously, and despite their differences, both alternatives to democracy identified by Runciman (that is, *liberated technologies* and *epistocracy*) help us to understand the centrality that algorithmic systems have acquired in many forms of decision-making. Algorithms are often considered by many as the embodiment of the long-dreamed-of possibility to transfer decisions to technical systems that can manage massive volumes of data to produce well-informed decisions, allegedly without individual biases and without the tensions and frictions inherent in politics.[8] 'Government algorithmic decision-making strongly emphasizes a culture of technical rationality, which emphasizes effectiveness and efficiency over ethical or normative concerns.'[9] Even if most algorithmic systems operate on the grounds of large data sets that, in the end, depend on the participation of millions of individuals, they are often perceived of not as mechanisms of collective intelligence, but as artefacts capable of delivering a superior and technical form of knowledge.

Algorithmic systems offer a way to deal with complex issues in a world marked by uncertainty and risk. They let us follow deforestation through satellite images and connect it to data about the temperature of the oceans to project future events and areas that might become unsuitable

---

[6] Brennan (2016).
[7] Talisse (2019) is an essential reference for the comprehension of the ways contemporary societies may be overdoing politics, while Rosanvallon (2008) sheds light on the quest for the *impolitique*, which empties the political dimension of public decisions.
[8] Silva (2017).
[9] Grimmelikhuijsen and Meijer (2022: 232).

for agriculture.[10] They allow us to re-examine the symptoms of millions of individuals to identify new correlations that may ease the diagnoses of rare diseases.[11] They make it possible to redesign strategies aimed at preventing terrorist attacks.[12] Ironically, they allow the emergence of highly precise weapons that can even decide who to kill and when to do it.[13] In a nutshell, they provide—or at least are sold as providing—solid grounds for defining courses of action in an extremely frightening world.

As we have argued throughout this book, in this process, algorithmic systems are becoming new institutions in contemporary society. They institutionalize epistocratic values, reconstructing shared ways in which humans make decisions and do things. Algorithms play a key role in setting the frames and the contexts that mark our interactions, and they increasingly do so in directions that embody epistocratic ideas. However, this epistocratic order of knowledge creates a series of new social and political dilemmas. John Danaher elaborates on the risks of this *algocracy*, which is the algorithmic realization of epistocracies, pointing to the difficulties of either resisting it or accommodating to it.[14] Hamid Akın Ünver also fears that algorithmic systems may foster authoritarian regimes in many ways.[15]

In this last chapter, we move one step forward in the comprehension of the political implications of thinking of algorithms as institutions. We understand that algorithms are a central dimension of contemporary societies and are here to stay. There is no way back to a pre-algorithmic world. However, in the same way that other institutions have been democratized throughout time, we believe that democracies now require—and depend on—the democratization of algorithms.[16]

Think about the history of parliaments, for instance. The idea of an assembly of voices supporting decision-making can be traced back to the Roman Senate and to a wide range of experiences in Russia, Japan, Norway, and Iceland in the Middle Ages.[17] The English case is particularly relevant for the purposes of our argument owing to its continuity in history. Assemblies of nobles consulted by monarchs have occurred since at least the tenth century,[18] and this *magnum concilium* had important roles not only in the

---

[10] See, e.g., Arefinia et al. (2022) for an application of algorithms to optimize crop patterns in the face of climate change.
[11] Garcelon et al. (2020) and Schaefer et al. (2020).
[12] Gundabathula and Vaidhehi (2018).
[13] See Asaro (2019).
[14] Danaher (2016).
[15] Akın Ünver (2018).
[16] Ford (2021).
[17] Dahl (2015).
[18] Maddicott (2010).

substantive consideration of public affairs but also in the institutionalization of channels for broad consensus building, even though sovereign power was owned by the monarch. Throughout subsequent centuries, this assembly would experience moments of empowerment and of weakening, but it was not until the end of the seventeenth century that it became the central piece of England's political life. The so-called Glorious Revolution marks the rise of a constitutional monarchy, which can be seen as a turning point in terms of the democratization of the institution in the years to come. In the following centuries, the House of Commons was progressively transformed only in terms not of its prerogatives but also of the procedures used to define who would occupy its seats and the roles such representatives would have in a complex structure with several institutional layers. In a nutshell, this parliament experienced a process of internal and external transformations that led to democratization.

Surely, a person could argue that this democratization is anaemic and incomplete. Money and status still have a tremendous influence in the way politics is conducted, affecting not only who occupies the seats of the House of Commons but also how decisions are often made. There are many asymmetries cutting across the polity, and signs of the manipulation of public opinion and disinformation can be found in many instances. Parliament is often incapable of delivering actual scrutiny of other institutions, and the majoritarian electoral system adopted in the UK is a continued source of misrepresentation of minorities. It seems undeniable, nonetheless, that the parliament as an institution has taken large steps towards democratization since its inception.

Looking at algorithmic systems, and conceiving of them as institutions, we can also imagine a similar movement towards democratization. These institutions are novel, they are confusing and opaque, they have ambivalent and incoherent consequences, and they are pervaded by deep power asymmetries and games. We are trying to make sense of them expeditiously as we witness their capacity to affect processes through which societies and individuals are changing rapidly. Yet, if algorithms may have been thought of as ways to foster epistocratic values and procedures, we might as well seek to bring them—and their consequences—closer to democratic values.

Someone may counter-argue that this is utopic and unrealistic. Democratizing political power, nevertheless, has never been easy. Who would have speculated the possibility of democratizing the English *magnum concilium*? The mere idea of submitting the power of the sovereign to other institutions would have seemed inconceivable during a significant portion of the Middle Ages, making the question itself anachronic. As argued by Ostrom, '"getting the institutions right" is a difficult, time-consuming, conflict-invoking process".[19] And, still, the institution—that is, parliament—has established rules and norms aligned with ideas of equality, popular consent, political representation, and checks and balances that were strengthened by modernity.

Someone may also counter-argue that algorithms and parliaments are not institutions of the same genus; it would be like comparing oranges and apples. After all, parliaments seem somehow less abstract and more concrete than algorithms. Algorithms are harder to grasp as they are dispersed in societies. It is one thing to redesign an institution such as a parliament to bring it closer to certain values and a very different thing to think of how to deal with a diffuse institutional arrangement with many different shapes, purposes, and applications.

This argument makes sense and points to the size of the challenges ahead of us. However, other diffuse institutions have also been transformed in some societies. Think about families, for instance: they are diffuse across the social fabric, assuming many shapes and forms. It is quite difficult to transform these institutions and to redesign them according to changing values, but feminist movements, to give one among the possible examples, have taken important steps in problematizing the asymmetries and forms of violence pervading families. They have fostered significant action that has affected the overall idea of family, with implications in many specific families and the behaviours and lives of individuals.

Likewise, historical institutionalism teaches us that institutions do change over time, despite their inertial tendencies. Algorithmic systems can therefore be resituated in a different political context to have their implications democratized. The critical juncture generated by the public problematization of the political consequences of algorithms in many instances provides a window of opportunity to promote change, to bring the design, deployment, and operation of algorithmic systems closer to democratic values. If algorithms are frequently thought of as a new Leviathan, subjugating individuals who transfer their freedoms to an external source of power and decision-making,[20] we should be thinking about possibilities to bring a more Rousseaunian type of contract back into the equation. Sovereignty should not be alienated, and citizens ought to discuss the public implications of issues that affect the collectivity.

To foster this shift, our argument requires two steps, the first being that this change needs a discussion about legitimacy. The democratization of

---

[19] Ostrom (1990: 14).
[20] König (2019).

institutions walks together with the debate about how to make legitimate decision-making in democratic contexts. Second, we will present a set of values lying at the heart of democracy that are necessary for the promotion of more democratic institutions. Our aim is to introduce key values to be considered in the process of democratizing algorithms.

Democratic Legitimacy and Institutions

The possibility of democracy is inherently linked to issues of legitimacy. If democracy, in broad terms, implies some form of self-government by a community of equals, its political institutions may be legitimized by citizens. In Suchman's definition, 'legitimacy is a generalized perception or assumption that the actions of an entity are desirable, proper, or appropriate within some socially constructed system of norms, values, beliefs, and definitions'.[21] In the famous definition of David Easton, legitimacy happens when a society's institutions correspond with the people's moral principles, implying diffuse support for the political action carried out by governments.[22]

Legitimacy can, however, be grounded on different principles, and such principles change over time. In one of his archaeologies of democracy, Pierre Rosanvallon devotes particular attention to the transformations in the way certain institutions have been legitimized to promote democracy. According to him, the ways through which polities have sought to promote social generality were significantly altered along the history of democracy.

First, modern democracies saw elections as the way to enact social generality, thereby legitimating the institutions responsible for decision-making. Rosanvallon points out that this argument requires a dual fiction: elections work as a synecdoque, transforming the part that proved to be majoritarian into the expression of the whole; and elections expand time by transforming a particular moment's result into a sign of authorization valid for a longer and predetermined period. Citizens soon realized, however, the need for another layer of legitimacy in democratic institutions, as elections became a form of competition between particular interests. Then bureaucracies were framed as a possible way to generate democratic legitimacy, owing to the expected impersonal routines and their alleged capacity to transcend particular political interests. While elections would provide a subjective test for those responsible for acting on the public's behalf, selecting a qualified body

[21] Suchman (1995: 574).
[22] Easton (1965).

of public servants would represent an objective test for the needed technical efficiency in delivering public services.

But elections and bureaucracies soon had to face public scepticism about their ability to deliver the social generality that legitimated them. For Rosanvallon, this double crisis of legitimacy led to institutional changes and attempts to pluralize the legitimating grounds of democracies. He diagnosed the emergence of three main alternative sources of legitimacy emerging at the end of the twentieth century: impartiality, reflexivity, and proximity. Impartiality grounds a form of *negative generality* that seeks distance from particular positions and becomes enacted in institutions such as regulatory agencies. Reflexivity embodies the *generality of multiplication*, pursuing the pluralization of perspectives in the complexification of issues of public relevance: 'Having increased their power everywhere, independent oversight authorities and constitutional courts have begun to change the way in which the question of democracy is framed.'[23] Last, proximity is related to a *generality of attention to particularity*, which is manifest in 'a new insistence on attentiveness, openness, fairness, compassion, recognition, respect, and presence'.[24] Such a principle of legitimacy is often institutionalized in participatory forums that promote the idea that decisions can be democratic only if they consider the variety of situations and singular perspectives experienced by citizens.

When we think about algorithms, we often think of them as institutions linked to two of the aforementioned factors. In a certain way, we may seek in algorithms legitimate justifications for their decisions mainly because of their technical efficiency (such as was expected from rational bureaucracies) and their impartiality (such as is expected from regulatory agencies). Algorithmic systems satisfy this condition to the extent that they produce decisions and perform tasks in a justifiably impartial manner.

Moreover, it is also possible to link algorithms to an idea of reflexivity, because they can manage colossal volumes of data, thus multiplying the perspectives considered in each decision and complexifying solutions. This helps to understand the current fascination with algorithmic systems: they gather features and promises that contemporary polities pursue with other institutions, and they are often presented as ways to replace other institutions.

There is, nevertheless, an important difference. While other institutions expected by democracies to deliver efficiency, impartiality, and reflexivity are linked to other sources of democratic legitimacy, algorithmic systems

---

[23] Rosanvallon (2011: 9).
[24] Rosanvallon (2011: 11).

almost never are. Bureaucracies, for instance, have at least two other forms of democratic control. First, bureaucrats must be selected through impartial and open competitions based on their technical knowledge. Second, efficient bureaucrats are subject to many forms of accountability, having to answer for their choices and the consequences of their actions if they violate any laws or generate losses for society. While algorithms employed by governments may be selected through open competition, they can generate constraints for future 'hires' owing to path dependence. In addition, algorithms with public implications go well beyond those employed by governments. Furthermore, algorithms are often not restricted by any forms of accountability, and their consequences go around without assessment and any sort of punishment in cases of inefficiency, injustice, and loss.

The impartiality delivered by regulatory agencies is also linked to forms of authorization and accountability. These agencies usually have a board of directors selected through public mechanisms and for predetermined mandates. Moreover, they have ombudsmen and channels for complaints and other forms of input from several stakeholders. Regulatory agencies are themselves regulated by detailed laws that define their specific attributions and limits for their actions. The markets they regulate depend on these definitions and follow the decisions taken by these agencies closely, contributing to their construction. The current view of algorithms looks nothing like regulatory agencies. Their impartiality is hard to follow or understand, and those affected by their consequences have a really hard time challenging the decisions taken through them. The opacity of algorithms is protected by trade secrets or the complexities of AI, which is often considered a form of unpredictable alchemy.

Last, the reflexivity of constitutional courts is grounded on the way these courts are constituted. Although rules vary from country to country, justices are usually nominated by governments and assessed by members of a parliament, who can approve or deny the nomination. Also, the publicity of the justice's actions is a central component of the reflexivity they may foster. The plurality of perspectives expressed in a constitutional court should nurture a public reflexivity around controversial topics of public interest. For this reason, justices must sustain their positions, provide justifications for what they advocate, and analyse the possible consequences of their decisions. Again, algorithmic systems are an animal of a highly different genus. Even if they can deal with various possibilities and simulate the results of a wide range of alternatives, they are restrained neither by the political dynamics of democratic politics nor by the public scrutiny of the to-and-fro of arguments. As a matter of fact, we have severe doubts whether we should actually describe their capacity to deal with different positions as a form of reflexivity. On the one hand, they may truly deliver complex solutions, taking into account many pieces of data with specific goals and objectives, but, on the other, they do not leave much room for the pause and reconsideration inherent to reflexivity.

In a nutshell, while algorithmic systems are a central piece of our contemporary institutional life, they lack the two main pillars of legitimation central to democracy: authorization and accountability. In different ways, and with diverse forms of combination between these two principles, elected politicians, bureaucrats, directors of regulatory agencies, and constitutional courts' justices are authorized to act on behalf of the collectivity and are held accountable to the political community. Decisions happening through algorithmic systems, in contrast, do not usually have clear mechanisms of authorization and accountability. Algorithms enjoy the benefits of the legitimacy expected from their outcomes, without the burdens inherent in democratic decision-making. They frame interactive settings and have deep collective consequences without passing through the tests of authorization or going through the controls that lie at the heart of other institutions with political implications in democratic regimes. That is, the institutionalization of algorithmic systems with different forms of public consequences rarely satisfies the criteria of democratic principles and values, with no clear procedures for their justification in the political community.

We claim that algorithmic institutions need to be democratized, but the meaning of this democratization requires further clarification. It obviously does not mean that the algorithms we use should be elected or that the experts designing algorithms and other citizens should have the same roles in the definition of how an algorithm should look. We do not define democracy as a majoritarian aggregation of opinions. In the case of algorithms, a critical reconceptualization of the meaning and practices of consent can point to ways forward in regard to authorization procedures. We do think, however, that the principle of accountability seems to be the key to democratize algorithms. This principle can, however, also lead to different paths. For this reason, in the following sections of this chapter, we will develop key democratic values that ought to be considered for a proper comprehension of possible avenues for a democratic accountability of algorithms.

Democratic Values

The literature on democratic theory is plural enough to encompass a wide range of definitions. Jean-Paul Gagnon has mapped more than two thousand different adjectives used to define democracies, demonstrating the amplitude and the vagueness of the concept.[25] Pluralists, elitists, agonists, radical, participatory, and deliberative democrats, to cite a few classic examples, have different starting points and different aims when they claim the need to protect or expand democracies. Yet, more scholars are trying to chart some common axes and agendas cutting across this field of investigation.

Morlino, for instance, conducted comparative analysis about the quality of democracies through eight dimensions: rule of law, electoral accountability, inter-institutional accountability, participation, competition, liberties, equality, and responsivity.[26] Mendonça also provided a framework grounded on seven dimensions that run across different theories of democracy: popular authorization for the exercise of representation; participation and self-government; monitoring and accountability; equality; plural competition; public debate; and the quest for the common good.[27] In contrast to Morlino, he sought to understand how these dimensions acquire diverse meanings in different theoretical conceptions of democracy. Diverse conceptions frame each of these dimensions differently and may even oppose some of them. Elitists, for instance, deny the notion of public good, although they discuss the topic, reinforcing its role as an axis of theoretical debate.

Similarly, Mark Warren has advocated a problem-based approach to democracy that seeks to overcome the rigid organization of models of democracy.[28] In Warren's view, a political system has to address three types of problems to become democratic: it must promote inclusion, it must enable the formation of collective agendas and wills, and it must generate collective decisions. Different practices may promote these central aims, which ground the idea of democracy. In a way, Warren's problem-based approach resembles John Dewey's call at the beginning of the twentieth century: a person should focus on the idea of democracy, instead of on the existent institutional machinery, to promote democracy. Institutions can operate in less or more democratic ways; the idea of democracy serves as the guideline to assess how to promote democratic processes. For Dewey, the idea of democracy is grounded in the capacity of a polity to deal collectively with public problems.[29] According to him, democracies require the emergence of publics around controversial issues. It is through communicative processes that citizens constitute publics, nurturing social reflexivity about

[25] Gagnon (2018).
[26] Morlino (2012).
[27] Mendonça (2018).
[28] Warren (2017).
[29] Dewey (1954).

shared problems. This process depends on the encounter of a wide range of perspectives, as social reflexivity involves a collective endeavour to test alternative hypotheses.

This broad idea of democracy may help us to think about the possibility of democratizing algorithms. Such democratization requires establishing public reflexivity around algorithms' consequences so that citizens find ways to deal with them. To be able to do so, certain values related to the aforementioned democratic dimensions must be promoted. As argued by Grimmelikhuijsen and Meijer, 'the legitimacy of algorithmic government increases when the outcomes of the use of an algorithm contribute to the realization of values that citizens consider important'.[30] In the following subsections, we map some of these values that are essential to algorithms' democratization.

Participation

Democratic legitimacy requires the actual engagement of those affected by a decision in its construction. This has been a basic corollary of democracy throughout history: self-government is essential to democracy, and, by self-government, we mean citizens should have an actual role in the production of decisions that affect them.[31] Empowerment is, therefore, a key component of participation. Citizens should have actual power and not merely a metaphorical and abstract consideration.

The value of participation has important implications to the democratization of algorithms. It reminds philosophers, computer scientists, lawyers, and social scientists that, even if they have a relevant role in the process, it is not only up to them to define if and how algorithms should be regulated, for example. Social movements and NGOs also have a key role in this process, especially in their struggle to transform invisible issues into public problems. They seek to expand engagement around issues often seen as too technical and opaque.

There is a growing call for the need for citizens' participation in the democratization of algorithms.[32] Robinson shows the centrality of the notion of openness in policy documents about AI adopted in Nordic countries that emphasize the centrality of citizens' participation in decision-making around AI technologies.[33] Grimmelikhuijsen and Meijer also highlight the need for

---

[30] Grimmelikhuijsen and Meijer (2022: 235).
[31] Pateman (1970).
[32] Lepri et al. (2018); König and Wenzelburger (2021); Mittelstadt et al. (2016); Grimmelikhuijsen and Meijer (2022).
[33] Robinson (2020).

participation in the development of algorithmic systems and policies in this area so as to assure input legitimacy in the functioning of the political system.[34] Participation is the bedrock of democracy, and, as was the case with many other institutions, the democratization of algorithms must count on citizens' engagement.

Equality

Democracies are communities of equals, which means that those considered to be members of the polity must have an equal say in the construction of the rules of this community. The Greeks operationalized democratic equality through the principles of isonomy and *isegoria*, using sortition to define the occupation of public functions and assuring that all citizens had the right to speak in assemblies. Modern democracies mainly use the idea of *one person, one vote* to realize equality.

The value of equality also means that decisions should not harm minorized groups, nor systematically and unjustifiably treat citizens unequally. A community of equals worthy of this name must cherish the struggle against unjustified asymmetries and foster equality as a value, counting its members in a symmetrical way, not only in the procedures employed to produce decisions, but also in the substance of these decisions. Algorithmic institutions can even contain biases if these biases promote redistributive forms of justice orientated by equity.

When we think about the democratization of algorithms, the value of equality has relevant ramifications that somehow overlap with those of participation. Equality implies first that citizens must be considered in the decisions affecting their lives. Even if corporations and experts have a technical type of knowledge and important resources to affect the design of algorithmic systems, the way such algorithms affect citizens demands that they have a say in the broader algorithmic infrastructure of societies and in the outcomes of specific algorithms.

The collective nature of algorithms' consequences invites a reflection about the possible ways in which they may harm minorities and feed vicious cycles of oppression. The democratization of algorithms requires not only procedures that enable the community of equals to participate in the definitions regarding how societies should deal with these systems but also mechanisms that systematically shed light on the way in which the outcomes of

---

[34] Grimmelikhuijsen and Meijer (2022: 236).

algorithmic systems may be generating or feeding unjustifiable inequalities. Democratized algorithms ought to foster inclusion and not exclusion.

In the literature about the political implications of algorithms, the democratic value of equality tends to appear under the label of fairness or in the attempts to problematize algorithmic biases. The concept of 'bias' may suggest, however, that unbiased decisions exist and that political choices may be overcome, thus nurturing the epistocratic frame we have previously criticized. Fairness is often reduced to the idea that decisions should treat citizens in the same way in the debates about algorithms, but equality may require unequal forms of treatment to be fair: 'The core question in this regard is, put simply, whether the ADM [Algorithmic Decision-Making] systems should reproduce patterns already existing in the data or actively intervene with reality through its treatments in order to gradually shape it toward a different state of society.'[35]

Pluralism

Democracies require the coexistence of a plurality of perspectives. There is no theory of democracy that attributes to majorities the right to eliminate their opponents. As Robert Dahl long ago explained, democratization involves a combination of inclusive participation and openness to the expression of dissent.[36] Pluralism is grounded in tolerance, acknowledging the democratic need for non-violent ways to deal with conflicts around power. In addition, power can provide mechanisms for the construction of better solutions through the consideration of many points of view.

Pluralism is particularly relevant when we think about the democratization of algorithms. Definitions for complex technological systems require a multiplicity of perspectives, not only because there are diverse interests at stake but also because no single actor has all the necessary information for the design of solutions to complex problems. Landemore showed the epistemic need for collective intelligence, following a route previously paved by authors such as John Stuart Mill and John Dewey.[37] She argued that better decisions can be achieved by encountering diverse perspectives to overcome informational asymmetries and biased perspectives. This plurality requires openness, and the democratization of digital technologies occurs when this multitude of perspectives is pushed into the public sphere.[38]

---

[35] König and Wenzelburger (2021: 7).
[36] Dahl (1971).
[37] Landemore (2013).
[38] Landemore (2021).

When we think, for instance, about democratic attempts to promote governance of the Internet, we notice the strengthening of multi-stakeholder approaches that emphasize the need of governments, private companies, civil society, and academics in the formulation of norms, principles, standards, and strategies to deal with vulnerabilities and risks. The plurality of views—in contexts such as those of the Internet Governance Forum (IGF), the Global Commission on the Stability of Cyberspace, and NetMundial—was essential to build more complex solutions capable of dealing with the specific interests and perspectives of different types of actors.[39] Sometimes leading to workable agreements and exposing hard-entrenched disagreements, these forums create mechanisms for a plural processing of collective issues.

Similarly, the democratization of algorithms requires the engagement of the multiple perspectives of actors who act through these algorithms and/or who are subject to their consequences. But different stakeholders may have diverse roles. We cannot expect experts, governments, and social movements to play the same role in the process of designing ways to deal with algorithms. We are not merely talking about divergent interests. The plurality of perspectives goes beyond interests, as Iris Young has demonstrated.[40] The fruitfulness of multi-stakeholder approaches is exactly the multiplicity of looks at a given phenomenon and the acknowledgement that dissent is inherent in democratic governance.

There are some attempts to create multi-stakeholder forms of governance of algorithms.[41] Maria Abdala and collaborators, for instance, argue that only actual agreements between diverse actors can make the governance of algorithms move from abstract principles towards concrete action:

> By establishing shared ground-rules, they [the multiple-stakeholders] can reduce the risks in both international and market competition, thereby supporting policy goals where global governance (the governance of increasingly automated decision systems) is needed. International standards could change the context in which AI is researched, developed, and implemented, simultaneously dealing with the geopolitical and cultural differences at hand and disseminating best practices at the global level.[42]

In this direction, the EU is establishing the European Centre for Algorithmic Transparency (ECAT) in Seville Spain. The centre seeks to bring together

---

[39] Kleinwächter and Almeida (2015).
[40] Young (2002).
[41] Webb et al. (2018).
[42] Abdala et al. (2020).

different actors to analyse algorithms and foster more democratic technological solutions:

> Scientists and experts working at the ECAT will cooperate with industry representatives, academia, and civil society organisations to improve our understanding of how algorithms work: they will analyse transparency, assess risks, and propose new transparent approaches and best practices.[43]

The focus of the centre on transparency leads us to the following value, which is crucial to the democratization of algorithms.

Accountability and Transparency

Accountability is a crucial element of democracies, if democracies mean that power must not be concentrated in one single institution or group of actors. Democracies require accountability in the sense that one institution is held accountable by others, having to justify the actions taken through it and being subject to eventual forms of punishment.[44] This is the heart of the idea of checks and balances, which allows the oversight of one institution by others and generates some form of equilibrium, avoiding the concentration of power. Transparency is a necessary condition for accountability, because the oversight and control of institutions depend on the availability of information about them and their actions.[45]

An important set of democratic theorists emphasizes the growing importance of accountability to contemporary democracies. John Keane, for instance, speaks of the rise of a *monitory democracy* in the second half of the twentieth century stemming from the growing importance of formal and informal networks of surveillance over political actors.[46] Rosanvallon speaks of mechanisms of *counter-democracy* that historically have contributed to the control of power. The mechanisms of negative sovereignty include not only vetoes but also the close monitoring and surveillance of institutions.[47]

The democratization of algorithms is heavily dependent on the establishment of forms of accountability.[48] Such a democratization requires clearer ways to hold actors accountable and make them responsible for the actual

---

[43] https://algorithmic-transparency.ec.europa.eu/index_en.
[44] Mulgan (2000); Bovens (2007).
[45] Filgueiras (2016).
[46] Keane (2013).
[47] Rosanvallon (2008).
[48] Kroll et al. (2017); Binns (2018).

consequences of algorithmic systems. To do so, transparency is always pointed out as a key element. If other institutions and actors cannot understand what is going on in the complex processes through which decisions are algorithmically made, accountability becomes impossible.

There are, however, significant difficulties in this regard. As previously argued, algorithms should not be thought of as black boxes that can be opened and whose secret content is awaiting disclosure. There are layers of complexity involving the unpredictable interrelations between algorithms and between humans and machines in the way AI works, making transparency a somehow awkward concept. There is not much to be revealed beneath the surface, because the surface is continuously unfolding and becoming something different.

Despite this apparent singularity, it should be reminded that other institutions operate similarly. Drawing from Ansell,[49] Rebecca Abers argues that quite often institutions coexist in ultracomplex structures marked by overlaps and contradictions.[50] It has never been easy to democratize institutions, and it has never been easy to understand the implications of their various interrelations. Perhaps it is the idea of what should be transparent that ought to change. Even if the design of an algorithm cannot become entirely transparent and comprehensible, a clearer comprehension of its results seems more attainable.

This helps solve another issue. Frequently it is argued that several algorithmic systems cannot be made more transparent: some algorithms are even protected by laws of trade secrecy, and, if these laws were eventually banned, they might cause pushbacks on technological developments. In addition, other algorithms need to remain opaque for reasons of national security. Were the operations of some algorithms fully disclosed, criminals and enemies might be able to twist them to serve their purposes, gaming with these algorithms in ways that would impede the realization of the tasks for which they were designed. Yet neither could decisions be made entirely transparent in an imaginary golden era of human action: 'In fact, human decision-makers are, ultimately, opaque; there are no ways to trace and discern their "internal" psychological processes used to arrive at a decision.'[51] Joanna Bryson spots exactly this point:

> Many claim that such accountability is impossible with AI, because of its complexity, or the fact that it includes machine learning or has some sort of autonomy.

[49] Ansell (2013).
[50] Abers (2021: 24).
[51] König and Wenzelburger (2021: 3).

However, we have been holding many human-run institutions such as banks and governments accountable for centuries. The humans in these institutions also learn and have autonomy, and the workings of their brains are far more inscrutable than any system deliberately built and maintained by humans. Nevertheless, we can determine credit and blame where necessary by maintaining accounts and logs of who does what and why.[52]

If we focus on the outcomes of decisions—analysing the algorithms instead of their design—the problem may be partially mitigated. Accountability does not necessarily need all forms of transparency, and the difficulty or undesirability of generating some forms of transparency should not imply an impossibility of holding actors and institutions accountable. König and Wenzelburger advocate this point when they argue that 'decision-making legitimacy is no longer rooted in internalized values and procedures but instead has to be tied to the acceptability of produced outputs'.[53]

We have said, however, that the focus on outcomes is only a partial solution. There is another layer of the problem that involves the decision of what should be protected and what should be disclosed. The fact that the design of some algorithms ought to be protected does not mean that all designs at all times must be secret. The definition of what should be made public is at the heart of democracies, most of which systematically face the trade-offs between secrecy and transparency. Regarding this dilemma, Simone Chambers argues that the definition itself of what should remain secret is political and should, therefore, be taken by democratic publics.[54] Some secrets are perfectly compatible with democracies, and what makes them legitimate is the construction of processes that publicly justify their need. This leads us to the next point of our discussion: the centrality of public debate.

Public Debate

Democracies depend on the capacity of the polity to process public issues through discursive exchanges. Discourses are the main medium for political participation and for the mediation of the conflicts running across the political community. Even if some aggregative mechanisms do not seem essentially discursive—such as voting—public discourses have been crucial to building these mechanisms' legitimacy.

[52] Bryson (2018).
[53] König and Wenzelburger (2021: 4).
[54] Chambers (2004).

In democratic theory, the role of public discussion has been emphasized in diverse traditions of thought. For different reasons, liberals, agonists, and participative democrats have shed light on the role played by public debates in democracies.[55] Deliberative democrats have reconstructed the whole concept of democracy around the centrality of public debates.[56] According to them, the public exchange of justifications is the main pillar of democratic legitimacy, and public deliberation can both foster epistemically complex solutions and promote a sense of community.[57]

The democratization of algorithmic systems is essentially linked to public debates or, in other words, to the enhancement of deliberative processes around algorithms.[58] Polities need to transform the operations and consequences of algorithms into issues of public concern, revealing their political dimension. While algorithms are seen as tools to rationalize decisions, they cannot be targeted properly by sociotechnical artefacts with political implications that shape individual behaviours and have collective consequences. It is only through public debate that the institutional nature of algorithms can be revealed and that ways to deal with them may emerge. The politicization of algorithms ultimately requires open and broad debate about them.

Publicity is a central feature of the debates necessary for democratization. As James Bohman argued long ago, publicity involves more than the establishment of a shared space of visibility for the appearance of issues of public concern, despite the centrality of this aspect.[59] Publicity also implies the emergence of certain constraints that allow the filtering of the muddy elements of argumentative processes, to use Jürgen Habermas's words,[60] or the fostering of the civilizing force of hypocrisy, to use Elster's concept.[61] Publicity is at the heart of the construction of public interest, enabling processes through which democratic citizens can process collective issues and make the unacceptability of certain arguments and outcomes visible. Publicity is constructed through communicative processes, as citizens build a shared public space for the reflection about issues of collective concern.

John Dewey advocated that democracies emerged when *communities of adventure* became *communities of enquiry*.[62] By this, he meant that democracies were a type of association that acknowledges the public implications of

---

[55] Mendonça (2018).
[56] Habermas (1996); Chambers (2003); Dryzek and Niemeyer (2010); Steiner (2012); Bächtiger et al. (2018); Ercan et al. (2022).
[57] Cooke (2000).
[58] Buhmann and Fieseler (2021).
[59] Bohman (1996).
[60] Habermas (2006).
[61] Elster (1998).
[62] Dewey (1954).

the coexistence of individuals—and their technologies—and started to think about ways to deal with these implications. It is through public debate that individuals can build shared ground and simulate alternatives to solve a collective problem. This debate ought to occur in the broad public sphere, which includes the traditional media, social media, and other arenas of broad visibility, but also in specific and empowered forums devoted to deal with the issue:

> all those who potentially suffer the negative effects of the processes and decisions of algorithmic systems should have equal access to a forum and a communicative process that aims to spotlight potential issues and facilitate argumentation with the aim of arriving at broadly acceptable decisions. Stakeholders need institutionalised *access to deliberative settings* to ensure they have a chance to voice their concerns, opinions, and arguments.[63]

Democratic innovations, hence, may have an important role in promoting discussions among those affected by algorithmic decision-making, but it is crucial to keep in mind the need to connect such innovations with wider (and wilder) discussions in the public sphere. As emphasized by Buhmann and Fieseler, critical journalism and civil society have a key role in promoting the connections that generate public and democratic discussion.

Liberty

Last, but not in any way least, democracies value freedoms. The modern reinvention of democracy in the eighteenth century is fundamentally linked to the idea of liberties. In this context, liberty essentially refers to forms of protection that citizens ought to have in relation to the state and to other citizens. Freedom of association, of opposition, of expression, and of belief are usually seen as part of the package of democratic liberties. Although the exact substance of each of these liberties is debatable, democracies depend on free individuals who can form and express their preferences.[64] Freedom is often seen as a condition for autonomy, which is itself crucial for the democratic formation of preferences and the aggregation of them.

Democratic liberties are not restricted, however, to this protective dimension. Democracies require freedom from coercion but also freedom to act and to be heard. Drawing from Isaiah Berlin's classic distinction, although

[63] Buhmann and Fieseler (2021: 3).
[64] Dahl (1971).

different from his argument, our comprehension of democracy entails both negative and positive liberties.[65] *Freedom from* and *freedom to* are necessary to the autonomous participation of citizens in the construction of the rules that govern their lives.

As we have seen throughout the book, algorithms can have deep consequences in the way liberties are experienced, often undermining possibilities of autonomous human agency.[66] Either through pervasive surveillance or through forms of manipulative recommendation, algorithms may damage the conditions for autonomous will formation. In addition, as many decisions are taken through algorithmic systems, citizens may lose sight of their freedom to act and to build the societies in which they live.

The democratization of algorithms requires more attention to the two types of liberty discussed by Berlin. First, data protection remains a central and unavoidable topic. While we agree with Sanches, who claims that privacy should not be seen as the unique driving value in discussions about digital technologies, it seems undeniable that mechanisms for the protection of information and personal data continue to be essential.[67] Data about individuals—and data produced by them—can be used by governments, adversaries, corporations, and other actors to inflict damage and undermine the possibilities of a safe existence. *Freedom from* can be curtailed because algorithmic systems may expose some individuals and make them traceable. Second, algorithmic systems have an impact on citizens' preferences and may undermine *freedom to*. For instance, when recommendation systems nurture echo chambers and spirals of silence or when campaigns of micro-targeting manage to induce specific forms of behaviour, we can speak of processes that may compromise autonomous action. Democratizing algorithms demands facing these issues. Many societies have fought hard to implement the conditions of liberty that allowed the emergence of our fragile (and problematic) democratic institutions. Continuous light should be placed on the consequences of algorithms over individual freedoms and collective liberties if democracies are to survive these difficult times!

Concluding Remarks

This chapter has argued that algorithms, as other institutions, must be democratized if democracies are to survive. To the extent in which algorithms

---

[65] Berlin (1958).
[66] Silva (2017).
[67] Sanches (2019).

acquire prominence and centrality in the organization of contemporary societies, their democratization emerges as a *sine qua* condition for the resilience of democracy as a political regime. Despite the fact that algorithms foster technocratic trends aligned with the rise of epistocratic alternatives to democracy, we argue that they can be democratized.

Such a democratization should not, however, be seen as an end state or achievable telos to be conquered. As the theories of democracy have extensively shown, democracy should be conceived of as a process or as a normative horizon that guides practices and allows the continuous criticism of existing institutions. Democratizing algorithms should not be thought of as a task that can be settled once and for all; rather, it is a horizon that should keep us alert to the many dilemmas and changes either happening or arriving in the future. Democratizing algorithms means that algorithmic systems should be thought of as issues of public concern that must be discussed systematically and dealt with collectively through democratic lenses. This endless process must be marked by the idea of democratic revisability, which reminds us that democracies advance through experimentation, trial and error, and progresses and setbacks. The democratization of algorithms requires bringing reflexivity back to the centre of the equation of how we govern ourselves.

Importantly, we should also emphasize that we were careful enough to speak about the need for a broad democratization of algorithms that goes beyond the systems employed by governments. While a great deal of debate is restricted to the need to democratize the algorithmic systems used in public services, we argue that many private systems may have public consequences that can contribute to democratic erosion. Seen as institutions that shape individual behaviours and have public consequences, algorithmic systems employed by diverse companies and with different purposes must be submitted to public scrutiny if democratic societies are to survive. From social-media platforms to systems used in the organization of employee schedules at work, we see several dangers to human autonomy, individual rights, collective enterprises, and the cultural fabric that is necessary for the survival of democracy.

Algorithmic Institutionalism offers a way forward to make sense of these phenomena and to think about the future of polities, politics, and policies. Pointing to the complex relations through which rules and norms that shape individual behaviours and that have collective outcomes are formed, it allows a nuanced comprehension of contemporary societies and argues that the democratization of algorithms is crucial to democracy, just as the democratization of other institutions have been in other moments of the history of humanity. Recognizing the institutional nature of algorithms is, therefore, a fruitful step to the comprehension of the complexities but also of the possibilities of the task that lies ahead of us.

The democratization of algorithms thought of as pervasive institutions in contemporary society requires a set of public actions that depend on the dimensions of polity, politics, and policy. First, in the polity dimension, algorithmic systems' design, deployment, and operation require evaluation—based on the principles listed—to build an order of legitimate interventions carried out in society. Principles are essential markers of values that guide the design and action of algorithms as institutions. Second, in the dimension of politics, political leaders need to be aware of algorithms' growing role in contemporary society. Party and civil-society leaders can be essential in mobilizing the community to build attention to public problems and the consequences of algorithmic systems. Finally, in the policy dimension, governments must take actions to regulate and foster democratic forms of governance of algorithmic systems, creating targeted policies to mitigate risks, monitor compliance, and steer digital development.

This leads us to a concluding question: are algorithmic institutions creating a new political order? Considering the cases previously analysed in the book, this is a process under construction, as we gradually shift towards a political order of algorithms. How to democratize this political order is challenging and requires dimensions of democracy consistent and coherent with values that instil legitimacy. It is possible for algorithmic systems to democratize existing political orders, establishing democratic decision-making mechanisms, advancing forms of pluralizing the knowledge of preferences, and shaping legitimate orders of decisions and governance. In a utopian future, digital technologies can be engines of profound democratic change.[68] However, this utopian future needs to be built, which requires critical thinking about the institutional role played by algorithms. The framework of Algorithmic Institutionalism seeks to provide adequate theoretical tools for this critical thinking. It allows us to understand nuances and consider multiple dimensions of the way algorithms play a role in the metamorphoses of societies. It also sheds light on the need to reconceive some elements of institutional theories, as we make clear in the final remarks following this chapter.

---

[68] Landemore (2021).

Final Remarks: A Needed Agenda

In this book, we have advanced the argument that algorithms are institutions that should be thought of as sociotechnical artefacts that shape individual behaviour and collective choices. As institutions, algorithmic systems have political and social consequences over diverse contexts of interaction. Algorithmic systems are a key component in processes of reorganizing societies, as they produce convenience for consumers and citizens and offer rationalizing solutions to companies and governments. In doing so, these political artefacts embody values and interpretative frameworks that shape the decisions affecting the fabric of social life.

As anticipated by Langdon Winner, these technical systems play a role similar to legislation, as they 'shape the basic pattern and content of human activity in our time. Thus, politics becomes (among other things) an active encounter with the specific forms and processes contained in technology.'[1] Such a perception is also shared by Lawrence Lessig, according to whom computer codes regulate human activity in the same way as do legal codes.[2]

The seminal works by Winner and Lessig offered the initial routes for understanding the place that algorithms occupy in contemporary societies. In many respects, both of them reproduce arguments from the old institutionalist tradition in which technologies play formal and legal roles. This book proposes a move beyond the earlier formal and legal issues around computational systems that paved the way to understanding them as institutions. We understand that algorithmic systems not only define the 'law' but should be read in more complex and nuanced ways through institutional theories. Algorithms are not just formal codes; they interact with layers of human agency and with other algorithms in complex assemblages that affect—in both formal and informal ways—the norms, rules, and contexts in which we live. They are an institutional infrastructure of contemporary existence.

Advancing the notion of Algorithmic Institutionalism, this book discusses how the pervasive presence of algorithms in societies has political consequences, reshaping power relations, creating new restraints

---

[1] Winner (1977: 323).
[2] Lessig (1999).

Algorithmic Institutionalism. Ricardo F. Mendonça, Fernando Filgueiras, and Virgílio Almeida, Oxford University Press.
© Ricardo F. Mendonça, Fernando Filgueiras, and Virgílio Almeida (2023). DOI: 10.1093/oso/9780192870070.003.0008

and opportunities for human action, and enacting historical processes and discursive dynamics through which we construct social reality.

Chapter 1 introduces the argument of Algorithmic Institutionalism, presenting some basic definitions and pointing to the growing pervasiveness of these sociotechnical systems in contemporary societies. It claims that algorithms play key roles in the processes of de-institutionalization and re-institutionalization through which societies change. Chapter 1 also argues that the lens of Algorithmic Institutionalism is particularly apt to avoid the series of dichotomies often used in attempts to theorize algorithmic societies. We conceive of algorithms as institutions, which means they lie somewhere between the poles of these dichotomies and are not animated autonomous agents or neutral tools. Instead, they are simultaneously structural and a form of agency, with individual and collective consequences. They are not deterministic factors of action nor entirely open to the novelty of unpredictable interactions.

Chapter 2 analyses different institutional theories, including sociological, rational choice, and historical and discursive institutionalism, to build a framework dedicated to understanding algorithmic institutions. The framework of Algorithmic Institutionalism requires attention to six dimensions: institution building and design; historical processes; rules and norms; power relations; gaming; and discursive dimensions. Once the framework is introduced, the book moves forward in the presentation of three focused operationalizations in areas of relevance that contemplate different levels of algorithmic systems. These operationalizations focus on a variety of cases that illustrate how the dimensions may be applied in specific areas of investigation.

Chapter 3 focuses on a specific subfield of algorithmic usage: security. The cases of predictive policing, the extensive use of FRTs, and the development of lethal autonomous weapons illustrate a multitude of social dilemmas related to the growing algorithmization of security. Algorithmic technologies employed in security are building a new type of Leviathan in which private organizations perform public functions. Algorithms are becoming institutions that implement security policies and changing routines in the state's coercive forces. In many situations, algorithms create authoritarian, unfair, and exclusionary action situations, impacting negatively on society. Algorithmic systems applied to security imply new dynamics of action and resistance.

Chapter 4 deals with various transformations in governments owing to their platformization through the growing use of algorithmic systems in the policy process. These systems are redesigning governmental structures and changing the routines of public administration and processes of policy formulation and implementation. Algorithmic systems create policy disruptions gradually, making critical public decisions with a high impact on society. They affect the logic of problem identification based on data and also change agenda-setting processes. Algorithmic systems automate implementation tasks, and, like other government institutions, they are crucial in the contemporary world, changing the way governments solve problems and shape political action.

Chapter 5 deals with the importance of recommendation systems, which sheds light on a wider technological mechanism running across many of the changes discussed throughout the book. These systems are employed in private and public sectors, commercial or affective relationships, industry, markets, and governments, to mention a few examples. Algorithmic recommendation systems rationalize human choices, delineating which options are available and visible, organizing and anticipating preferences of citizens and consumers. Furthermore, they drive consumer choices, generating opportunities for business optimization. The pervasiveness of algorithmic recommendation systems creates diverse moral and political challenges, as evidenced in their usages in social-media platforms and in key services, such as identifying those entitled to receive organ donations.

Finally, Chapter 6 draws on the previous discussions to argue that algorithmic systems are emerging as institutions deeply connected to a movement in the direction of epistocratic regimes, where technical knowledge is seen as the grounds to overcome politics and democracy. In the face of the valorization of epistocracy, algorithms play a role in shaping technical decisions and configuring new power relations. People, whether consciously, deliberately, or inadvertently, use systems that influence how they work, communicate, consume, participate in the public sphere, build public goods, appreciate culture, and build social relationships. Likewise, this political order of algorithms produces new social outcomes, creating new forms of injustice, dilemmas, and problems. Chapter 6 argues that the survival of democracies requires the democratization of these central institutions of contemporary societies called algorithms. This democratization should be thought of as a normative horizon that guides practices and allows continuous criticism of existing institutions. To be democratic, algorithms must be inserted in political dynamics orientated by the values of participation, equality, pluralism, accountability, public debate, and liberty. Democratization should be thought of not as an end state but as an ongoing process that revolves around the idea of democracy adapting to different and ever-changing contexts.

Additionally, throughout this book we advocate that the lenses of institutionalist theories are fruitful to make sense of algorithms, grasping what they are and how they operate in sociopolitical terms. Institutional theories provide innovative elements for understanding these sociotechnical artefacts and their consequences. They offer concepts and a tradition of investigations of similarly complex phenomena, driving our attention to important dimensions of algorithmic systems. With the aid of institutional theories, we can look at rationalization processes, rules and norms, institutional isomorphism, path dependence, and critical junctures, thereby shedding new light on the algorithmization of societies. The central preoccupation with legitimacy and democracy in institutional theories may even foster advancements in the steps needed to migrate towards more democratic algorithms.

If the understanding of algorithms can benefit from institutional theories, we also argue that institutional theories can benefit from the study of algorithms, rethinking some of these concepts and elements. Algorithms are a particular kind of institution, and their specificities invite reflection about central concepts such as agency, rationality, reflexivity, responsibility, and accountability pervading institutional theories. Algorithms can push the boundaries of institutional organization usually discussed by sociological institutionalism and radically change the contexts of discursive production focused on by discursive institutionalists. Algorithms push path dependence to a new level and claim that there is a need to rethink models of rational agency. Moreover, they may have drastic consequences in institutional change, working not only as exogenous technological shocks, but also as endogenous driving forces in the dynamics of institutional transformation. We did not deepen these points throughout the book, but we highlight them as an agenda for future studies that can evolve once the first step has been taken: acknowledging that algorithms are institutions.

This theoretical disruption indicates a wide field of applications that look at how these institutions solve problems, shape decisions, carry out organizational tasks, allocate resources, affect social relationships, assign meanings to collective action, and define what is prohibited, allowed, or facilitated in the interactions between humans and machines. Algorithmic Institutionalism provides a rich theoretical framework to make sense of a changing world in uncertain times.

References

Abdala, M. B., Ortega, A., and Pomares, J. (2020). 'Managing the Transition to a Multi-Stakeholder Artificial Intelligence Governance'. Real Institute Elcano. Policy brief. https://www.realinstitutoelcano.org/en/analyses/managing-the-transition-to-a-multi-stakeholder-artificial-intelligence-governance/.

Abers, R. (2021). *Ativismo institucional: Criatividade e luta na burocracia brasileira*. Brasília: Editora UnB.

Agudo, U., and Matute, H. (2021). 'The Influence of Algorithms on Political and Dating Decisions', *PLoS ONE*, 16/4: e0249454. https://doi.org/10.1371/journal.pone.0249454.

Aguirre, K., Badran, E., and Muggah, R. (2019). 'Future Crime: Assessing Twenty-First Century Crime Prediction', *Igarapé Institute Strategic Note*, 33: 4. https://igarape.org.br/wp-content/uploads/2019/07/2019-07-03-NE_33_Future_Crime-V2.pdf.

Ahmad, K., Doja, M. N., Udzir, N. I., and Singh, M. P. (2019). *Emerging Security Algorithms and Techniques*. Boca Raton: Taylor & Francis.

Airoldi, M. (2022). *Machine habitus: Toward a Sociology of Algorithms*. Cambridge: Polity Press.

Akın Ünver, H. (2018). 'Artificial Intelligence, Authoritarianism and the Future of Political Systems'. Centre for Economics and Foreign Policy Studies. https://www.jstor.org/stable/resrep26084.

Al Jazeera (2022). 'Facial Recognition Taken to Court in India's Surveillance Hotspot', 20 January. https://www.aljazeera.com/news/2022/1/20/india-surveillance-hotspot-telangana-facial-recognition-court-lawsuit-privacy.

Allen, D. (2019). 'Farmers are Using AI to Spot Pests and Catch Diseases—and Many Believe it's the Future of Agriculture', *Business Insider*, 8 November. https://www.businessinsider.com/farmers-artificial-intelligence-in-agriculture-catch-disease-pests.

Allen, D. W. (2005). 'Marriage as an Institution: A New Institutional Economic Approach'. Unpublished manuscript, Department of Economics, Simon Fraser University. http://www.sfu.ca/~allen/Allen%20marriage%20institution.pdf.

Almeida, V., Filgueiras, F., Mendonça, R.F. (2022). Algorithms and Institutions: How Social Sciences can Contribute to Governance of Algorithms. *IEEE Internet Computer*, 26 (2), 42–46. https://doi.org/10.1109/MIC.2022.3147923.

Alnemr, N. (2021). '*Defending Deliberative Democracy in an Algorithmic Society: Building Deliberative Capacity through Contesting Algorithmic Harms*'. Unpublished manuscript.

Alves, M. A. S., and Andrade, O. M. (2022). 'Autonomia individual em risco? Governamentalidade algorítmica e a constituição do sujeito', *Cadernos da Metrópole*, 24/55: 1007–23. https://doi.org/10.1590/2236-9996.2022-5507.

Alves, G., Rodrigues, R. M., Santos, I. de A., and Nascimento, T. (2022). 'Brazilian Favelas Need Racial Justice, not Facial Recognition', *Southern Voice*, 25 July. https://southernvoice.org/brazilian-favelas-need-racial-justice-not-facial-recognition/.

Amnesty International (2022). 'Myanmar: The Social Atrocity: Meta and the Right to Remedy for the Rohingya', *Amnesty International*, 29 September 2022. Index Number: ASA 16/5933/2022.

Amoore, L. (2006). 'Biometric Borders: Governing Mobilities in the War on Terror', *Political Geography*, 25/3: 336–51. https://doi.org/10.1016/j.polgeo.2006.02.001.

Amoore, L. (2008). 'Governing by Identity', in C. Bennett and D. Lyon (eds), *Playing the Identity Card: Surveillance, Security, and Identification in Global Perspective*. London: Routledge, 21–36.

Amoore, L. (2014). 'Security and the Incalculable', *Security Dialogue*, 45/5: 423–39. https://doi.org/10.1177/0967010614539719.

Amoore, L. (2020). *Cloud Ethics: Algorithms and the Attributes of Ourselves and Others*. Durham, NC: Duke University Press.

Amoore, L. (2021). 'The Deep Border', *Political Geography*, 96: 1–9. https://doi.org/10.1016/j.polgeo.2021.102547.

Ananny, M. (2016). 'Toward an Ethics of Algorithms: Convening, Observation, Probability, and Timeliness', *Science, Technology & Human Values*, 41/1: 93–117. https://doi.org/10.1177%2F0162243915606523.

Aneesh, A. (2006). *Virtual Migration: The Programming of Globalization*. Durham, NC: Duke University Press.

Angwin, J., Larson, J., Mattu, S., and Kirchner, L. (2016). 'Machine Bias: There's Software Used across the Country to Predict Future Criminals: And it's Biased against Blacks', *ProPublica*, 23 May. www.propublica.org/article/machine-bias-risk-assessments-in-criminal-sentencing.

Ansell, C. (2013). 'Ecological Explanation', in G. Berk, D. C. Galvan, and V. Hattam (eds), *Political Creativity: Reconfiguring Institutional Order and Change*. Philadelphia: University of Pennsylvania Press, 55–77.

Aquino, J. P. D. (2022). 'Segurança Pública no Ceará: Finalmente, as estatísticas de mortes violentas sofrem efetivas reduções', in Fórum Brasileiro de Segurança Pública, *Anuário Brasileiro de Segurança Pública: 2018–2021*. São Paulo: FBSP/Konrad Adenauer Stiftung, 71–79.

Aradau, C., and Blanke, T. (2022). *Algorithmic Reason: The New Government of Self and Other*. Oxford: Oxford University Press.

Aral, S., and Eckles, D. (2019). 'Protecting Elections from Social Media Manipulation', *Science*, 365/6456: 858–61. https://doi.org/10.1126/science.aaw8243.

Arefinia, A., Bozorg-Haddad, O., Ahmadaali, K., Zolghadr-Asli, B., and Loàiciga, H. A. (2022). 'Cropping Patterns Based on Virtual Water Content Considering Water and Food Security under Climate Change Conditions', *Natural Hazards*, 114: 1709–21. https://doi.org/10.1007/s11069-022-05443-3.

Arkin, R. C., Kaelbling, L., Russell, S., Sadigh, D., Scharre, P., Selman, B., and Walsh, T. (2019). 'A Path towards Reasonable Autonomous Weapons Regulation', *IEEE Spectrum*. https://spectrum.ieee.org/a-path-towards-reasonable-autonomous-weapons-regulation.

Arrow, K. (1950). 'A Difficulty in the Concept of Social Welfare', *Journal of Political Economy*, 58/4: 328–346. https://doi.org/10.1086/256963.

Arthur, W. B. (1989). 'Competing Technologies, Increasing Returns, and Lock-in by Historical Events', *Economic Journal*, 99/394: 116–131. https://doi.org/10.2307/2234208.

Asaro, P. (2019). 'Algorithms of Violence: Critical Social Perspectives on Autonomous Weapons', *Social Research: An International Quarterly*, 86/2: 537–55. https://doi.org/10.1353/sor.2019.0026.

Austin, J. L. (2001). 'The Concept of Security', *Review of International Studies*, 23: 5–26. https://doi.org/10.1017/S0260210597000053.

Avritzer, L. (2019). *O pêndulo da democracia no Brasil*. São Paulo: Todavia.

Axelrod, R. (1984). *The Evolution of Cooperation*. New York: Basic Books.

Bachrach, P., Baratz, M.S. (1962). Two Faces of Power. *American Political Science Review*, 56 (4), 947–952. https://doi.org/10.2307/1952796

References

Bächtiger, A., Dryzek, J. S., Mansbridge, J., and Warren, M. (2018). *The Oxford Handbook of Deliberative Democracy*. Oxford: Oxford University Press.

Baeza-Yates, R., and Fayyad, U. M. (2021). 'The Attention Economy and the Impact of Artificial Intelligence', in H. Werthner, E. Prem, E. A. Lee, and C, Ghezzi (eds), *Perspectives on Digital Humanism*. Berlin: Springer, 123–34. https://doi.org/10.1007/978-3-030-86144-5_18.

Baldwin, D.A. (1997). The Concept of Security. *Review of International Studies*, 23 (1), 5–26.

Bateson, G. (2000). 'A Theory of Play and Fantasy', in G. Bateson, *Steps to an Ecology of Mind*. Chicago: University of Chicago Press, 177–193.

Beer, D. (2017). 'The Social Power of Algorithms', *Information, Communication & Society*, 20/1: 1–13. https://doi.org/10.1080/1369118X.2016.1216147.

Béland, D. (2019). *How Ideas and Institutions Shape the Politics and Public Policy*. Cambridge: Cambridge University Press.

Benjamin, R. (2019). *Race after Technology*. New York: Polity Press.

Benn, C., and Lazar, S. (2022). 'What's Wrong with Automated Influence', *Canadian Journal of Philosophy*, 52/1: 125–48. https://doi.org/10.1017/can.2021.23.

Berger, P. L., and Luckmann, T. (1967). *The Social Construction of Reality: A Treatise on the Sociology of Knowledge*. Garden City, NY: Doubleday Anchor.

Bergman, R., and Mazzetti, M. (2022). 'The Battle for the World's Most Powerful Cyberweapon', *New York Times*, 28 January. https://www.nytimes.com/2022/01/28/magazine/nso-group-israel-spyware.html.

Berlin, I. (1958). *Two Concepts of Liberty: An Inaugural Lecture Delivered before the University of Oxford on 31 October 1958*. Oxford: Clarendon Press.

Binns, R. (2018). 'Algorithmic Accountability and Public Reason', *Philosophy & Technology*, 31/4: 543–56. https://doi.org/10.1007/s13347-017-0263-5.

Bischoff, P. (2022). *Facial Recognition Technology (FRT): 100 Countries Analyzed*. Comparitech, January, 24, 2022. Retrieved from: https://www.comparitech.com/blog/vpn-privacy/facial-recognition-statistics/

Black, I. (2013). 'NSA Spying Scandal: What we Have Learned', *Guardian*, 10 June. https://www.theguardian.com/world/2013/jun/10/nsa-spying-scandal-what-we-have-learned.

Bohman, J. (1996). *Public Deliberation: Pluralism, Complexity and Democracy*. Cambridge, MA: MIT Press.

Bommasani, R., et al. (2021). 'On the Opportunities and Risks of Foundation Models', *arXiv*, preprint arXiv:2108.07258.

Bovens, Mark (2007). 'Analysing and Assessing Accountability: A Conceptual Framework', *European Law Journal*, 13: 447–68.

Brayne, S. (2017). 'Big Data Surveillance: The Case of Policing', *American Sociological Review*, 82/5: 977–1008. https://doi.org/10.1177%2F0003122417725865.

Brayne, S. (2021). *Predict and Surveil: Data, Discretion, and the Future of Policing*. New York: Oxford University Press.

Brennan, J. (2016). *Against Democracy*. Princeton: Princeton University Press.

Browne, S. (2015). *Dark Matters*. Durham, NC: Duke University Press.

Bruns, A. (2019). *Are Filter Bubbles Real? Digital Futures*. Cambridge: Polity Press.

Bryson, J. (2018). 'AI & Global Governance: No One Should Trust AI'. https://cpr.unu.edu/publications/articles/ai-global-governance-no-one-should-trust-ai.html.

Buchanan, J., and Tullock, G. (1962). *The Calculus of Consent. Logical Foundations of Constitutional Democracy*. Ann Arbor: University of Michigan Press.

Bucher T. (2012). 'Want to Be on the Top? Algorithmic Power and the Threat of Invisibility on Facebook', *New Media & Society*, 14/7: 1164–80.

Bucher, T. (2018). *If... Then: Algorithmic Power and Politics*. Oxford: Oxford University Press.

Buhmann, A., and Fieseler, C. (2021). 'Towards a Deliberative Framework for Responsible Innovation in Artificial Intelligence', *Technology in Society*, 64: 1–7.

Burrell, J., and Fourcade, M. (2021). 'The Society of Algorithms', *Annual Review of Sociology*, 47/1: 213–37.

Byrnes, M. (2014). 'Nightfall: Machine Autonomy in Air-to-Air Combat', *Air and Space Power Journal*, 28/3: 48–75.

Calo, R., and Rosenblat, A. (2017). 'The Taking Economy: Uber, Information, and Power', *Columbia Law Review*, 117 (6). Retrieved from: https://columbialawreview.org/content/the-taking-economy-uber-information-and-power/

Caplan, R., and boyd, D. (2018). 'Isomorphism through Algorithms: Institutional Dependencies in the Case of Facebook', *Big Data & Society*, 5/1: 1–12. https://doi.org/10.1177%2F2053951718757253.

Capoccia, G. (2015). 'Critical Junctures and Institutional Change', in J. Mahoney and K. Thelen (eds), *Advances in Comparative Historical Analysis*. Cambridge: Cambridge University Press, 147–79.

Caramani, D. (2017). 'Will vs Reason: The Populist and Technocratic Forms of Political Representation and their Critique to Party Government', *American Political Science Review*, 111/1: 54–67. https://doi.org/10.1017/S0003055416000538.

Cardoso, B. B. (2020). 'The Implementation on Emergency Aid as an Exceptional Measure of Social Protection', *Brazilian Journal of Public Administration*, 54/4: 1052–1063. https://doi.org/10.1590/0034-761220200267x.

Centeno, M. A. (1993). 'The New Leviathan: The Dynamics and Limits of Technocracy', *Theory and Society*, 22/3: 307–35. https://doi.org/10.1007/BF00993531.

Chambers, S. (2003). 'Deliberative Democratic Theory', *Annual Review of Political Science*, 6/1: 307–26.

Chambers, S. (2004), 'Behind Closed Doors: Publicity, Secrecy, and the Quality of Deliberation'. *Journal of Political Philosophy*, 12: 389–410. https://doi.org/10.1111/j.1467-9760.2004.00206.x

Chambers, S. (2021). 'Truth, Deliberative Democracy, and the Virtues of Accuracy: Is Fake News Destroying the Public Sphere?', *Political Studies*, 69/1: 147–63. https://doi.org/10.1177/0032321719890811.

Chatterjee, C., and Sokol, D. D. (2021). 'Data Security, Data Breaches, and Compliance', in B. Rooij and D. D. Sokol.(eds), *The Cambridge Handbook of Compliance*. Cambridge: Cambridge University Press, 936–48. https://doi.org/10.1017/9781108759458.064.

Chen, C., Surette, R., and Shah, M. (2021). 'Automated Monitoring for Security Camera Networks: Promise from Computer Vision Labs', *Security Journal*, 34: 389–409. https://doi.org/10.1057/s41284-020-00230-w.

Chen, L., Mislove, A., and Wilson, C. (2015). 'Peeking beneath the Hood of Uber', *Proceedings of the 2015 Internet Measurement Conference*. New York: Association for Computing Machinery, 495–508. https://doi.org/10.1145/2815675.2815681.

Cinelli, M., Morales, G., Galeazzi, A., Quattrociocchi, W., and Starnini, M. (2021). 'The Echo Chamber Effect on Social Media', *Proceedings of the National Academy of Sciences*, 118/9: e2023301118. https://doi.org/10.1073/pnas.2023301118.

Cobbe, J., and Singh, J. (2019). 'Regulating Recommending: Motivations, Considerations, and Principles', *European Journal of Law and Technology*, 10/3: 1–37.

Competition & Market Authority (2021). *Algorithms: How they Can Reduce Competition and Harm Consumers*. https://www.gov.uk/government/publications/algorithms-how-they-can-reduce-competition-and-harm-consumers/algorithms-how-they-can-reduce-competition-and-harm-consumers.

Connolly, R. (2020). 'Why Computing Belongs within the Social Sciences', *Communications of the ACM*, 63/8: 54–9. https://doi.org/10.1145/3383444.
Cooke, M. (2000). 'Five Arguments for Deliberative Democracy', *Political Studies*, 48/5: 947–69. https://doi.org/10.1111/1467-9248.00289.
Cotter, K. (2019). 'Playing the Visibility Game: How Digital Influencers and Algorithms Negotiate Influence on Instagram', *New Media & Society*, 21/4: 895–913. https://doi.org/10.1177/1461444818815684.
Couldry, N., and Mejias, U. (2019). 'Data Colonialism: Rethinking Big Data's Relation to the Contemporary Subject', *Television & New Media*, 20/4: 336–49. https://doi.org/10.1177/1527476418796632.
Couldry, N., and Mejias, U. A. (2021). 'The Decolonial Turn in Data and Technology Research: What Is at Stake and where Is it Heading?', *Information, Communication & Society*. https://doi.org/10.1080/1369118X.2021.1986102.
Crawford, K. (2016). 'Can an Algorithm be Agonistic? Ten Scenes from Life in Calculated Publics', *Science, Technology & Human Values*, 41/1: 77–92. https://doi.org/10.1177/0162243915589635.
Crawford, K. (2021). *The Atlas of AI: Power, Politics, and the Planetary Costs of Artificial Intelligence.* New Haven: Yale University Press.
Crouch, C. (2004). *Post-Democracy.* Cambridge: Polity Press.
Culpepper, P. D., and Thelen, K. (2021). 'Are we All Amazon Primed? Consumers and the Politics of Platform Power', *Comparative Political Studies*, 53/2: 288–318. https://doi.org/10.1177%2F0010414019852687.
Curato, N., Hammond, M., and Min, J. (2019). *Power in Deliberative Democracy.* New York: Palgrave Macmillan.
Dahl, R. A. (1971). *Polyarchy: Participation and Opposition.* New Haven: Yale University Press.
Dahl, R. A. (2015). *On Democracy.* New Haven: Yale University Press.
Dai, X. (2020). 'Enforcing Law and Norms for Good Citizens: One View of China's Social Credit System Project', *Development*, 63: 38–43. https://doi.org/10.1057/s41301-020-00244-2.
Danaher, J. (2016). 'The Threat of Algocracy: Reality, Resistance and Accommodation', *Philosophy & Technology*, 29: 245–68. https://doi.org/10.1007/s13347-015-0211-1.
Dave, P. (2022). 'US Cities are Backing off Banning Facial Recognition as Crime Rises', *Reuters*, 12 May. https://www.reuters.com/world/us/us-cities-are-backing-off-banning-facial-recognition-crime-rises-2022-05-12/#:~:text=From%202019%20through%202021%2C%20about,protests%20gave%20the%20arguments%20momentum.
Davis, A. R. (2015). 'A Conceptual Framework for Understanding Path Dependency and Technology Option Evaluation when Valuing IT Opportunities', *International Journal of Business and Social Science*, 6/1: 34–42.
De Vries, P., and Schinkel, W. (2019). 'Algorithmic Anxiety: Masks and Camouflage in Artistic Imaginaries of Facial Recognition Algorithms', *Big Data & Society*, 6/1: 1–12. https://doi.org/10.1177%2F2053951719851532.
Dekoninck, H., and Schmuck, D. (2022). 'The Mobilizing Power of Influencers for Pro-Environmental Behavior Intentions and Political Participation', *Environmental Communication*, 16/4: 458–72. https://doi.org/10.1080/17524032.2022.2027801.
Deloitte (2016). *D01—Study on the Public Sector Data Strategies, Policies and Governance.* https://joinup.ec.europa.eu/sites/default/files/custom-page/attachment/2020-06/DIGIT%20-%20D01%20-%20Study%20on%20public%20sector%20data%20strategies%2C%20policies%20and%20governance%20Task%203%20Workshop%20Version_1.pdf.
Dewey, J. (1954). *The Public and its Problems.* Chicago: The Swallon.

Diakopoulos, N. (2020) 'Transparency', in M. Dubber, F. Pasquale, and S. Das (eds.), *Oxford Handbook of Ethics and AI*. Oxford: Oxford University Press, 197–213.
DiMaggio, P., and Powell, W. (1983). 'The Iron Cage Revisited: Institutional Isomorphism and Collective Rationality in Organizational Fields', *American Sociological Review*, 48/2: 147–60. https://doi.org/10.2307/2095101.
Donahoe, E., Metzger, M.M. (2019). Artificial intelligence and human rights. *Journal of Democracy*, 30 (2), 115–126.
Dressel, J., and Farid, H. (2018). 'The Accuracy, Fairness, and Limits of Predicting Recidivism', *Science Advances*, 4: aao5580. https://www.science.org/doi/10.1126/sciadv.aao5580
Drott, E., 'Fake Streams, Listening Bots, and Click Farms: Counterfeiting Attention in the Streaming Music Economy', American Music 1 July 2020; 38 (2): 153–175. https://doi.org/10.5406/americanmusic.38.2.0153
Dryzek, J. S. (2000). *Deliberative Democracy and Beyond: Liberals, Critics, Contestations*. New York: Oxford University Press.
Dryzek, J. S., Bächtiger, A., Chambers, S., Cohen, J., Druckman, J. N., Felicetti, A., Fishkin, J. S., Farrell, D. M., Fung, A., Gutmann, G., Landemore, H., Mansbridge, J., Marien, S., Neblo, M. A., Niemeyer, S., Setälä, M., Slothuus, R., Suiter, J., Thompson, D., and Warren, M. E. (2019). 'The Crisis of Democracy and the Science of Deliberation', *Science*, 363/6432: 1144–6. https://doi.org/10.1126/science.aaw2694.
Dryzek, J. S., and Niemeyer, S. (2010). *Foundations and Frontiers of Deliberative Governance*. Oxford: Oxford University Press.
Dunleavy, P., and Margetts, H. (2013). 'The Second Wave of Digital-Era Governance: A Quasi-Paradigm for Government on the Web', *Philosophical Transactions of the Real Society*, 371/1987: 1–17. https://doi.org/10.1098/rsta.2012.0382.
Dunleavy, P., Margetts, H., Bastow, S., and Tinkler, J. (2006). 'New Public Management is Dead—Long Live Digital-Era Governance', *Journal of Public Administration Research and Theory*, 16/3: 467–94. https://doi.org/10.1093/jopart/mui057.
Easton, D. (1965). *A System Analysis of Political Life*. New York: John Wiley.
EBC (2022). '80% das prisões errôneas por reconhecimento facial no RJ são de negros', Radio Agência Nacional, 12 January. https://agenciabrasil.ebc.com.br/radioagencia-nacional/justica/audio/2022-01/80-das-prisoes-erroneas-por-reconhecimento-facial-no-rj-sao-de-negros.
Ekbia, H. (2015). 'Heteronomous Humans and Autonomous Agents: Toward Artificial Relational Intelligence', in J. Romportl, E. Zackova, and J. Kelemen (eds), *Beyond Artificial Intelligence: Topics in Intelligent Engineering and Informatics*. Cham: Springer, 63–77. https://doi.org/10.1007/978-3-319-09668-1_5.
Ekstrand, M. D., Riedl, J. T., and Konstan, J. A. (2011). 'Collaborative Filtering Recommender Systems', *Foundations and Trends in Human–Computer Interaction*, 4/2: 81–173.
Elster, J. (1998). 'Deliberation and Constitution Making', in J. Elster (ed.), *Deliberative Democracy*. Cambridge: Cambridge University Press, 97–122:
Elster, J. (2000). 'Arguing and Bargaining in Two Constituent Assemblies', *University of Pennsylvania Journal of Constitutional Law*, 2: 345–419.
Entman, R. (1993). 'Framing toward Clarification of a Fractured Paradigm', *Journal of Communication*, 10: 155–73.
Epstein, R., and Robertson R. E. (2015). 'The Search Engine Manipulation Effect (SEME) and its Possible Impact on the Outcomes of Elections', *Proceedings of the National Academy of Sciences USA*, 112: E4512–E4521.
Ercan, S., Asenbaum, H., Curato, N., and Mendonca, R. (2022). *Research Methods in Deliberative Democracy*. Oxford: Oxford University Press.

Ercan, S., and Gagnon, J. P. (2014). 'The Crisis of Democracy: Which Crisis? Which Democracy?', *Democratic Theory*, 1/2: 1–10.

Etzioni, A., and Etzioni, O. (2017). 'Pros and Cons of Autonomous Weapons Systems', in A. Etzioni (ed.), *Happiness is the WRONG METRICS*. Berlin: Springer Open, 253–63.

Eubanks, V. (2018). *Automating Inequality: How High-Tech Tools Profile, Police, and Punish the Poor*. New York: St Martin's Press.

Ezrachi, A., and Stucke M. (2016). *Virtual Competition: The Promise and Perils of the Algorithm-Driven Economy*. Cambridge, MA: Harvard University Press.

Fairclough, N. (2001). *Discurso e mudança social*. Brasília: Ed. Unb.

Fairclough, N. (2003). *Analysing Discourse: Textual Analysis for Social Research*. New York: Routledge.

Filgueiras, F. (2016). 'Transparency and Accountability: Principles and Rules for the Construction of Publicity', *Journal of Public Affairs*, 16/2: 192–202. https://doi.org/10.1002/pa.1575.

Filgueiras, F., and Almeida, V. (2021). *Governance for the Digital World: Neither More State nor More Market*. London: Palgrave Macmillan.

Finkel, E. F., Bail, C. A., Cikara, M., Ditto, P. H., Iyengar, S., Klar, S., Mason, L., McGrath, M. C., Nyhan, B., Rand, D. G., Skitka, L. J., Tucker, J. A., Van Bavel, J. J, Wang, C. S., and Druckman, J. N. (2020). 'Political Sectarianism in America', *Science*, 370: 533–6.

Firmino, R. J., Kanashiro, M., Bruno, F., Evangelista, R., and Nascimento, L. C. (2013). 'Fear, Security, and the Spread of CCTV in Brazilian Cities: Legislation, Debate, and the Market', *Journal of Urban Technology*, 20/3: 65–84. https://doi.org/10.1080/10630732.2013.809221.

Fischer, F. (1990). *Technocracy and the Politics of Expertise*. Newbury Park, CA: Sage.

Fischer, F. (2015). 'In Pursuit of Usable Knowledge: Critical Policy Analysis and the Argumentative Turn', in F. Fischer, D. Torgerson, A. Durnova, and M. Orsini (eds), *Handbook of Critical Policy Studies*. Cheltenham: Edward Elgar, 47–66.

Fischer, F. (2017). *Climate Crisis and the Democratic Prospect: Participatory Governance in Sustainable Communities*. Oxford: Oxford University Press.

Fisher, E. (2022). 'Do Algorithms Have a Right to the City? Waze and Algorithmic Spatiality', *Cultural Studies*, 36/1: 74–95. https://doi.org/10.1080/09502386.2020.1755711.

Fisher, M., and Taub, A. (2019). 'How YouTube Radicalized Brazil', *New York Times*, 11 August. https://www.nytimes.com/2019/08/11/world/americas/youtube-brazil.html.

Foderaro, L. (2017). 'Navigation Apps Are Turning Quiet Neighborhoods into Traffic Nightmares', *New York Times*, 24 December. https://www.nytimes.com/2017/12/24/nyregion/traffic-apps-gps-neighborhoods.html.

Ford, B. (2021). 'Technologizing Democracy or Democratizing Technology? A Layered-Architecture Perspective on Potentials and Challenges', in L. Bernholz, H. Landemore, and R. Reich (eds), *Digital Technology and Democratic Theory*. Chicago: University of Chicago Press, 274–310.

Forst, R. (2019). 'Two Bad Halves Don't Make a Whole: On the Crisis of Democracy', *Constellations*, 26/3: 378–83.

Foucault, M. (1979). 'Truth and Power: An Interview with Michel Foucault', *Critique of Anthropology*, 4/13–14: 131–7. https://doi.org/10.1177/0308275X7900401311.

Foucault, M. (1980) *Power/knowledge*, New York: Pantheon Books.

Foucault, M. (1995). *Discipline and Punish: The Birth of the Prison*. New York: Vintage Books.

Foucault, M. (2008). *The Birth of Biopolitics: Lectures at the College de France, 1978–1979*. Basingstoke: Palgrave Macmillan.

Frischmann, B., and Selinger, E. (2018). *Re-Engineering Humanity*. Cambridge: Cambridge University Press.

Fukuyama, F. (2015). *Political Order and Political Decay: From the Industrial Revolution to the Globalization of Democracy*. New York: Farrar Straus Giroux.

Gabbatt, A. (2014). 'Protesters Rally for "the Day we Fight Back" against Mass Surveillance', US, *Guardian*, 11 February. https://www.theguardian.com/world/2014/feb/11/day-fight-back-protest-nsa-mass-surveillance.

Gagnon, J.-P. (2018). '2,234 Descriptions of Democracy: An Update to Democracy's Ontological Pluralism', *Democratic Theory*, 5/2: 92–113.

Gandra, A. (2021). 'Pesquisa do IBGE mostra enfraquecimento do mercado de trabalho em 2020', 3 December. Rio de Janeiro, Brasil: Agência Brasil. https://agenciabrasil.ebc.com.br/economia/noticia/2021-12/pesquisa-do-ibge-mostra-enfraquecimento-do-mercado-de-trabalho-em-2020.

Garcelon, N., Burgun, A., Salomon, R., and Neuraz, A. (2020). 'Electronic Health Records for the Diagnosis of Rare Diseases', *Kidney International*, 97/4: 676–86. https://doi.org/10.1016/j.kint.2019.11.037.

Gaw, F. (2021). 'Algorithmic Logics and the Construction of Cultural Taste of the Netflix Recommender System', *Media, Culture & Society*, 44/4: 706–25. https://doi.org/10.1177/01634437211053767.

Gerards, J. (2019). 'The Fundamental Rights Challenges of Algorithms', *Netherlands Quarterly of Human Rights*, 37/3: 205–9. https://doi.org/10.1177/0924051919861773.

Gidaris, C. (2020). 'The Carceral Airport', *Public*, 30/60: 76–91. https://doi.org/10.1386/public_00007_7.

Giest, S. (2017). 'Big Data for Policymaking: Fad or Fast Track?' *Policy Sciences*, 50/3: 367–82. https://doi.org/10.1007/s11077-017-9293-1.

Gilbert, K. (2022). 'Cupid's Code: Tweaking an Algorithm Can Alter the Course of Finding Love Online', *Stanford GSB*, 9 February. https://www.gsb.stanford.edu/insights/cupids-code-tweaking-algorithm-can-alter-course-finding-love-online.

Gillespie, T. (2014). 'The Relevance of Algorithms', in T. Gillespie, P. Boczkowski, and K. Foot (eds), *Media Technologies*. Cambridge, MA: MIT Press, 167–193.

Goffman, E. (1986). *Frame Analysis: An Essay on the Organization of Experience*. Boston: Northeastern University Press.

Gomez-Uribe, C. A., and Hunt, N. (2015). 'The Netflix Recommender System: Algorithms, Business Value, and Innovation', *ACM Transactions on Management Information Systems (TMIS)*, 6/4: 1–19. https://doi.org/10.1145/2843948.

Gorwa, R., Binns, R., and Katzenbach, C. (2020). 'Algorithmic Content Moderation: Technical and Political Challenges in Automation of Platform Governance', *Big Data & Society*, 7/1: 1–15. https://doi.org/10.1177/2053951719897945.

Graaf, S. (2018). 'In Waze we Trust: Algorithmic Governance of the Public Sphere', *Media and Communication*, 6/4: 153–62.

Green, B. J. (2021). 'The Contestation of Tech Ethics: A Sociotechnical Approach to Ethics and Technology in Action', *Journal of Social Computing*, 2/3: 209–25. https://scholar.harvard.edu/files/bgreen/files/21-jsc-intro.pdf.

Greer, J. M. (2014). *Decline and Fall: The End of Empire and the Future of Democracy in 21st Century America*. Gabriola Island: New Society Publisher.

Grimmelikhuijsen, S., and Meijer, A. (2022). 'Legitimacy of Algorithmic Decision-Making: Six Threats and the Need for a Calibrated Institutional Response', *Perspectives on Public Management and Governance*, 5/3: 232–42. https://doi.org/10.1093/ppmgov/gvac008.

Gundabathula, V. T., and Vaidhehi, V. (2018). 'An Efficient Modelling of Terrorist Groups in India using Machine Learning Algorithms', *Indian Journal of Science and Technology*, 11/15: 1–10.

References

Gunningham, N., and Sinclair, D. (2019). *Designing Smart Regulation*. Paris: OECD. https://www.oecd.org/env/outreach/33947759.pdf.

Habermas, J. (1996). *Between Facts and Norms: Contributions to a Discourse Theory of Law and Democracy*. Cambridge, MA: MIT Press.

Habermas, J. (2006). 'Political Communication in Media Society: Does Democracy Still Enjoy an Epistemic Dimension? The Impact of Normative Theory on Empirical Research', *Communication Theory*, 16/4: 411–26.

Hacker, J. S, Pierson, P., and Thelen, K. (2015). 'Drift and Conversion: Hidden Faces of Institutional Change', in J. Mahoney and K. Thelen (eds), *Advances in Comparative Historical Analysis*. Cambridge: Cambridge University Press, 180–208.

Haggerty, K. D., and Ericson, R. V. (2000). 'The Surveillant Assemblage', *British Journal of Sociology*, 51/4: 605–22. https://doi.org/10.1080/00071310020015280.

Hall, P. A. (1992). 'The Movement from Keynesianism to Monetarism: Institutional Analysis and British Economic Policy in the 1970s', in S. Steinmo, K. Thelen, and F. Longstreth (eds), *Structuring Politics*. Cambridge: Cambridge University Press, 90–113.

Hall, P. A., and Taylor, R. C. R. (1996). 'Political Science and the Three New Institutionalisms', *Political Studies*, 44/5: 952–973. https://doi.org/10.1111%2Fj.1467-9248.1996.tb00343.x.

Harcourt, B. E. (2015). *Exposed: Desire and Disobedience in the Digital Age*. Cambridge, MA: Harvard University Press.

Hay, C. (2008). 'Constructivist Institutionalism', in R. A. W. Rhodes, S. Binder, and B. Rockman (eds), *The Oxford Handbook of Political Institutions*. Oxford: Oxford University Press, 56–74.

Hay, C. (2016). 'Good in a Crisis: The Ontological Institutionalism of Social Constructivism', *New Political Economy*, 21/6: 520–35. https://doi.org/10.1080/13563467.2016.1158800.

Helberger, N. (2019). 'On the Democratic Role of News Recommenders', *Digital Journalism*, 7/8: 993–1012. https://doi.org/10.1080/21670811.2019.1623700.

Henderson, P., Chugg, B., Anderson, B., and Ho, D. E. (2021). 'Beyond Ads: Sequential Decision-Making Algorithms in Public Policy', 13 December. https://arxiv.org/abs/2112.06833.

Hill, K. (2020). 'Wrongfully Accused by an Algorithm', *New York Times*, 24 June. https://www.nytimes.com/2020/06/24/technology/facial-recognition-arrest.html.

Hobbes, T. (1996). *Leviathan*, ed. R. Tuck. Cambridge: Cambridge University Press.

Holst, C. (2012). 'What is epistocracy?', in S. A. Øyen, T. Lund-Olsen, and N. S. Vaage (eds), *Sacred Science?* Wageningen: Wageningen Academic Publishers.

Hong, Y. (2017). *Networking China: The Digital Transformation of the Chinese Economy*. Urbana: University of Illinois Press.

Hood, C., and Margetts, H. (2007). *The Tools of Government in the Digital Age*. London: Palgrave.

Hosseinmardi, H., Ghasemian, A., Clauset, A., Mobius, M., Rothschild, D. M., and Watts, D. J. (2021). 'Examining the Consumption of Radical Content on YouTube', *Proceedings of the National Academy of Sciences*, 118/32. https://doi.org/10.1073/pnas.2101967118.

Human Security Unit (2010). *Training Manual: Human Security Regional Training*. New York: United Nations.

Huszár, F., Ktena, S., O'Brien, C., Belli, L., Schlaikjer, A., and Hardt, M. (2022). 'Algorithmic Amplification of Politics on Twitter', *Proceedings of the National Academy of Sciences*, 119/1: e2025334119. https://doi.org/10.1073/pnas.2025334119.

Illouz, E. (2011). *O amor nos tempos do capitalismo*. Rio de Janeiro: Zahar.

Introna, L. D., and Nissenbaum, H. (2014). 'Facial Recognition Technology: A Survey of Policy and Implementation Issues'. Center for Catastrophe Preparedness and Response, New York University. https://ssrn.com/abstract=1437730.

Jakesch, M., Garimella, K., Eckles, D., and Naaman, M. (2021). 'Trend Alert: A Cross-Platform Organization Manipulated Twitter Trends in the Indian General Election', *Proceedings of the ACM on Human–Computer Interaction*, 5 (CSCW2). https://doi.org/10.1145/3479523.

Javorsky, E., Tegmark, M., and Helfand I. (2019). 'Lethal Autonomous Weapons', *BMJ*, 364: l1171. https://doi.org/10.1136/bmj.l1171.

Jepperson, R. (1991). 'Institutions, Institutional Effects, and Institutionalism', in W. Powell and P. DiMaggio (eds), *The New Institutionalism in Organizational Analysis*. Chicago: University of Chicago Press, 143–63.

Jonas, J., and Harper, J. (2006). 'Effective Counterterrorism and the Limited Role of Predictive Data Mining', *Policy Analysis*, 584: 1–11.

Joyce, K., Smith-Doerr, L., Alegria, S., Bell, S., Cruz, T., Hoffman, S. G., Noble, S. U., and Shestakofsky, B. (2021). 'Toward a Sociology of Artificial Intelligence: A Call for Research on Inequalities and Structural Change', *Socius: Sociological Research for a Dynamic World*, 7: 1–11. https://doi.org/10.1177/2378023121999581.

Just, N., and Latzer, M. (2017). 'Governance by Algorithms: Reality Construction by Algorithmic Selection on the Internet', *Media, Culture & Society*, 39/2: 238–58. https://doi.org/10.1177/0163443716643157.

Kalyvas, A. (2019). 'Whose Crisis? Which Democracy? Notes on the Current Political Conjuncture', *Constellations*, 26/3: 384–90.

Kantrowitz, A. (2016). 'Racist Twitter Bot Went Awry due to "Coordinated Effort" by Users, Says Microsoft', *BuzzFeed News*, 24 March. https://www.buzzfeednews.com/article/alexkantrowitz/microsoft-blames-chatbots-racist-outburst-on-coordinated-eff.

Karuna, P., Purohit, H., Ganesan, R., and Jajodia, S. (2018). 'Generating Hard to Comprehend Fake Documents for Defensive Cyber Deception', *IEEE Intelligent Systems*, 33/5: 16–25. https://doi.org/10.1109/MIS.2018.2877277.

Kattel, R., and Mergel, I. (2019). 'Estonia's Digital Transformation: Mission Mystique and the Hiding Hand', in P. t'Hart and M. Compton (eds), *Great Policy Success*. Oxford: Oxford University Press, 143–160.

Kayser-Bril, N. (2020). 'In a Quest to Optimize Welfare Management, Denmark Built a Surveillance Behemoth', *Algorithm Watch*, 6 August. https://algorithmwatch.org/en/udbetaling-danmark/.

Keane, J. (2013). *Democracy and Media Decadence*. Cambridge: Cambridge University Press.

Keane, J. (2020). *The New Despotism*. Cambridge, MA: Harvard University Press.

Kearns, M., and Roth, A. (2020). *The Ethical Algorithm: The Science of Socially Aware Algorithm Design*. New York: Oxford University Press.

Kehl, D., Guo, P., and Kessler, S. (2017). *Algorithms in the Criminal Justice System: Assessing the Use of Risk Assessments in Sentencing*. Responsive Communities Initiative, Berkman Klein Center for Internet & Society, Harvard Law School. http://nrs.harvard.edu/urn-3:HUL.InstRepos:33746041.

Kelleher, J. (2019). *Deep Learning*. Cambridge, MA: MIT Press.

Kellogg, K., Valentine, M., and Christin, A. (2020). 'Algorithms at Work: The New Contested Terrain of Control', *Academy of Management Annals*, 14/1: 366–410. https://doi.org/10.5465/annals.2018.0174.

Kleinwächter, W., and Almeida, V. (2015). 'The Internet Governance Ecosystem and the Rainforest', *IEEE Internet Computing*, 19/2: 64–7.

Knuth, D. (1968). *The Art of Computer Programming*, i. *Fundamental Algorithms*. New York: Addison-Wesley.

König, P. D. (2019). 'Dissecting the Algorithmic Leviathan: On the Socio-Political Anatomy of Algorithmic Governance', *Philosophy & Technology*, 33/4: 467–85. https://doi.org/10.1007/s13347-019-00363-w.

König, P. D., and Wenzelburger, G. (2021). 'The Legitimacy Gap of Algorithmic Decision-Making in the Public Sector: Why it Arises and how to Address it', *Technology in Society*, 67: 1–10.

Koning, E. A. (2016). 'The Three Institutionalisms and Institutional Dynamics: Understanding Endogenous and Exogenous Change', *Journal of Public Policy*, 36/4: 639–64. http://www.jstor.org/stable/26336727.

Kramer, A. D. I., Guillory, J. E., and Hancock, J. T. (2014). 'Experimental Evidence of Massive-Scale Emotional Contagion through Social Networks', *Proceedings of National Academy of Science*, 111: 8788–90.

Krasner, S. D. (1988). 'Sovereignty: An Institutional Perspective', *Comparative Political Studies*, 21/1: 66–94. https://doi.org/10.1177/0010414088021001004.

Kreif, N., and DiazOrdaz, K. (2019). 'Machine Learning in Policy Evaluation: New Tools for Causal Inference', *Economics and Finance—Oxford Research Encyclopedia*, 1–40. https://doi.org/10.1093/acrefore/9780190625979.013.256.

Kroll, J. A., Huey, J., Barocas, S., Felten, E. W., Reidenberg, J. R., Robinson, D. G., and Yu, H. (2017). 'Accountable Algorithms', *University of Pennsylvania Law Review*, 165: 633–705. https://scholarship.law.upenn.edu/penn_law_review/vol165/iss3/3.

Kurlantzick, J. (2013). *Democracy in Retreat: The Revolt of Middle Class and the Worldwide Decline of Representative Government*. New Haven: Yale University Press.

Lancet Editorial (2016). 'Organ Donation Depends on Trust', *Lancet*, 387/10038: 2575. https://doi.org/10.1016/S0140-6736(16)30886-8.

Landemore, H. (2013). *Democratic Reason: Politics, Collective Intelligence, and the Rule of the Many*. Princeton: Princeton University Press.

Landemore, H. (2021). 'Open Democracies and Digital Technologies', in L. Bernholz, H. Landemore, and R. Reich (eds), *Digital Technology and Democratic Theory*. Chicago: University of Chicago Press, 62–89.

Lasswell, H. D., and Kaplan, A. (2017). *Power and Society: A Framework for Political Inquiry*. New York: Routledge.

Latour, B. (1992). 'Where are the Missing Masses? The Sociology of a Few Mundane Artifacts', in W. E. Bijker and J. Law (eds), *Shaping Technology/Building Society: Studies in Sociotechnical Change*. Cambridge, MA: MIT Press, 225–258.

Lee, M., Kusbit, D., Metsky, E., and Dabbish, L. (2015). 'Working with Machines: The Impact of Algorithmic and Data-Driven Management on Human Workers', *Proceedings of the 33rd Annual ACM Conference on Human Factors in Computing Systems*. New York: Association for Computing Machinery, 1603–12. https://doi.org/10.1145/2702123.2702548.

Lemos, A., and Pastor, L. (2020). 'Algorithmic Experience: Action and Data Practice on Instagram Platform', *Contemporânea*, 39/2: 133–46.

Lepri, B., Oliver, N., Letouzé, E., et al. (2018). 'Fair, Transparent, and Accountable Algorithmic Decision-Making Processes', *Philosophy & Technology*, 31: 611–27. https://doi.org/10.1007/s13347-017-0279-x.

Lessig, L. (1999). *Code and Other Laws of Cyberspace*. New York: Basic Books.

Levi, M. (1997). 'A Model, a Method and a Map: Rational Choice in Comparative and Historical Analysis', in M. I. Lichbach and A. S. Zuckerman (eds), *Comparative Politics: Rationality, Culture and Structure*. Cambridge: Cambridge University Press, 19–41.

Levi, M., and Smith, R. G. (2021). *Fraud and its Relationship to Pandemics and Economic Crises: From Spanish Flu to Covid-19*. Canberra: Australian Institute of Criminology. https://www.aic.gov.au/publications/rr/rr19.

Levitsky, S., and Ziblatt, D. (2018). *How Democracies Die*. New York: Crown Publishing.

Li, E. (2021). 'Europe's Next Steps in Regulating Facial Recognition Technology', *Columbia Journal of Transnational Law*, 7 November. https://www.jtl.columbia.edu/bulletin-blog/europes-next-steps-in-regulating-facial-recognition-technology#:~:text=On%20October%206th%2C%202021%2C%20the,of%20private%20facial%20recognition%20databases.

Lima, M. S. M., and Delen, D. (2020). 'Predicting and Explaining Corruption across Countries: A Machine Learning Approach', *Government Information Quarterly*, 37/1: 1–15.

Lindblom, C. E. (1984). *The Policy-Making Process*. Englewood Cliffs, NJ: Prentice Hall.

Liptak, A. (2017). 'Sent to Prison by a Software Program's Secret Algorithms', *New York Times*, 1 May. https://www.nytimes.com/2017/05/01/us/politics/sent-to-prison-by-a-software-programs-secret-algorithms.html.

Lukes, S. (2005). *Power: A Radical View*. London: Palgrave Macmillan.

Lyon, D. (2014). 'Surveillance, Snowden, and Big Data: Capacities, Consequences, Critique', *Big Data & Society*, 1/2: 1–13. https://doi.org/10.1177%2F2053951714541861.

McCarthy, O. J. (2019). 'AI & Global Governance: Turning the Tide on Crime with Predictive Policing'. https://cpr.unu.edu/publications/articles/ai-global-governance-turning-the-tide-on-crime-with-predictive-policing.html.

McCubbins, M. D., and Schwartz, T. (1984). 'Congressional Oversight Overlooked: Police Patrols versus Fire Alarms', *American Journal of Science*, 28: 165–79. https://doi.org/10.2307/2110792.

Maddicott, J. R. (2010). *The Origins of the English Parliament, 924–1327*. Oxford: Oxford University Press.

Mahoney, J., and Thelen, K. (2010). 'A Theory of Gradual Institutional Change', in J. Mahoney and K. Thelen (eds), *Explaining Institutional Change: Ambiguity, Agency, and Power*. Cambridge: Cambridge University Press, 1–37.

Marasciulo, M. (2022). 'How Anitta Megafans Gamed Spotify to Help Create Brazil's First Global Chart-Topper'. https://restofworld.org/2022/anitta-fans-spotify-brazil-global-chart/.

March, J. G., and Olsen, J. P. (1975). 'The Uncertainty of Past: Organizational Learning under Ambiguity', *European Journal of Political Research*, 3/2: 147–71. https://doi.org/10.1111/j.1475-6765.1975.tb00521.x.

March, J. G., and Olsen, J. P. (1984). 'The New Institutionalism: Organizational Factors in Political Life', *American Political Science Review*, 78/3: 734–49. https://doi.org/10.2307/1961840.

March, J. G., and Olsen, J. P. (1989). *Rediscovering Institutions: The Organizational Basis of Politics*. New York: Free Press.

March, J. G, and Olsen, J. P. (2006). 'Elaborating the New Institutionalism', in R. Rhodes, S. Binder, and B. Rockman (eds), *The Oxford Handbook of Political Institutions*. Oxford: Oxford University Press, 3–20.

March, J. G., and Olsen, J. P. (2009). 'The Logic of Appropriateness', in R.E. Goodin (ed.), *The Oxford Handbook of Political Science*. Oxford: Oxford University Press, 478–497.

Margetts, H. (2012). 'New Players: Government Contracting of Information Technology', in H. Margetts, *Information Technology in Government*. New York: Routledge, 140–76.

Margulies, P. S. (2016). 'Surveillance by Algorithm: The NSA, Computerized Intelligence Collection, and Human Rights', *Florida Law Review*, 68/4: 1045–1117.

Matinde, V. (2017). 'Ghanaian Blockchain Company Looks to Verify Land Ownership', *IDG Connect*, 10 February. https://www.idgconnect.com/article/3577192/ghanaian-blockchain-company-looks-to-verify-land-ownership.html.

Matthews, J., Babaeianjelodar, M., Lorenz, S., Matthews, A., Njie, M., Adams, N., Krane, D., Goldwaite, J., and Hughes, C. (2019). 'The Right to Confront your Accusers: Opening the Black Box of Forensic DNA Software', *Proceedings of the 2019 AAAI/ACM Conference on AI, Ethics, and Society*, 321–7. https://doi.org/10.1145/3306618.3314279.

Meijer, A. (2014). 'Transparency', in M. Bovens, R. E. Goodin, and, T. Schillemans (eds), *The Oxford Handbook of Public Accountability*. Oxford: Oxford University Press, 507–524.

Meijer, A., Lorenz, L., and Wessels, M. (2021). 'Algorithmization of Bureaucratic Organizations: Using Practical Lens to Study how Context Shapes Predictive Policing Systems', *Public Administration*, 81/5: 1–10. https://doi.org/10.1111/puar.13391.

Meijer, A., and Wessels, M. (2019). 'Predictive Policing: Review of Benefits and Drawbacks', *International Journal of Public Administration*, 42/12: 1031–9. https://doi.org/10.1080/01900692.2019.1575664.

Melville, P., and Sindhwani, V. (2017). 'Recommender Systems', in C. Sammut and G. I. Webb (eds), *Encyclopedia of Machine Learning and Data Mining*. Boston: Springer, 1056–1066. https://doi.org/10.1007/978-1-4899-7687-1_964.

Mendonça, R. F. (2018). 'Dimensões democráticas nas jornadas de junho: Reflexões sobre a compreensão de democracia entre manifestantes de 2013', *Revista Brasileira de Ciências Sociais*, 33/98: e339707.

Mendonça, R. F. (2020). 'Can Deliberative Democracy Help Democracy in Dangerous Times?'. Western Political Science Association Meeeting, Los Angeles/online.

Mendonça, R. F., Abreu, M., and Sarmento, R. (2021). 'Repertórios discursivos e as disputas políticas contemporâneas', *Novos estudos CEBRAP*, 40/1: 33–54. https://doi.org/10.25091/s01013300202100010002.

Mendonça, R. F., Filgueiras, F., and Almeida, V. (2023). 'The Infrapolitics of Algorithmic Gaming', *Communications of the ACM*.

Mendonça, R. F., and Simões, P. G. (2012). 'Enquadramento: Diferentes operacionalizações analíticas de um conceito', *Revista Brasileira de Ciências Sociais*, 27/79: 187–235. https://doi.org/10.1590/S0102-69092012000200012.

Metz, C., and Satariano, A. (2020). 'An Algorithm that Grants Freedom, or Takes it away'. *New York Times*, 6 February. https://www.nytimes.com/2020/02/06/technology/predictive-algorithms-crime.html.

Meyer, J., and Rowan, B. (1977). 'Institutionalizing Organizations: Formal Structure as Myth and Ceremony', *American Journal of Sociology*, 83/2: 340–63. https://doi.org/10.1086/226550.

Milano, S., Taddeo, M., and Floridi, L. (2020). 'Recommender Systems and their Ethical Challenges', *AI & Society*, 35: 957–67. https://doi.org/10.1007/s00146-020-00950-y/.

Mittelstadt, B. D., Allo, P., Taddeo, M., Wachter, S., and Floridi, L. (2016). 'The Ethics of Algorithms: Mapping the Debate', *Big Data & Society*, 3/2. https://doi.org/10.1177/2053951716679679.

Mohamed, S., Png, M.-T., and Isaac, W. (2020). 'Decolonial AI: Decolonial Theory as Sociotechnical Foresight in Artificial Intelligence', *Philosophy and Technology*, 33/4: 659–84. https://doi.org/10.1007/s13347-020-00405-8.

Möhlmann, M., and Henfridsson, O. (2019). 'What People Hate about Being Managed by Algorithms, According to a Study of Uber Drivers', *Harvard Business Review*, 30 August.

Morlino, L. (2012). *Changes for Democracy: Actors, Structures, Processes*. Oxford: Oxford University Press.

Mounk, Y. (2018). *The People vs Democracy*. Cambridge, MA: Harvard University Press.

Mulgan, R. (2000). '"Accountability": An Ever-Expanding Concept?', *Public Administration*, 78/3: 555–73. https://doi.org/10.1111/1467-9299.00218.

References

Najibi, A. (2020). 'Racial Discrimination in Face Recognition Technology', *Harvard Blog Science Policy*, Special Edition: Science Policy and Social Justice, 24 October. https://sitn.hms.harvard.edu/flash/2020/racial-discrimination-in-face-recognition-technology/.

Napoli, P. M. (2013). 'The Algorithm as Institution: Toward a Theoretical Framework for Automated Media Production and Consumption', *McGannon Center Working Paper Series*, 26. https://fordham.bepress.com/mcgannon_working_papers/26.

Napoli, P. M. (2014). 'Automated Media: An Institutional Theory Perspective on Algorithmic Media Production and Consumption', *Communication Theory*, 24/3: 340–60. https://doi.org/10.1111/comt.12039.

Neumann, J. V., and Morgerstern, O. (2021). *Theory of Games and Economic Behavior*. New York: Interbooks.

Neyland, D. (2019). *The Everyday Life of an Algorithm*. London: Palgrave Macmillan. https://doi.org/10.1007/978-3-030-00578-8.

Nguyen, D., and Hekman, E. (2022). 'The News Framing of Artificial Intelligence: A Critical Exploration of how Media Discourses Make Sense of Automation', *AI & Society*, early view, 1–15. https://doi.org/10.1007/s00146-022-01511-1.

Nisan, N., Roughgarden, T., Tardos, E., and Vazirani, V. V. (2007). *Algorithmic Game Theory*. Cambridge: Cambridge University Press.

Noble, S. U. (2018). *Algorithms of Oppression: How Search Engines Reinforce Racism*. New York: New York University Press. https://doi.org/10.2307/j.ctt1pwt9w5.

Norris, P., and Inglehart, R. (2019). *Cultural Backlash: Trump, Brexit and Authoritarian Populism*. Cambridge: Cambridge University Press.

North, D. (1990). *Institutions, Institutional Change, and Economic Performance*. New York: Cambridge University Press.

Nyhan, B. (2021). 'YouTube Still Hosts Extremist Videos: Here's who Watches them', *Washington Post*, 10 March. https://www.washingtonpost.com/outlook/2021/03/10/youtube-extremist-supremacy-radicalize-adl-study/.

O'Neil, C. (2016). *The Weapons of Math Destruction: How Big Data Increases Inequality and Threatens Democracy*. New York: Crown Publishing.

Obermeyer, Z., Powers, B., Vogeli, C., and Mullainathan, S. (2019). 'Dissecting Racial Bias in an Algorithm Used to Manage the Health of Populations', *Science*, 366/6464: 447–53.

OECD (2014). *Recommendation of the Council on Digital Government Strategies*. Paris: OECD. https://www.oecd.org/gov/digital-government/Recommendation-digital-government-strategies.pdf.

OFCOM (2012). *Measuring Media Plurality: Ofcom's Advice to the Secretary of State for Culture, Olympics, Media and Sport*. London: OFCOM. https://www.ofcom.org.uk/__data/assets/pdf_file/0031/57694/measuring-media-plurality.pdf.

Ohme, J. (2021). 'Algorithmic Social Media Use and its Relationship to Attitude Reinforcement and Issue-Specific Political Participation: The Case of the 2015 European Immigration Movements', *Journal of Information Technology & Politics*, 18/1: 36–54. https://doi.org/10.1080/19331681.2020.1805085.

Orren, K., and Skowronek, S. (1994). 'Beyond the Iconography of Order: Notes for a New Institutionalism', in L. C. Dodd. and C. Jillson (eds), *The Dynamics of American Politics*. Boulder, CO: Westview, 314–320.

Ostrom, E. (1990). *Governing the Commons: The Evolution of Institutions of Collective Action*. Cambridge: Cambridge University Press.

Ostrom, E. (1999). 'A Behavioral Approach to the Rational Choice Theory of Collective Action: Presidential Address', *American Political Science Review*, 92/1: 1–22. https://doi.org/10.2307/2585925.

Ostrom, E. (2005). *Understanding Institutional Diversity*. Princeton: Princeton University Press.

Park, A. (2019). 'Injustice ex machina: Predictive Algorithms in Criminal Sentencing'. *UCLA Law Review*. https://www.uclalawreview.org/injustice-ex-machina-predictive-algorithms-in-criminal-sentencing/.

Parsons, T. (1949). *The Structure of Social Action*. New York: Free Press.

Pasquale, F. (2015). *The Black Box Society: The Secret Algorithms that Control Money and Information*. Cambridge, MA: Harvard University Press.

Pateman, C. (1970). *Participation and Democratic Theory*. Cambridge: Cambridge University Press.

Perrin, A., and Anderson, M. (2019). 'Share of US Adults Using Social Media, Including Facebook, Is Mostly Unchanged since 2018', Pew Research Center. https://www.pewresearch.org/fact-tank/2019/04/10/share-of-u-s-adults-using-social-media-including-facebook-is-mostly-unchanged-since-2018/.

Perry, W. L., McInnis, B., Price, C. C., Smith, S., and Hollywood, J. S. (2013). *Predictive Policing: The Role of Crime Forecasting in Law Enforcement Operations*. Santa Monica: RAND Corporation. https://www.rand.org/pubs/research_reports/RR233.html.

Peters, B. G. (2019). *Institutional Theory in Political Science: The New Institutionalism*. Cheltenham: Edward Elgar.

Petre, C., Duffy, B. E., and Hund, E. (2019). '"Gaming the System": Platform Paternalism and the Politics of Algorithmic Visibility', *New Media + Society*, 5/4: 1–12. https://doi.org/10.1177%2F2056305119879995.

Phillips, N., Lawrence, T. B., and Hardy, C. (2004). 'Discourse and Institutions', *Academy of Management Review*, 29/4: 635–52.

Pierson, P. (2000). 'Increasing Returns, Path Dependence and the Study of Politics', *American Political Science Review*, 94: 251–67.

Pierson, P. (2004). *Politics in Time: History, Institutions and Social Analysis*. Princeton: Princeton University Press.

Pierson, P., and Skocpol. T. (2002). 'Historical Institutionalism in Contemporary Political Science', in I. Katznelson and H. V. Milner (eds), *Political Science: State of Discipline*. New York: Norton, 693–721.

Pollard, M. (2020). 'Even Mask Wearers Can Be ID'd, China Facial Recognition Firm Says'. https://www.reuters.com/article/us-health-coronavirus-facial-recognition/even-mask-wearers-can-be-idd-china-facial-recognition-firm-says-idUSKBN20W0WL.

Popper, K. R. (2002a). *The Poverty of Historicism*. New York: Routledge.

Popper, K. R. (2002b). *The Logic of Scientific Discovery*. New York: Routledge.

Portland Communications (2018). 'How Africa Tweets 2018'. https://portland-communications.com/pdf/How-Africa-Tweets-2018.pdf.

Przeworski, A. (2019). *Crises of Democracy*. Cambridge: Cambridge University Press.

Rabushka, A., and Shepsle, K. (2009). *Politics in Plural Societies: A Theory of Democratic Instability*. New York: Longman.

Rajchman, J. (1991). 'Foucault's Art of Seeing', *Philosophical Events: Essays of the '80s*. New York: Columbia University Press, 68–102.

Rajvanshi, A. (2022) 'From Arranged Matches to Tinder Hook-ups: How the Apps Changed Dating in India', *ABC News, Australia*. https://www.abc.net.au/news/2022-07-17/how-dating-apps-india-helped-young-widow-believe-in-second-love/101242852.

Rancière, J. (1999). *Dis-Agreement: Politics and Philosophy*. Minneapolis: University of Minnesota Press.

Ratcliffe, Rebecca (2019). 'How a Glitch in India's Biometric Welfare System Can Be Lethal', *Guardian*. https://www.theguardian.com/technology/2019/oct/16/glitch-india-biometric-welfare-system-starvation.

Rebello, A. (2020). 'Da placa de carro ao CPF', *Intercept*, 21 September. https://theintercept.com/2020/09/21/governo-vigilancia-cortex/.

Ribeiro, M. H., Ottoni, R., West, R., Almeida, V. A., and Meira Jr, W. (2020). 'Auditing Radicalization Pathways on YouTube', *Proceedings of the 2020 Conference on Fairness, Accountability, and Transparency*, 131–41. https://doi.org/10.1145/3351095.3372879.

Rinta-Kahila, T., Someh, I. A., Gillespie, N., Indulska, M., and Gregor, S. (2022). 'How to Avoid Algorithmic Decision-Making Mistakes: Lessons from the Robodebt Debacle'. University of Queensland. https://stories.uq.edu.au/momentum-magazine/robodebt-algorithmic-decision-making-mistakes/index.html.

Robinson, D. (2022a). 'The Kidney Transplant Algorithm's Surprising Lessons for Ethical A.I.', *Slate*, 31 August. https://slate.com/technology/2022/08/kidney-allocation-algorithm-ai-ethics.html.

Robinson, D. (2022b). *Voices in the Code: A Story about People, their Values, and the Algorithm they Made*. New York: Russell Sage.

Robinson, S. C. (2020). 'Trust, Transparency, and Openness: How Inclusion of Cultural Values Shapes Nordic National Public Policy Strategies for Artificial Intelligence (AI)', *Technology in Society*, 63: 1–15. https://doi.org/10.1016/j.techsoc.2020.101421.

Rosanvallon, P. (2008). *Counter-Democracy: Politics in an Age of Distrust*. Cambridge: Cambridge University Press.

Rosanvallon, P. (2011). *Democratic Legitimacy: Impartiality, Reflexivity and Proximity*. Princeton: Princeton University Press.

Rose, J., and Jones, M. (2005). 'The Double Dance of Agency: A Socio-Theoretic Account of How Machines and Humans Interact', *Systems, Signs & Actions*, 1/1: 19–37.

Rosenblat, A., and Stark, L. (2016). 'Algorithmic Labor and Information Asymmetries: A Case Study of Uber's Drivers', *International Journal of Communication*, 10 (30 July), 3758–84. http://dx.doi.org/10.2139/ssrn.2686227.

Rosenfeld, M., Thomas, R., and Hausen, S. (2019). 'Disintermediating your Friends: How Online Dating in the United States Displaces Other Ways of Meeting', *Proceedings of National Academy of Science*, 116/36: 17753–8. https://doi.org/10.1073/pnas.1908630116.

Rotaru, V., Huang, Y., Li, T., et al. (2022). 'Event-Level Prediction of Urban Crime Reveals a Signature of Enforcement Bias in US Cities', *Nature Human Behavior*, 6: 1056–68. https://doi.org/10.1038/s41562-022-01372-0.

Rouvroy, A. (2011). 'Technology, Virtuality and Utopia: Governmentality in an Age of Autonomic Computing', in M. Hildebrandt and A. Rouvroy (eds), *Law, Human Agency and Autonomic Computing: The Philosophy of Law Meets the Philosophy of Technology*. London: Routledge, 119–140.

Rouvroy, A. (2016) 'Algorithmic Governmentality: Radicalisation and Immune Strategy of Capitalism and Neoliberalism?' *La Deleuziana—Online Journal of Philosophy*, 3: 30–36.

Rouvroy, A. (2018). 'Governing without Norms: Algorithmic Governmentality', *Psychoanalytical Notebooks*, 32: 99–102.

Rouvroy, A., and Berns, T. (2013). 'Algorithmic Governmentality and Prospects of Emancipation', *Réseaux*, 177/1: 163–96.

Roy, D., and Dutta, M. (2022). 'A Systematic Review and Research Perspective on Recommender Systems', *Journal of Big Data*, 9/59: 1–36. https://doi.org/10.1186/s40537-022-00592-5.

Royal Society (2017). *Machine Learning: The Power and Promise of Computers that Learn by Example*. https://royalsociety.org/~/media/policy/projects/machine-learning/publications/machine-learning-report.pdf.

Rubel, A., Castro, C., and Pham, A. (2021). *Algorithms and Autonomy: The Ethics of Automated Decision Systems*. Cambridge: Cambridge University Press.

Runciman, D. (2018). *How Democracy Ends*. New York: Basic Books.

Russell, S. (2019). *Human Compatible: Artificial Intelligence and the Problem of Control.* New York: Viking.
Russell, S. (2022). 'Why We Need to Regulate Non-State Use of Arms', 18 May. https://www.weforum.org/agenda/2022/05/regulate-non-state-use-arms/#:~:text=Stuart%20Russell&text=An%20emerging%20arms%20race%20between,while%20the%20technology%20rapidly%20advances.
Russell, S., and Norvig. P. (2021). *Artificial Intelligence: A Modern Approach. Pearson Series in Artifical Intelligence.* Hoboken: Pearson Education Limited.
Sadowski, J. (2019). 'When Data Is Capital: Datafication, Accumulation, and Extraction', *Big Data & Society,* 6/1: 1–12.
Sanches, R. (2019). 'Economia política digital: Um ensaio crítico sobre as condições para a vida democrática no contemporâneo'. *MA Dissertation in Political Science.* Belo Horizonte: UFMG.
Santiso, C. (2021). *Digitalisation as an Anticorruption Strategy: What Are the Integrity Dividends of Going Digital?* https://www.caf.com/en/knowledge/views/2021/08/digitalisation-as-an-anticorruption-strategy-what-are-the-integrity-dividends-of-going-digital/.
Santos, F. P., Lelkes, Y., and Levin, S. A. (2021). 'Link Recommendation Algorithms and Dynamics of Polarization in Online Social Networks', *Proceedings of National Academy of Science,* 118: e2102141118.
Schaefer, J., Lehne, M., Schepers, J., et al. (2020). 'The Use 0f Machine Learning in Rare Diseases: A Scoping Review', *Orphanet Journal of Rare Diseases,* 15: 145. https://doi.org/10.1186/s13023-020-01424-6.
Schank, R. C., and Abelson, R. (1977). *Scripts, Plans, Goals, and Understanding.* Hillsdale, NJ: Earlbaum Association.
Scharpf, F. (1997). *Games Real Actors Play: Actor-Centered Institutionalism in Policy Research.* Boulder, CO: Westview Press.
Scharre, P. (2018). *Army of None: Autonomous Weapons and the Future of War.* New York: Norton.
Schmidt, V. A. (2008). 'Discursive Institutionalism: The Explanatory Power of Ideas and Discourse', *Annual Review of Political Science,* 11: 303–26. https://doi.org/10.1146/annurev.polisci.11.060606.135342.
Schmidt, V. A. (2010). 'Taking Ideas and Discourse Seriously: Explaining Change through Discursive Institutionalism as the Fourth "New Institutionalism"', *European Political Science Review,* 2/1: 1–25. https://doi.org/10.1017/S175577390999021X.
Schmidt, V. A. (2011). 'Speaking of Change: Why Discourse is Key to the Dynamics of Policy Transformation', *Critical Policy Studies,* 5/2: 106–26. https://doi.org/10.1080/19460171.2011.576520.
Schrage, M. (2020). *Recommendation Engines.* Cambridge, MA: MIT Press.
Scott, J. C. (1990). *Domination and the Arts of Resistance.* New Haven: Yale University Press.
Scott. W. R. (2014). *Institutions and Organizations: Ideas, Interests and Identities.* Thousand Oaks, CA: Sage.
Seaver, N. (2013). 'Knowing Algorithms', *Media in Transition,* 8. https://digitalsts.net/wp-content/uploads/2019/03/26_Knowing-Algorithms.pdf.
Selznick, P. (1949). *TVA and the Grass Roots.* Berkeley and Los Angeles: University of California Press.
Shepsle, K. (1989). 'Studying Institutions: Lessons from the Rational Choice Approach', *Journal of Theoretical Politics,* 1/2: 131–47. https://doi.org/10.1177%2F0951692889001002002.
Silva, S. P. (2017). 'Algoritmos, comunicação digital e democracia: dimensões culturais e implicações políticas nos processos de Big Data', in J. P. Mehl and S. Silva (eds), *Cultura*

digital, internet e apropriações políticas: Experiências, desafios e horizontes. Rio de Janeiro: Letra e Imagem, 29–43.
Silva, T. (2022). *Racismo algorítmico: Inteligência artificial e discriminação nas redes digitais*. Sao Paulo: Edições Sesc.
Silverstone, R. (2012). *Why Study the Media?* New York: Sage Publications.
Simon, H. A. (1976). *Administrative Behavior: A Study of Decision-Making Processes in Administrative Organization*. New York: Free Press.
Simon, H. A. (1996). *The Sciences of the Artificial*. Cambridge, MA: MIT Press.
Simon, H. A., and Newell, A. (1958). 'Heuristic Problem-Solving: The Next Advance in Operation Research', *Operations Research*, 6/1: 1–10.
Skeem, J., and Lowenkamp, C. (2020). 'Using Algorithms to Address Trade-offs Inherent in Predicting Recidivism', *Behavioural Science Law*, 38/3: 259–78. https://doi.org/10.1002/bsl.2465.
Skocpol T. (1992). *Protecting Soldiers and Mothers: The Political Origins of Social Policy in the United States*. Cambridge, MA: Belknap.
Slater, M. (2021). 'Lawful but Corrupt: Gaming and the Problem of Institutional Corruption in the Private Sector'. Working Paper Number 11–060, Harvard Business School.
Snip, I. (2017). 'Georgia: Authorities Use Blockchain for Developing Land Register', *Eurasianet*, 19 April. https://eurasianet.org/georgia-authorities-use-blockchain-technology-for-developing-land-registry.
Solsman, J. (2018). 'YouTube's AI is the Puppet Master over Most of what you Watch', *CNET*, 10 January. https://www.cnet.com/tech/services-and-software/youtube-ces-2018-neal-mohan/.
Sorkin, A. R. (2010). *Too Big to Fail: The Inside Story of how Wall Street and Washington Fought to Save Financial System—and Themselves*. New York: Penguin Books.
Steiner, J. (2012). *The Foundations of Deliberative Democracy: Empirical Research and Normative Implications*. Cambridge: Cambridge University Press
Steinmo, S. (2019). 'Historical Institutionalism: The Cognitive Foundations of Cooperation', *Public Performance & Management Review*, 44/5: 1140–59. https://doi.org/10.1080/15309576.2019.1694548.
Stinchcombe, A. L. (1997). 'On the Virtues of the Old Institutionalism', *Annual Review of Sociology*, 23: 1–18. https://doi.org/10.1146/annurev.soc.23.1.1.
Stokel-Walker, C., and Van Noorden. R. (2023). 'What ChatGPT and Generative AI Mean for Science', *Nature*, 614/7947: 214–16. https://doi.org/10.1038/d41586-023-00340-6.
Stray, J., Halevy, A., Assar, P., Hadfield-Menell, D., Boutilier, C., Ashar, A., Beattie, L., Ekstrand, M., Leibowicz, C., Sehat, C. M., and Johansen, S. (2022). 'Building Human Values into Recommender Systems: An Interdisciplinary Synthesis'. https://arxiv.org/abs/2207.10192.
Suchman, M. C. (1995). 'Managing Legitimacy: Strategic and Institutional Approaches', *Academy of Management Review*, 20/3: 571–610.
Sunstein, C. (2022). 'Governing by Algorithm? No Noise and (Potentially) Less Bias', *Duke Law Journal*, 71/6: 1175–1205. https://scholarship.law.duke.edu/dlj/vol71/iss6/1.
Sweeney, L. (2013). 'Discrimination in Online Ad Delivery', *Queue*, 11/3: 10–29.
Talaviya, T., Shah, D., Patel, N., Yagnik, H., and Shah, M. (2020). 'Implementation of Artificial Intelligence in Agriculture for Optimisation of Irrigation and Application of Pesticides and Herbicides', *Artificial Intelligence in Agriculture*, 4: 58–73. https://doi.org/10.1016/j.aiia.2020.04.002.
Talisse, R. (2019). *Overdoing Democracy: We Must Put Politics in its Place*. Oxford: Oxford University Press.
Thelen, K. (1999). 'Historical Institutionalism in Comparative Politics', *Annual Review of Political Science*, 2/1: 369–404. https://doi.org/10.1146/annurev.polisci.2.1.369.

Thurnher, J. (2012). 'Legal Implications of Fully Autonomous Targeting', *Joint Force Quarterly*, 67/4: 77–84.
Tufekci, Z. (2018). 'YouTube, the Great Radicalizer', *New York Times*, 10 March. 2018/03/10/opinion/sunday/youtube-politics-radical.html, 2018.
Turing, A. (1950). 'Computing Machinery and Intelligence', *Mind—A Quarterly Review of Psychology and Philosophy*, 59/236: 433–60.
United Nations (2019). *Report of the Special Rapporteur on Extreme Poverty and Human Rights*. New York: General Assembly of the United Nations. https://digitallibrary.un.org/record/3834146?ln=en.
United Nations Development Program, Oxford Poverty and Human Development Initiative (2023). *Global Multidimensional Poverty Index*. Unstacking global poverty: Data for high impact action. New York: UNDP and OPHDI. Retrieved from: https://hdr.undp.org/content/2023-global-multidimensional-poverty-index-mpi#/indicies/MPI.
Urbinati, N. (2019). *Me the People: How Populism Transforms Democracy*. Cambridge, MA: Harvard University Press.
Valença, L (2021). 'Além de Pegasus, Carlos Bolsonaro queria sistema para monitorar o Planalto', *UOL*, 3 August. https://noticias.uol.com.br/politica/ultimas-noticias/2021/08/03/alem-do-pegasus-carlos-bolsonaro-previa-sistema-para-monitorar-planalto.htm.
Valente, R. (2020). 'Ação sigilosa do governo mira professores e policiais antifascistas', *UOL*, 24 July. https://noticias.uol.com.br/colunas/rubens-valente/2020/07/24/ministerio-justica-governo-bolsonaro-antifascistas.htm.
Van Gorp, B. (2006). 'The Constructionist Approach to Framing: Bringing Culture Back in', *Journal of Communication*, 57/1: 60–78. https://doi.org/10.1111/j.0021-9916.2007.00329.x.
Van Rompay, T. J. L., Vonk, D. J., and Fransen, M. L. (2009). 'The Eye of the Camera: Effects of Security Cameras pn Prosocial Behavior', *Environment and Behavior*, 41/1: 60–74. https://doi.org/10.1177/0013916507309996.
Vardi, M. (2022). 'ACM, Ethics, and Corporate Behavior', *Commun. ACM*, 65/3 (March), 5. https://doi.org/10.1145/3516423.
Varshney, L. (2020). 'Respect for Human Autonomy in Recommender Systems', Third FAccTRec Workshop on Responsible Recommendation. https://arxiv.org/abs/2009.02603.
Van Poell, T., and van Dijck, J. (2014). 'Social Media and Journalistic Independence', in J. Bennett and N. Strange (eds), *Media Independence: Working with Freedom or Working for Free?* New York: Routledge, 182–201.
Veale, M., and Brass, I. (2019). 'Administration by Algorithm? Public Management Meets Public Sector Machine Learning', in K. Yeung and M. Lodge (eds), *Algorithmic Regulation*. Oxford: Oxford University Press, 121–149.
Verdegem, P. (2022). 'Dismantling AI Capitalism: The Commons as an Alternative to the Power Concentration of Big Tech', *AI & Society*, early view. https://doi.org/10.1007/s00146-022-01437-8.
Verhoest, K. (2013). 'Agencification Processes and Agency Governance: Organizational Innovation at a Global Scale?', in P. Valkama, S. J. Bailey, and A. V. Anttiroiko (eds), *Organizational Innovation in Public Service.s*. London: Palgrave Macmillan, 49–71. https://doi.org/10.1057/9781137011848_4.
Wagner, C., Strohmaier, M., Olteanu, A., Kiciman, E., Contractor, N., and Eliassi-Rad, E. (2021). 'Measuring Algorithmically Infused Societies', *Nature*, 595: 197–204. https://doi.org/10.1038/s41586-021-03666-1.
Wang, P., and Huang, Q. (2022). 'Digital Influencers, Social Power and Consumer Engagement in Social Commerce', *Internet Research*, early view, 1–15. https://doi.org/10.1108/INTR-08-2020-0467.

References

Warren, M. (2017). 'A Problem-Based Approach to Democratic Theory', *American Political Science Review*, 111/1: 39–53. https://doi.org/10.1017/S0003055416000605.

Webb, H., Koene, A., Patel, M., and Vallejos, E. P. (2018). 'Multi-Stakeholder Dialogue for Policy Recommendations on Algorithmic Fairness', *SMSociety '18: Proceedings of the 9th International Conference on Social Media and Society*, 395–9.

Weber, M. (1978). *Economy and Society*. Berkeley and Los Angeles: University of California Press.

Weingast, B. R. (2002). 'Rational Choice Institutionalism', in I. Katznelson and H. V. Milner. (eds), *Political Science: State of Discipline*. New York: Norton.

Weizenbaum, J. (1976). *Computer Power and Human Reason: From Judgment to Calculation*. San Francisco: W. H. Freeman.

Wenzelburger, G., König, P., Felfeli, J., and Achtiziger, A. (2022). 'Algorithms in Public Sector: Why Contexts Matter?', *Public Administration*, early view, 1–39. https://doi.org/10.1111/padm.12901.

West, J. D., and Bergstrom, C. T. (2021). 'Misinformation in and about Science', *Proceedings of National Academy of Science*, 118/15: e1912444117.

Wharton, E. (2020). 'Promoting a "Perfect" Pride: How Spotify's Pride Playlists Construct LGBTQ Culture and Identities'. 10.13140/RG.2.2.14177.12643.

Wilson, J. Q. (1989). *Bureaucracy What Government Agencies Do and why they Do it*. New York: Basic Books.

Wilson, W. (1956). *Congressional Government: A Study in American Politics*. Boston: D. C. Health.

Winner, L. (1977). *Autonomous Technology: Technics-out-of-Control as a Theme of Political Thought*. Cambridge, MA: MIT Press.

Winner, L. (1980). 'Do Artifacts Have Politics?' *Daedalus*, 109/1: 121–36.

Winston, P. H. (1992). *Artificial Intelligence*. New York: Addison-Wesley.

Wolf, M., Miller, M., and Grodzinsky, F. (2017). 'Why We Should Have Seen that Coming: Comments on Microsoft's Tay "Experiment", and Wider Implications', *ORBIT Journal*, 1/2: 1–12. https://doi.org/10.29297/orbit.v1i2.49.

Yee, K., Tantipongpipat, U., and Mishra, S. (2021). 'Image Cropping on Twitter: Fairness Metrics, their Limitations, and the Importance of Representation, Design, and Agency', *Proceedings of the ACM Human-Computer Interaction*, 5 (CSCW2), article 450. https://doi.org/10.1145/3479594.

Yeung, K. (2017). '"Hypernudge": Big Data as a Mode of Regulation by Design', *Information, Communication & Society*, 20/1: 118–36. https://doi.org/10.1080/1369118X.2016.1186713.

Yeung, K. (2018). 'Algorithmic Regulation: A Critical Interrogation', *Regulation & Governance*, 12: 505–23. https://doi.org/10.1111/rego.12158.

Young, I. M. (2002). *Inclusion and Democracy*. Oxford: Oxford University Press.

Završnik, A. (2019). 'Big Data: What Is it and why Does it Matter for Crime and Social Control?', in A. Završnik (ed.), *Big Data, Crime, and Social Control*. London: Routledge, 3–28.

Završnik, A. (2021). 'Algorithmic Justice: Algorithms and Big Data in Criminal Justice Settings', *European Journal of Criminology*, 18/5: 623–42. https://doi.org/10.1177/1477370819876762.

Zuboff, S. (2019). *The Age of Surveillance Capitalism: The Fight for a Human Future at the New Frontier of Power*. New York: Public Affairs.

Zysman, J. (1994). 'How Institutions Create Historically Rooted Trajectories of Growth', *Industrial and Corporate Change*, 3/1: 243–83. https://doi.org/10.1093/icc/3.1.243.

Index

For the benefit of digital users, indexed terms that span two pages (e.g., 52–53) may, on occasion, appear on only one of those pages.

A

Abers, Rebecca 141
accountability 6, 13, 61, 68, 122, 132–133, 135, 140–142, 150, 151
accuracy 6, 8, 50, 54–55, 65–66, 85, 113, 123–124
action scripts 23–24, 27–28, 30–32, 47–48, 50, 66–68, 72, 84–86, 93–95, 123
action situations 23–25, 30–31, 49, 95, 107, 149
administration 32, 79, 81–86, 88, 89, 93–94, 98–100, 117–118, 149–150
affordances 16, 19, 20–21, 40–41, 44, 51, 73, 115
agencification 82
agency 2, 10–11, 13, 14, 19–21, 35, 39–40, 45, 47–49, 52, 62, 64, 72, 76, 85, 100–103, 114, 118–119, 149, 151
   human agency 2, 11, 13–14, 20–21, 50, 92, 145, 148
   sociotechnical agency 2
   algorithmic agency 11–12, 14, 18
   machine agency 11, 15–16
Ahmad, Khaleel 63
artificial intelligence (AI) 8, 10–11, 13, 20, 53–54, 57–58, 61, 62–65, 74, 111, 133, 136–137, 139, 141
   Generative AI 13–14
   artificial neural networks 9, 54–55
   artificial agents 29
algocracy 46, 128
algorithmic
   algorithmic decision-making 4, 10, 12, 19, 22, 67, 80, 88, 90, 127, 138, 144
   algorithmic interactions 1
   algorithmic-based companies 5
   algorithmic management 5–7
   algorithmic platforms 10, 35, 125
   algorithmic agency 11–12, 14
   algorithmic spatiality 12
   algorithmic societies 41, 44, 51–52, 55, 59–60, 77, 103. 106–107, 149
   algorithmic power 46–47
   algorithmic governmentality 46–47, 58
   algorithmic security 59–60
   algorithmic regulation 90–92
   algorithmic transparency 100, 139–140
   algorithmic biases 138
   algorithmic recommenders 85–86, 105–112, 115–121, 123–124, 150
algorithmization 83, 85, 102, 149, 151
Allen, Daniel 64, 106
Almeida, Virgílio 81, 139
Alves, Marco A.S. 46–47
Amazon 10, 31, 60, 109, 111–112, 116–117
Amnesty International 122
Amoore, Louise 11, 14, 48–49, 54–57, 87, 94–95
Anderson, Monica 104–105
Andrade, Otávio M. 46–47
Aneesh, Aneesh 23–24, 46
Angwin, Julia 61, 65
anonymization 71, 96
Aradau, Claudia 9, 11, 86
arena 19–21, 66, 70, 76–77, 99, 100, 143–144
argument 2, 40–41, 51, 72–73, 76–77, 97–99, 111, 122, 128–129, 133–134, 143–145, 148
   symbolic argument 32
   practical argument 73
   technocratic argument 99
   perlocutionary argument 100
Arrow, Kenneth 32–33
artefacts 10–12, 14, 15–17, 20, 21, 23, 26, 33–34, 41–45, 47, 48, 50, 72, 77, 127, 143, 148, 151
assembly 128–129
asymmetries 6, 45, 47–48, 59, 65, 68, 129–130, 137–138
attitudes 46–47, 54
audiences 51, 115, 121

audit 97–99, 114
  auditing 2, 80
austerity 84, 88, 89, 98–99
Australia 94, 96–99
authoritarianism 35, 69, 76
authority 15, 33–34, 78, 101–102
authorization 131–135
autonomous 1, 20–21
  autonomous cars 8
  autonomous agents 10–11, 20, 149
  autonomous weapons systems 54, 64–65, 73–74, 78, 149
  autonomous individuals 59, 144–145
  autonomous human agency 145
Auxílio Brasil 79, 87, 89

B

Bachrach, Peter 45
Bächtiger, Andre 143
Baratz, Morton S. 45
Bateson, Gregory 23
Beer, David 12–13, 47
behavioural 27–28, 33–34, 54, 58–59
  behavioural data 111–112
behaviourism 27
Benjamin, Ruha 44, 68
Benn, Claire 104, 109, 118–119
Bergman, Ronen 69–70
Berlin, Isaiah 144–145
Berns, Thomas 46–47
bias 1, 6, 13–14, 61, 65–66, 76, 82–83, 87, 111, 114–115, 127, 137–138
  political and social bias 10, 112
  racial bias 40–44, 59, 62, 65–66, 68, 73, 87–88
Binns, Reuben 140–141
biometric technologies 54
biometric data 62, 72, 92–93
black boxes 5, 141
black peoples 13, 36–37, 40–41, 59, 65–67, 82–83
  black bodies 59
Blanke, Tobias 9, 11, 86
blockchain 91
Bohman, James 143
Bolsonaro 64, 69, 104
Boston 5, 55
bots 120–121
Bovens, Mark 140
boyd, danah 26, 31–32

Brass, Irina 48–49, 81
Brayne, Sarah 54, 66, 67
Brazil 53, 61–62, 65, 69, 75, 79, 87, 91–92, 100, 104–105
Brennan, Jason 19–20, 127
Browne, Simone 59
Bryson, Joanna 141
bubble 7–8
  filter bubble 115–116
  closed-loop bubble 50
Bucher, Taina 12–14, 47, 116
Buhmann, Alexander 143–144
bureaucracy 26–27, 31, 85, 93, 95
bureaucratic 6, 10–11, 30, 31, 33–34, 82, 85–86, 88–89, 94–95, 101–102
  bureaucratic agents 31, 33–34, 85, 95
business 12, 19, 31, 37, 38, 43, 49, 110–112, 116–117, 121, 122, 150

C

capitalism 58–59, 83–84, 111–112, 123–124
Caplan, Robyn 26, 31–32
CCTV 53–54, 75
Ceará 61–62, 65
censorship 71–72, 120, 123–124
chatbots 11, 13–14, 95
ChatGPT 14
Chen, Le 5, 54–55
civil society 99, 116, 126, 139–140, 144, 147
climate change 40, 127–128
Cobbe, Jennifer 108, 111–112, 121
code 10–14, 16, 24, 27–28, 32, 41–42, 46, 73, 98, 99, 114, 148
coercion 31, 45, 54, 144–145
commons 34–35
Comparitech 53–54
COMPAS 36, 60, 61, 67
competition 28, 96–97, 111, 131–133, 135, 139
compliance 6, 80, 82, 90, 91–92, 147
Connolly, Randy 12–13, 22–23
consent 111–112, 129–130, 134
consistency 32–33, 36, 37–38
constitutional 26–27, 128–129, 132, 133–134
conversion 37–38, 43
cooperation 34–35
Couldry, Nick 59, 68, 87, 111–112
Covid-19 56–57, 96–97
Crawford, Kate 14, 40–41

crime 54–57, 61–62, 65–66, 73, 75
critical juncture 22, 36–38, 43–44, 86, 89, 114, 130, 151
Culpepper, Pepper 36–37, 88
culture 10, 12, 16, 27, 123, 127, 150
Curato, Nicole 126

D
Dahl, Robert A. 128–129, 138, 144
Danaher, John 46, 83, 128
data colonialism 59, 111–112
dating 10, 18–19, 44, 105–106, 109, 123
decision-making 4, 6, 7, 12, 33–34, 42–43, 46, 50, 68, 80–81, 84, 85, 90, 94–95, 102, 107, 110–111, 113, 118–119, 126–132, 134, 136–137, 142, 144, 147
democracy 19–20, 68, 104–105, 110, 126–127, 130–132, 134, 135–138, 140, 143–147, 150, 151
democratization 3, 17–18, 103, 128–131, 134, 136–141, 143, 145–147, 150
de-democratization 126
Denmark 55, 97, 98–100
design 3–4, 7–8, 23, 26, 41–44, 51, 54, 76, 77, 80, 82–83, 105–106
    algorithm design 7–8, 24, 34–35, 37–38, 41–43, 60, 61–63, 65–66, 85, 86, 89–90, 99, 109, 111–113, 117, 122, 130, 137, 141, 142, 147
    system designers C 17, 20
    institutional design 23, 26, 37, 41, 57–58, 60, 61–62, 66, 77, 84, 85–86, 93–94, 102, 138
    policy design 82, 89–90, 92–93, 101
determinism 21–22, 49
Dewey, John 135–136, 138, 143–144
DiMaggio, Paul 31, 63
discourse 26, 38–41, 45–48, 50–51, 73–75, 77, 97–100, 102, 118, 121–123, 127, 142
discrimination 1, 6, 13–14, 68, 122–124
discursive 3–4, 26, 29, 39, 40–41, 50–52, 60, 72, 75, 97–101, 110, 121–122, 142, 148–149, 151
    discursive institutionalism, 26, 38–41, 48, 50, 72, 122
    discursive interactions 39, 51
    discursive frames 39–40, 72, 97–98
disidentification 71
distrust 87–88, 94–95
diversity 29, 33–34, 40–41, 47–48

drift 37–38, 43
Drott, Eric 120
Dryzek, John 38–39, 126
Dunleavy, Patrick 81, 84

E
Easton, David 27, 131
echo chambers 115–116, 119, 145
Eckles, Dean 119
economy 36–37, 79, 88–90, 120, 123–124
    sharing economy 5–6
    market economy 6
    algorithm-drive economy 31
    digital economy 98, 109
    attention economy 112
ecosystem 1, 6, 115–117, 119
Ekstrand, Michael D. 108
election 119–121, 125, 131–132
Elster, Jon 67, 143
enforcement 9, 44–45, 54, 57–58
environmental 80, 91–92, 119–120, 126
epistemology 23–25
epistocracy 127, 150
    epistocratic 20, 127, 128–129, 138, 150
Epstein, Robert 10
equality 129–130, 135, 137–138, 150
equity 113, 137
Ercan, Selen 126, 143
ethical 20, 73–75, 109, 112–114, 127
ethnic 87–88, 114–115, 122
Etzioni, Amitai 73–74
Etzioni, Oren 73–74
Eubanks, Virginia 80–81, 88, 95
experts 60–61, 73–74, 84, 92–93, 120–122, 134, 137, 139–140
exploitation 6, 111–112
extremist 10, 104–105, 117–119, 121, 123–124

F
Facebook 10, 12, 31–32, 60, 109, 111–112, 117, 119, 122
facial recognition (FRT) 5, 53–55, 59, 60–63, 65, 66–67, 69, 72–73, 75–77, 92–93, 149
Fairclough, Norman 39–40
fairness 6, 65–66, 85, 116, 122, 132, 138
fake news 121
feedback 11–12, 16, 36–37, 82–83, 87–89, 99, 101–102

Fieseler, Christian 144
Filgueiras, Fernando 81, 140
Finkel, Eli J. 122–123
Fischer, Frank 51, 94–95, 126
Fisher, Eran 12, 104
Ford, Bryan 48–49, 128
World Economic Forum 84, 98
Foucault, Michel 45–47, 57–58, 117–119
frames 23–24, 27–28, 30–31, 35–37, 39–41, 50–51, 66, 72, 88–89, 93–95, 97–99, 102, 109, 121–122, 128
framework 2–4, 16, 17–18, 22–23, 26, 29, 40, 41, 44, 45, 50, 51–52, 55, 59–60, 66, 76–77, 81, 84–85, 87, 92, 97–98, 100–101, 103, 110, 114, 116, 135, 147–149, 151
fraud 5, 91, 95–99

G

game 17, 28, 34–35, 39–40, 50–51, 121, 126, 129
   rule-governed game 17, 28
   game theoretical models 33–34
   cooperative games 34–35
gaming 3–4, 26, 41, 49, 50, 59–60, 96, 110, 120–121, 123–124, 141, 149
gender 13, 87–88
geopolitical 70, 98–99, 139
Georgia 91
Gerards, Janneke 68
Germany 55, 100, 104–105
Giest, Sarah 80, 82
Gillespie, Tarleton 48–49
Goffman, Erving 23
governance 14, 19–20, 40–41, 48–49, 58, 84–85, 122, 147
   regulatory governance 90, 92
   governance of algorithmic systems 114, 139, 147
   content-governance 116
   multi-stakeholder governance 122, 139
   Internet governance 139
   democratic governance 139
government 1–2, 4, 16, 24–25, 31, 32, 34, 35, 43, 53–57, 64, 69, 76, 79–91, 93–103, 110–112, 123–125, 127, 131–133, 139, 145–150
   government platforms 81–82, 85–86, 88–90, 94–98, 100–101
   digital government 85, 87, 93–94, 98, 136

   self-government 135–136
governmentality 46–49
   algorithmic governmentality 58
Grimmelikhuijsen, Stephan 127, 136–137

H

Habermas, Jürgen 143
Hacker, Jacob 37–38, 43
Hall, Peter 29–31, 39
Harcourt, Bernard 71, 118
harm 13, 68, 73–75, 119, 137–138
hate speech 38, 110, 116, 121, 123–124
Hay, Colin 23, 27–28, 39, 40
health 19, 44, 56–57, 82–83, 94, 107, 113, 125
healthcare 80, 82–83, 112, 114
Henderson, Peter 80, 82–83
Henfridsson, Ola 6–7
Hobbes, Thomas 45, 56, 77
Hong, Yu 86
Hood, Christopher 82
Hosseinmardi, Homa 105
Huang, Qian 119–120
human-machine assemblages 7
human-machine interactions 16–17
human interactions 15, 18, 20–21, 38–39, 41–42, 107, 115, 123–124
human rights 1, 9, 56, 66, 68–69, 73–75, 89, 91, 95, 96, 99, 126, 146

I

identification 24, 56–57, 71, 92–93, 95, 96, 102, 149–150
   image-identification algorithms 11
identity 13
   virtual identity 71
impartiality 132–133
implementation 80, 82, 85–90, 102, 149–150
inclusion 135–138
India 53–55, 69, 75, 92–93, 105, 120–121
industry 31, 73–74, 85, 110–112, 139–140, 150
inequalities 1, 47–48, 68, 82–83, 92, 137–138
influencers 104, 115, 119–121, 123–124
information 6, 9, 10, 15, 44, 53–54, 64, 72, 80, 87, 90, 97–98, 102, 105–112, 117–118, 138, 140, 145
infrastructure 9, 15, 21, 81, 83–84, 86, 87, 107, 137, 148
injustice 76, 82–83, 87, 89, 132–133

innovation 21, 39, 41, 43, 79, 88, 89, 101, 111, 144
   democratic innovations 144
Instagram 117, 119
Institutionalism 1–3, 24–25, 38–39, 43, 47–48, 66, 77, 102
   new institutionalism 26–30, 32–33, 41, 50, 52
   old institutionalism 26–27
   sociological institutionalism 26, 30–32, 39, 48
   historical institutionalism 26, 35–39, 48, 88, 114–115, 123–124, 130, 151
   rational choice institutionalism 26, 32–36, 48
   discursive institutionalism 26, 38–41, 48, 50, 72, 122, 149
institutionalization 18, 23, 30–31, 84, 89, 91, 128–129, 134
   de-institutionalization 18–19, 149
   reinstitutionalization 18–19, 149
instrument 17, 45, 46–47, 93, 110–111, 116
   instrumentalization 56, 58–59, 110–111
   instrumentalism 20
interfaces 5, 16–18, 29, 35, 41–42
interpretative 87, 121–122, 148
Introna, Lucas 53–54
isomorphism 63, 76, 93–95, 100–102, 151
Israel 70

J
Japan 55, 100, 128–129
journalism 31–32, 144
Joyce, Kelly 66, 87
justice 10, 19–20, 89, 116, 133–134, 137
justifications 1, 67, 132–134, 143

K
Keane, John 48–49, 69, 115–116, 140
knowledge 1, 6–7, 12–13, 17, 22–24, 45–47, 54–55, 66, 69, 82, 85–86, 94–95, 112, 118, 127, 128, 132–133, 137, 147, 150
König, Pascal 46, 130, 136–138, 141, 142
Krasner, Stephen 36, 43

L
labour 6, 28–29, 41–42, 46
Landemore, Hélène 138, 147
language 8, 11, 13–14, 17, 77
Latin America 53–54, 61, 98–99

law 9, 26–27, 49, 57–58, 66–67, 77, 87, 100, 132–133, 135, 141
Lazar, Seth 104, 109, 118–119
Lee, Min 5–6
legal 80, 106, 148
legitimacy 3, 49, 56, 92, 130–134, 136–137, 142, 143, 147, 151
Lessig, Lawrence 2, 15–16, 148
Levi, Margaret 36, 96–97
Leviathan 46, 56, 77, 130, 149
LGBTQ 18–19, 120–121
liberty 95, 118–119, 144, 145, 150
Lima, Marcio 91
Lukes, Steven 45
Lyon, David 54–55, 66

M
machine-learning 3, 8–9, 12, 38, 54–55, 62, 77, 99, 111
Mahoney, James 37–38
management 5–7, 9, 46–47, 58
manipulation 48–49, 92, 101–102, 118–119, 129
March, James 11, 18, 27–28, 40–41, 57
Margetts, Helen 61, 82, 84
market 6, 60, 77, 83–84, 86, 91–92, 96–97, 105, 117, 139
marriage 105–106, 125
masks 62–63, 72
Matthews, Jeanna 68
Mazzetti, Mark 69–70
McCarthy, Odhran 54–55
McCubbins, Mathew 33–34
mechanisms 20, 63, 85, 93, 110–111, 116, 121, 127, 133–134, 137–140, 142, 145, 147
   surveillance mechanisms 35, 57, 58–59, 92
   mechanisms of enforcement 44–46, automated mechanisms 50
   content governance mechanisms 116
   engagement mechanisms 120
   bureaucratic mechanisms 31
   coordinating mechanisms 32–33
Meijer, Albert 54–55, 83, 85, 127, 136–137
Mejias, Ulises 59, 68, 87, 111–112
Microsoft 11, 60
military 55–57, 61, 64, 66, 73–74
minorities 75, 129, 137–138
misinformation 13–14, 38

Mohamed, Shakir 59
Möhlmann, Mareike 6–7
moral 20, 22, 35, 66, 103, 112–114, 131, 150
Myanmar 122–124

N
Napoli, Philip 2, 17, 31–32, 48–49
Nash equilibria 34–35
Netflix 10, 109
network 2–3, 11–12, 31, 45–46, 69, 75, 99, 122–123, 140
Newell, Allen 16–17
NGOs 61–62, 126, 136
Niemeyer, Simon 143
Nissenbaum, Helen 53–54
Niterói 104
Noble, Safiya 44, 66, 68
North, Douglass 28, 32–33, 48, 66
NSA 66–67, 99–100
NSO 69–70
nudge 49, 90, 92, 101–102
Nyhan, Brendan 104–105

O
O'Neil, Cathy 14, 50–51, 54–55, 65–66
Obermeyer, Ziad 82–83
OECD 32, 84, 85, 90
OFCOM 115–116
Olsen, Johan 11, 18, 27–28, 40–41, 57
opacity 14, 95, 116, 133
opinion 75, 99, 107, 109, 110, 113, 115, 119, 121–123, 127, 129, 134, 143–144
oppression 58–59
organ 112–114, 122
organizations 2
organizational 31–32, 81, 82, 93–94, 115–116
  organizational leadership 30
  organizational work 30–31, 85, 96, 151
  organizational structure 30–31
  organizational change 31, 48–49, 102
  organizational networks 31
  organizational archetypes 32
  organizational convergences 86
Ostrom, Elinor 28, 32–34, 129–130
oversight 114, 132, 140

P
pandemic 18–19, 56–57, 62–63, 79, 80, 87–88, 90, 96–97, 107

Park, Andrew 37, 42–43
parliament 126, 128–130, 133–134
participation 10, 46, 85, 94–95, 114, 119–120, 122, 127, 135, 136–138, 142, 144–145, 150
Pasquale, Frank 14
path-dependence 22, 35–37, 43, 66, 76, 87–89, 100–102, 114–115, 132–133, 151
Pegasus 69–70
Peters, B. Guy 26, 29, 30–31
Phillips, Nelson 121–122
Pierson, Paul 36, 39, 43, 66, 89, 101–102
platformization 24–25, 80–83, 85, 86, 88, 89–90, 93–95, 98, 100–102, 149–150
polarization 10, 109, 119, 122–124
policymaking 80–81, 83, 84, 93–94, 97–98, 100–102, 126
policy agenda 82
policy implementation 62–63, 82
policy evaluation 99, 102
political order 4, 19–20, 52, 56–57, 147, 150
polity 129, 135–137, 142, 147
Popper 22–24
poverty 79, 92–93, 95
Powell, Walter 31, 63, 93–94
power 12–13, 17, 19–20, 26–27, 29, 30, 33–34, 37, 45–49, 70, 71, 76, 78, 93, 95–96, 100–102, 105, 106–107, 109, 117–120, 123–124, 130, 132, 136, 138, 140
  colonial power 59
  concentration of power 140
  decision-making power 95, 118–119
  police power 73
  political power 88, 129–130,
  power asymmetries 6, 47–48, 129,
  power dynamics 93–94, 112, 123–124,
  power relations 2–4, 17, 22, 26, 27–29, 34, 39, 41, 48–49, 52, 59–60, 68, 70, 93–95, 100, 110, 119, 120, 123–124, 148–150,
  power structures 20, 86, 95, 102
  sovereign power 128–129
  technocratic power 68, 76, 92–95
predictive policing 54–55, 59, 60, 62, 63, 65–67, 73, 75–77, 149
preference 16–17, 27, 32–33, 35, 36
principal-agent 33–34
principles 1, 23, 131–132, 134, 137, 139, 147
prison 57
prisoner's dilemma 34–35

privacy 7–8, 13–14, 50, 58, 66–68, 99–100, 145
public integrity 82, 84, 98–99
public sphere 40–41, 51, 72–75, 77, 97–99, 138, 143–144, 150

R
racism 44, 123–124
radical 10, 74, 104–105, 134–135
   radicalization 58, 104–105, 123
Ratcliffe, Rebecca 92–93
rational-choice 11, 34–36, 49
rationality 23–24, 30–35, 45–47, 94–95, 107, 110, 127, 151
rationalization 9, 23–24, 30–31, 88–89, 93, 100–101, 107, 151
recidivism 54, 60, 75
reflexivity 16, 20, 43, 132–136, 146, 151
reform 22–23, 35, 66–67, 80–81, 84, 87, 98
regulation 12, 14, 40–41, 48–49, 74, 75, 90, 95, 100
   content regulation 38
   algorithmic regulation 90–92
   technocratic regulation 92
   market regulation 96–97
reinforcement learning 8–9, 16
Renovabio 91–92
resistance 45, 49, 72, 75, 76, 95, 96–97, 102, 149
resource 1–3, 14, 27–29, 45, 47–48, 54–55, 69, 73–75, 91, 96, 107, 111–112, 119, 137, 151
Ribeiro, Manoel 10, 104–105
right-wing 104–105
risk 9, 18–19, 27–28, 61, 65–66, 74, 75–76, 82–83, 90, 92, 95, 99, 109, 115–116, 127–128, 139–140, 147
   risk-assessment 65, 67, 73, 75, 76–77
Robertson, Ronald 10, 14
Robinson, David 112, 114–115, 122
Robinson, Stephen 136–137
Robodebt 94, 96
Rohingya 122–124
Rosanvallon, Pierre 126–127, 131–132, 140
Rosenblat, Alex 6
Rosenfeld, Michael 18–19, 105–106
routines 23–24, 79, 85, 96, 98–99, 131–132, 149–150
Rouvroy, Antoinette 46–49, 58
Runciman, David 48–49, 126–127

Russell, Stuart 8, 10–11, 54, 57, 74
Russia 53–54, 69, 70, 128–129

S
Sadowski, Jathan 111–112
Sanches, Rafael 58, 145
Santos, Fernando 122–123
Saudi Arabia 69
Scharre, Paul 57, 66
Schmidt 57, 66
Scott, W. Richard 17, 34
Scott, James 71
search engines 8, 11, 111, 115
security assemblages 76
Selznick, Philip 30
sensors 72
Shepsle, Kenneth A. 32–33
Silva, Tarcízio 42–44, 62, 127, 145
Silverstone, Roger 15
Simon, Herbert A. 16–17, 41–42, 110
Singh 108, 111–112, 121
Skocpol, Theda 36
Smith, Russell 96–97
Snowden, Edward 66–67, 99–100
social interaction 17, 24, 40, 48–49, 51, 67, 76
social media 2, 10–11, 16, 17, 31–32, 38, 44, 47, 50, 66–67, 104–105, 109, 110, 115–116, 118–119, 122–124, 143–144, 146, 150
social movements 126, 136, 139
software 8–9, 11–12, 54, 58, 60–63, 67, 69–70, 73–77, 122
Sokol, Daniel 82–83
Solsman, Joan 104, 109
sovereignty 130, 140
Spotify 10, 109, 120–121
spyware 69
standards 14, 16–17, 20, 31–32, 55, 57, 82, 83–85, 139
state 53–54, 56–57, 61–62, 65, 73, 75, 78, 85, 86, 90, 93, 95, 98–99, 102, 115–116, 144, 146, 149
   authoritarian states 58–59
   rogue states 74
   state capacity 82
   welfare state 95, 97
strategies 14, 16–17, 28, 31–32, 35, 36–37, 45–46, 49, 54–57, 66, 71–72, 84–85, 92, 102, 120, 123–124, 127–128, 139

gaming strategy 50
strategy of surveillance 57
security strategies 59
operational strategies 83
streaming 16, 50, 109, 117–118
subject 46–47, 58, 65, 115
subjectivities 57–58, 70
surveillance 57–62, 64, 65–66, 69, 71, 73, 76, 92, 96–97, 100–102, 140, 145
   surveillance assemblages 67, 73–74, 77
   surveillance capitalism 58–59

T
Tay 11
Taylor, Rosemary C.R. 29–31
technocracy 94–95
Thelen, Kathleen 22, 29, 32–33, 35–37, 41, 48, 88
TikTok 109, 111–112, 117, 119
Tinder 10, 18–19, 44, 105–106
trade secrecy 141–142
transparency 6–7, 13, 19–20, 92, 99, 114, 122, 139–142
trust 73, 88, 109, 122, 123–124, 126
truth 45–47, 68
Tufekci, Zeynep 117–118
Turing, Alan 15–16, 57
Twitter 10, 13, 109, 116, 119–122

U
Uber 5–7, 96–97
UK 87–88, 96–97, 104–105, 115–116, 129
uncertainty 8–9, 33, 43, 46–48, 113, 127–128
United Nations 40, 56, 70, 95
UNOS 113–114, 122
Ünver, Akin H. 128
urban 12, 57, 67, 80, 90

V
Valente, Rubens 64
Vardi, Moshe 111
Veale, Michael 48–49, 81
Verhoest, Koen 82
violations 13–14, 66–68, 73
violence 67, 73, 77, 122, 123–124, 130
visibility 31–32, 105, 115–121, 123–124, 143–144
vision 57–58, 64

W
war 64–67, 107, 126
Warren, Mark 135–136
Waze 12
web 8
   dark web 71
Webb 139
Weber, Max 30–31, 45, 93
Weingast, Barry 33
Weizenbaum, Joseph 17
Wenzelburger, Georg 88, 136–138, 142
Wessels, Martijn 54–55, 75
West, Jevin D. 107
Wharton, Emily 120–121
Wilson, Woodrow 26–27
Wilson, James Q. 87–88
Winner, Langdon 15–16, 148
Winston, Patrick H. 10–11

Y
Yee, Kyra 13
Yeung, Karen 48–49, 91, 92
Young, Iris M. 139
YouTube 10, 12, 104–105, 109, 117–119, 122

Z
Završnik, Aleš 54, 66, 71
Zuboff, Shoshana 14, 58–59, 111
Zysman, John 36–37, 88–89